OTHER BOOKS BY SCOTT MACDONALD

Saving Investa: How an Ex-factory Worker Helped Save One of Australia's Iconic Companies (2016)

Think Like a Dog: How Dogs Teach Us to Be Happy in Life and Successful at Work (2019)

EDUCATION WITHOUT DEBT

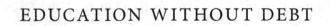

EDUCATION WITHOUT DEBT

Giving Back and Paying It Forward

Scott MacDonald

INDIANA UNIVERSITY PRESS

This book is a publication of

Indiana University Press
Office of Scholarly Publishing
Herman B Wells Library 350
1320 East 10th Street
Bloomington, Indiana 47405 USA

iupress.org

Manufactured in the United States of America

First printing 2020

Cataloging information is available from the Library of Congress.

ISBN 978-0-253-05143-1 (hardback)
ISBN 978-0-253-05144-8 (paperback)
ISBN 978-0-253-05145-5 (web PDF)

*In memory of Professor David Brower, my good
friend and teacher, and his wife, Lou Ann.*

*In memory of Lacey Lumpkin, a graduate student
at the University of North Carolina who helped research parts of this book and passed far too young.*

To the donors who make education more affordable.

*To the teachers who mentor, train, and share their knowledge de-
spite low financial compensation and often challenging conditions.*

*To the students who benefit from those above and will
someday share their gain with those who follow.*

Profits from the sale of this book will support
scholarships for need-eligible students.

CONTENTS

7   What Schools Are Doing to Reduce
    Student Debt   *77*

    My Story: Tattooed Tales / Hannah Locklear   *92*

PART 4. Giving Back

8   The Importance of Philanthropy   *101*

9   Giving Back / Milt Stewart   *110*

10 John Kuykendall and Davidson College   *116*

    My Story: Getting an Education and Giving Back
    in Africa / Edward Kabaka   *122*

PART 5. Stories from Scholarship Donors

11 Barnard Scholarship: Not Just about the Money /
    David Barnard   *129*

12 Robert J. Lake Scholarship: In Memory of
    My Father / Gilmour Lake   *133*

13 Changing a Life to Change the World /
    Dwight Worden   *135*

14 On Reflection / Judy Benson   *141*

    My Story: Searching for Financial Aid /
    Anya Thompson   *142*

PREFACE

AFTER MY FATHER DIED WHEN I WAS VERY YOUNG, MY MOTHER worked at an insurance company and then a bank. It was always clear that my family could not afford to help me pay for college, but it was also always expected that I would go to college. When I enrolled at Indiana University (IU) in Bloomington in the fall of 1965, things were quite different than they are today. Tuition was $30 per credit hour, or $360 to $450 per semester depending on whether I took twelve or fifteen course hours. As I recall, room and board at the university's aged Wright Quadrangle was about $500 per semester. I could go to school for less than $2,000 per school year.

During high school, I worked and saved money. The factory in Cicero, Illinois, where I worked paid a bit less than two dollars per hour; if I worked a normal shift, I could make about eighty dollars per week, and with occasional overtime I averaged about one hundred dollars per week. Working twenty weeks a year, including summer vacation and spring and winter breaks, I could make enough to pay for tuition and room and board.

At college, I waited tables and worked for a fraternity, earning funds for incidental expenses and supplementing my factory wages. Like many of my generation, I was able to work my way through college, largely because quality education was affordable.

During my sophomore year, my mother suffered a financial setback, and my savings were needed at home. I asked the staff at the financial aid office at IU for help, and they arranged a student loan for me so I could finish the school year. Without the loan, I would have been unable to continue my education.

During my junior year, I dropped out of school and joined the marines. I was tired of always being short of money and was dealing with personal challenges. My service with the marines was cut short due to a knee injury, but I had saved a year of wages. I then returned to work at the factory in Cicero, even though I had a pronounced limp. Subsequently, I returned to IU and completed my undergraduate degree.

With help from the US Department of Veterans Affairs and two scholarships, I was able to attend the University of North Carolina (UNC) and obtain a master's degree. Without financial aid, I never would have been able to continue my education. During holidays and other breaks, I continued to work at the factory—except for the summer between my two years of graduate school, when I had a well-paying internship at the National Capital Planning Commission in Washington, DC.

On graduating from UNC, I obtained a good job at a consulting firm in Washington, DC, which paid me $11,500 a year—a large sum in my mind at the time. Without a master's degree and my internship experience, that job would have been unavailable to me. With my good income, I was able to pay off my student loan relatively quickly.

My situation, which was fairly typical at the time, was much different from what young men and women experience today. Indiana University now costs about $25,000 a year for an in-state student and closer to $46,000 for an out-of-state student. I was an out-of-state student (from Illinois) and would not have been able to go to IU under a cost structure like today's.

The factory in Cicero closed long ago. If I were a student today, I likely would seek work at a retail store and earn $8 to $10 an hour. Working forty hours a week would generate a maximum of $400, and retail industry employers often schedule staff for fewer than forty hours so they don't have to pay benefits. If I were able to work twenty weeks a year, I could earn $8,000 before paying taxes. Even against an in-state educational cost of $25,000, that would not go far. This is the challenge young people face today, and it is very different from the challenge my generation faced in earlier times.

Compared to when I attended school, today's circumstances appear even worse when examined further. During graduate school, I was able to obtain a well-paying internship, as did almost all my classmates. Recently, I visited UNC and talked with Noreen McDonald, the department chair for the Department of City and Regional Planning. She explained that most internships today are unpaid. Students need work experience but are not typically paid when acquiring it. Carol Quillen, the president of Davidson College, told me a similar story, and I witnessed the growth of unpaid internships myself when I was president of New Plan Excel Property Trust in New York several years ago. When asked to approve a summer internship program, I asked how much it would cost. The response was, "Nothing." Interns worked for free because they needed the experience on their resumes.

The economics of acquiring a college education have shifted dramatically. Without financial aid, only the affluent can obtain an education. And even with aid, typically only the affluent can obtain internships that provide the work and professional experience needed to secure good jobs after graduation. The need to work and make money during summer vacations is not compatible with unpaid internships.

The imbalance between what someone can earn and save and the cost of education has led to an explosion of student debt, as documented in this book and elsewhere. I was able to pay off my student debt after working for a couple of years; today's graduates are looking at many years of payments, which affects their ability to buy a house, start a family, and begin accumulating life's necessities and pleasures.

I have had a successful career that has included becoming CEO, president, or managing director of several companies and working on real estate projects throughout the world. I have become wealthy; I live in a beautiful home in Southern California and enjoy a comfortable lifestyle. But as I look back, none of this would have happened if I had not received a good education. And I would not have had the opportunities that an education affords if I had not received financial aid when I needed it.

Education was important to my success; it provided me with personal and career opportunities as well as access to jobs and income. In recognition of this, it became my mission to give back by setting up scholarship programs for need-eligible students at several universities, including IU and the UNC. It is my hope that others will join me in doing the same so young people can access the opportunities that my generation were able to realize in earlier years.

Scott MacDonald
Macdonaldscholars.com

"We'd be happy to give your son a
student loan as soon as you pay off yours."

EDUCATION WITHOUT DEBT

INTRODUCTION

I T WAS LATE AFTERNOON AFTER A BUSY AND STRESSFUL DAY WHEN MY desk phone rang. I was CEO of the Investa Property Group in Sydney, one of Australia's largest property companies, with ownership of billions of dollars of commercial and residential real estate. We also had about $4.5 billion in debt and no clear ability to repay. Every day was stressful, but the company paid me a lot of money to figure out how to solve its problems and help it survive until the economy improved.

I had an excellent assistant, Elpie Vanos, but usually answered my own phone if I was not in a meeting. It was 2009, and we still used landlines. I looked at the ringing phone and thought for a moment: Was it a banker wanting to be repaid, an irate tenant who was failing in the global financial crisis and wanted out of their lease, a broker wanting a higher commission? It didn't really matter; I picked up the phone.

"Are you the Scott MacDonald who set up scholarships at Davidson College?" a young woman asked.

"Yes," I replied, not knowing where the conversation was going. Several years earlier, when my son Andrew had been a student at Davidson, I'd wanted to give back. My investors and I had sold a company in Houston that I was CEO of at the time, and I had been well rewarded; I had some money that I didn't need. I met with the Davidson development staff, including Eileen Keeley, and we created a new scholarship program. I agreed to endow up to four scholarships for need-eligible students, and the recipients would agree to undertake community service projects to help others in need. I called the scholarships Giving Back and Paying It Forward. The model was based on an existing Bonner Scholars program at Davidson managed by the Center for Civic Engagement and led by Stacey Riemer, but my program offered more money and greater flexibility than the Bonner program.

I did not keep in touch with the program or Davidson after my son Ross graduated. My contribution had simply been a thank-you to Davidson for educating my two sons and a means of giving back to students who needed money to attend college. I did not expect anything in return. So I was surprised to hear the question asked of me in faraway Sydney, Australia.

"Mr. MacDonald, my name is Olivia Tait, and I was a MacDonald Scholar at Davidson. It changed my life. I wanted to call and say thank you so much. I am working in Sydney, and the alumni office told me you're working here too."

I arranged to take young Olivia out to dinner one night, and she told me her amazing story. She had grown up initially in Switzerland with her mother; her father had died before she was born. Because of her mother's health problems, they had moved to South Carolina for a while, and then Olivia had lived in South Australia before ending up in college at Davidson. She had attended precollege schools in Switzerland, the United States (South Carolina), and Australia.

Because of her mother's poor health and inability to work regularly, Olivia had qualified for financial aid. Without financial support, she could not have attended college. At Davidson, she received substantial aid and was the recipient of a MacDonald Scholarship. As a MacDonald Scholar, she was required to undertake community service projects each semester, and Olivia worked on several projects, including helping at Aida Jenkins School, which offered programs for children from predominately poor families.

In her junior or senior year, she undertook a signature project, which is typical of MacDonald Scholars. Her project was to fund the development and operation of an elementary school in a village in Ethiopia. She had a friend who was working for an NGO (nongovernmental organization—a.k.a. a nonprofit charity) in Africa and explained to Olivia that there were typically no elementary schools in villages in Ethiopia. There were schools in the cities, but in smaller villages children were illiterate and went uneducated. Olivia, probably twenty years old at the time, decided she would address the problem by building a school.

She learned that the cost of building a simple school was $5,000; the villagers would help with construction, but there was still the cost of materials. Also, the cost of operating a school was about $5,000 a year; it did not make sense to build a school and then not staff or operate it. She needed to raise $5,000 initially and then $5,000 per year for the subsequent years.

Olivia was not deterred. She called a photographer friend and arranged to use his inventory of children's pictures from around the world. Then she sent letters to the schools she had attended in South Carolina, Australia, and Switzerland and requested poems and sayings from their students. She created a beautiful book out of the children's pictures and poems and talked a local printer into publishing; she called the book *Animi*. She sold it for fifty dollars out of her dorm room and the back of her car and through a website that her mother set up and managed. When she had raised $5,000, the school was built, and when she raised another $5,000 the school opened and has been operating ever since. I was so impressed that I bought fifty of her books and gave them to my employees.

I was stunned that with time, effort, and financial support, a college kid could change the world. There are children in that village of Ethiopia who can read and write today and look forward to a future because of one young woman's determination. When I returned from Australia in 2013, I called Eileen Keeley at Davidson and asked to meet with other MacDonald Scholars; I was curious what else was happening as a result of freeing students from work requirements and unleashing their enthusiasm and energy to improve the world.

I met with existing and former MacDonald Scholars over dinner, and one after another told me how meaningful the experience of being in this program was—particularly helping others and not having to worry about paying for college. They generally agreed that they had benefited as much from helping people as those whom they had helped. They also talked about the close relationships they had developed while working together on service projects. Almost everyone claimed it was a life-changing experience.

Based on the amazing feedback from Davidson, I called the University of North Carolina (UNC), where I had attended graduate school. I had kept in touch with Emil Maliza, the chair of the City and Regional Planning Department, and Shawne Grabbs of UNC's development office. Shawne set up meetings with university officials to discuss establishing a MacDonald Scholars program at UNC. With substantial input from the Office of Scholarships, Admissions, and the Carolina Center for Public Service, we established both a MacDonald Scholars program and a MacDonald Fellows program to provide needed expenses to support community service activities. Three to four students in each class currently endeavor to make the world a better place while incurring less student debt, and early results have been impressive.

Next, I contacted Indiana University (IU) in Bloomington, where I had received my bachelor's degree. I had met the president, Michael McRobbie, when he was visiting Australia a few years before, and he introduced me to the IU Foundation staff. It turned out that Curt Simic, who had supervised my involvement with the IU Student Foundation when I had been a student, had become president of the IU Foundation and subsequently president emeritus. With foundation staff including Abby O'Neal, and with encouragement from university officials including Provost Lauren Robel, we created a MacDonald Scholars program at IU. The participating students, like their counterparts at Davidson and UNC, are remarkable for their enthusiasm for, commitment to, and persistence in improving the lives of others. And they are thankful for the opportunities their scholarships have provided.

Programs have been subsequently established at the University of Michigan and the University of San Diego. The program differs from school to school, but all share a common theme: need-eligible students receive grants, which reduce their student debt burden and help other people through a defined service program. I meet annually with the student recipients, and their accomplishments continue to amaze me. And like my students, I feel the benefit of helping others secure an education, access better future opportunities, and do good deeds along the way. I receive far more pleasure from these students than I would from owning another house, a yacht, or other material possessions.

However, I can do only so much. The crisis of student debt in the United States has become acute, with most students and graduates now burdened by college-related debt, including some loans that will last a lifetime. This indebtedness limits an individual's future choices, adversely impacts personal and societal decisions, delays marriages and families, and reduces economic growth and opportunity. It limits the availability of education as a path to a better life for many Americans.

Something must be done, but elected officials, government employees, and university administrators are making little progress. The chapters that follow depict the growing crisis in student debt in both personal terms and hard statistics. Interspersed are stories of hope—the amazing things people can accomplish when given the resources to obtain an education.

PART 1
THE CRISIS OF STUDENT DEBT

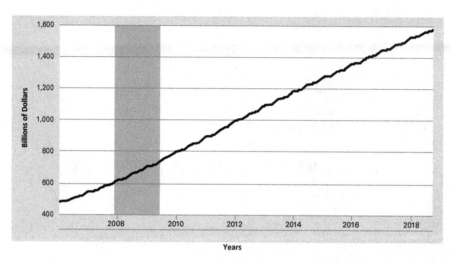

Figure 1.1. Student loans owned and securitized, outstanding. Shaded area indicates US recessions. *Source: Board of Governors of the Federal Reserve System (US)*, myf.red/g/noV2.

1

THE RISING LEVEL OF STUDENT DEBT
AND SOCIETAL IMPLICATIONS

IN 2018, THE AMOUNT OF STUDENT DEBT IN THE UNITED STATES passed the $1.5 trillion mark. There is more outstanding student debt than any other type of debt except home mortgages. There is more student debt than auto loan debt; there is more student debt even than credit card debt.

The amount of student debt has escalated quickly and continues to rise in dramatic fashion. Figure 1.1, provided by the Federal Reserve Bank, depicts the dramatic rise in total student debt in the last several years.

In 2019, approximately 70 percent of college students graduated with significant student debt. The number of students graduating with student loans are as follows: about 66 percent of graduates from public colleges, about 75 percent of graduates from private nonprofit colleges, and about 88 percent of graduates from for-profit colleges.[1] Over 44 million Americans collectively hold nearly $1.5 trillion in student debt. Roughly one in four Americans is paying off student loans.[2]

The author thanks Indiana University student Samantha Young for assistance with research and the preparation of drafts of this chapter.

I went to college and in turn, accrued about $70,000 in student loans both private and public. I went to school to become a teacher. I worked four jobs in college to alleviate how much I needed to take out in loans. It has since been four years that I graduated and after paying around $600 a month every month for four years, that adds up to around $28,000 I have paid toward my loans. My current balance is now $65,000. So because of interest rates that are close to 10 percent on several of my loans, the near $30,000 I have paid only results in a credit of $5,000. This is madness. How can I keep up with this? And for how long?[3]

Emilie, Minnesota

Student loans are a major source of financial aid for students. In the 2016–17 academic years, loans accounted for 24 percent of the funds used by undergraduate students and 53 percent of the funds used by graduate students.[4] While the total amount of federal loans has decreased in recent years, federal loans to undergraduates have increased by 25 percent since 2005–6.

In 2018, the average student borrower had more than $37,000 in student loans when he or she graduated—a $20,000 increase from thirteen years ago.[5] At public colleges, the average debt is approximately $25,550; for private nonprofit schools, it is $32,300; and at for-profit colleges, the average debt is almost $40,000.

Ashley Castelli, who is a middle school language arts teacher, had to borrow $42,000 to receive her bachelor's degree. Even though she has been paying off her loans for six years, she has been able to pay only the interest every month.[6] On average, it takes ten years to pay off a student loan.

Student loans are the only debt that cannot be extinguished in bankruptcy. Under laws passed by Congress and signed by the president in 1976, 1978, and 1984, student loans are not eligible for discharge by bankruptcy filings except in extreme "hardship" situations, which are difficult to prove. This is unlike credit card debt, auto loans, personal loans, obligations to service providers like doctors, and unpaid expenses. Students who take student loans from government or private lenders, and parents who cosign such loans, will be obligated to repay the loans regardless of future financial circumstances. Repayment terms of certain government loans can be adjusted in certain circumstances, however.

Despite the difficulty in discharging a student loan, defaulting is an ever-worsening problem. In 2016, nearly 1.1 million students defaulted on their loans for the first time, accounting for $19 billion in loans.[7] Every thirty seconds a new student defaults on his or her loan. In the time it took to read this paragraph, a student defaulted on a loan.

After a payment is overdue by 90 days, the loan will be reported as delinquent to credit bureaus. Federal student loans are usually not considered in default until a payment is 270 days past due. Despite this nine-month delay, defaults are rising quickly. About 11.5 percent of borrowers default within three years of having to make a payment. More than 5 million borrowers began repaying loans on October 1, 2013; about 581,000 had defaulted by September 30, 2016.

I grew up in poverty and started working when I was 14. I went to college to find a brighter future and then to graduate school. I have over $120,000 in student loan debt. I work as a mental health therapist and will never be able to pay off my loans—making the possibility of a brighter future impossible. I'm tired. I've been working over half my life and have never been able to get ahead enough to breathe. My debt gives me anxiety.[8]

Badia, California

Increasing debt is associated with an increase in the five-year default rate for students. For borrowers entering repayment in 2008–9, the five-year default rate was 28 percent, an increase from the 16 percent rate of the 1998–99 cohort.[9] Even though defaulting on a student loan has such long-lasting and severe consequences, more than one in four student borrowers default on their loans. More than one in four borrowers will have damaged credit ratings affecting their ability to buy houses. More than one in four borrowers may have tax refunds withheld and wages garnished. More than one in four borrowers can be brought to legal action. And that rate increases when looking at public two-year and for-profit universities. The five-year default rate is 38 percent for the 2008–9 cohort at public two-year universities and 47 percent at for-profit universities. Excluding private loans, almost half of the students who borrowed money to attend for-profit universities in that time period defaulted on their loans within five years.[10]

> *I'm a special education teacher who will never own anything because I have $160,000 in student loan debt, mostly private loans. Navient is no help, and I struggle every day worrying and stressing over it. I was the first in my family to ever go to college but little did I know it was the worst [decision]. This was the mistake of my life.*[11]
>
>   Kristin, New Jersey

Default rates also vary depending on the size of the loan. Interestingly, the highest default rates are among students with the lowest loan balances. For defaulters who entered repayment in 2010–11, 35 percent had loans under $5,000. Only 4 percent of defaulters had loans more than $40,000. As students stay in school longer and complete their degrees, more debt accumulates.[12] However, job prospects and wages are improved for students with degrees. Graduates with high school degrees make on average $30,000 a year. Those with bachelor's degrees make an average of $50,000 a year, and those with graduate degrees earn an average of $65,000 a year.[13] As debt increases, so does a student's ability to pay that debt back if they stay in school and obtain a degree.

In the third quarter of 2016, defaulted loans accounted for 10 percent of the federal education loan portfolio. That is equivalent to approximately $130 billion in loans that students gave up on paying. That amount would pay for nearly two years of discretionary funding for the US Department of Education.[14]

For-profit colleges have a particularly bad track record on student defaults. Students who attend for-profit colleges are more likely to incur debt, will typically have more debt, and are much more likely to default on loans. Most students who borrow money and attend for-profit colleges will default on their loans, as did 52 percent of student borrowers who attended for-profit schools and borrowed money in 2003.[15] This is twice the level of defaults for community colleges and more than twice the level of private and public nonprofit schools. The level of for-profit school defaults is forecast to rise to 70 percent over time. Of the ten institutions with the largest amount of student debt awarded, eight are for-profit schools.[16]

Defaulted loans can affect more than just a student's education. When a student goes into default, he or she loses any eligibility for additional federal student aid, and schools can withhold his or her academic transcripts. It will also affect how the loan is paid back. When a student defaults, the entire balance of the loan and interest is immediately due. The student can no longer defer his or her loans, and he or she is unable to choose a repayment plan. Defaulting also negatively impacts the student's credit rating.[17] The consequences of defaulting on student loans are severe and long-lasting, yet student debt and defaults continue to rise.

Not only does student debt affect the federal budget, but it also affects the nation's economy. Consider the rate of home purchases. A 2014 study showed that among twenty-three- to twenty-five-year-old college graduates, almost 5 percent more students with no debt owned homes than did students with debt. While homeownership rates were nearly equal among thirty-three- to thirty-five-year-olds, this is likely to change as debt levels and default rates continue to rise.[18]

Student debt levels also appear to be influencing lifestyle decisions including delaying marriage, taking higher-paying jobs instead of lower-paying public service jobs, and deferring consumer purchases. An article in the *Wall Street Journal* attributes slower jewelry sales to millennials having other priorities, including paying off debt. Tracy Hoover, a twenty-six-year-old engineer in Tennessee, said in the article, "Everyone I know is still paying off student loans. I think a lot of my generation doesn't really prioritize jewelry."[19] The same concept likely applies to other discretionary purchases.

The federal government has tried to make loan repayment easier for student borrowers. There are multiple repayment plans available for federal loans, all with different advantages. Under the standard repayment plan, all payments are a fixed amount, and the loan will be paid off in up to ten years. The graduated repayment plan is similar but with lower payments at first and then higher payments later on, which will cost student borrowers more over time. The extended repayment plan can have either fixed or graduated payments for up to twenty-five years and may be available for students who owe more than $30,000. There are also multiple income-based repayment plans, which use the student's subsequent income level to determine the monthly payment.[20]

Payments can also be simplified by consolidating multiple loans into one, and the repayment plan itself can be changed. Even the payment due date may be changed, depending on circumstances. Some students can also postpone their payments through deferment or forbearance. However, any postponement of payments generally results in ultimately larger loan balances, as interest can still accrue when the loan is not being actively paid back.[21] For students such as Lauren Pena, entering specifically designated public service or teaching in eligible schools means loan forgiveness may even be possible. Pena started with $30,000 in loans, and eleven years later she has only $6,000 left to pay, in part because she taught Spanish—a high-need subject—in a Title I school, and so some of her loans were forgiven.[22]

Despite more flexible payment options, the rising magnitude of student debt and the increasing burden of loans on a large and growing number of individuals appear unsustainable. More debt, more defaults, more financial distress, and an impaired economy all result from the current situation, and all are becoming more acute with each passing day.

2

MORE STORIES OF STUDENT DEBT

I am a 62-year-old retired teacher, so I never made a lot of money, but my wife and I always paid our bills and put away money for retirement. When it came time to send our four children to college, we made too much money to get full financial aid. We now have close to one half million dollars in student debt in our names that paid for tuition for our children. Our oldest now gives us more than $1,400 a month to pay off her college debt. Thankfully she has a job, and, luckily, she has the least amount of debt. But this enormous monthly payment means she lives at home and cannot participate in the economy the way a professional not burdened with such debt could otherwise. The other three are still in school, so they are still acquiring debt. The only way to help them start out their young professional lives without such a financial burden would be for my wife and I to spend all of our retirement savings. Either way, our family will be financially crippled for decades. We cannot be unique in this . . . this same situation must exist for thousands of families, and that number is only going to grow.

Doug, New Jersey

The stories in this chapter were publicly posted by individuals on the website studentdebtcrisis.org, accessed on January 17, 2019. Last names and the dates of posting have been omitted here.

I grew up in a very poor family with a mother raising three kids on her own. She held down multiple jobs just so we would have food to eat. By the time I was sixteen years old, I was on my own financially. I got my own jobs after school and worked really hard to buy a car and insurance, my own clothes, and anything else I needed.

When it came time to pick a college, I found a home at a small, private, liberal arts school a couple of hours from home. I had no prior knowledge of how loans worked and the massive burden I would be taking on as I was the first in my whole family to go to college. My mother simply could not take much in the way of parent-plus loans because she was still struggling to make ends meet. But this school was my dream, and I had no idea what the real world would be like once I graduated. In my generation, I was brought up hearing you had to get a college degree to be anything and ever really make anything of yourself. I totally bought into all of it.

Once I graduated from college, I started working full time at my alma mater and made a small salary. I then made the decision to go on to a graduate program and get a master's degree. I packed up everything that would fit in my tiny Ford Escort hatchback and moved to Mississippi without knowing a soul.

After all was said and done and my master's was earned, I now sit with a debt of approximately $98,000. I will never be able to pay that off in my lifetime with what I make. I am thirty-seven years old and will be completely crippled with this debt for the rest of my life unless something miraculous happens.

April, Tennessee

I'm 27 and married to my twenty-nine-year-old husband. He went to DeVry and got a master's degree there. They got in trouble for defrauding students, and he didn't get any of the settlement from the FTC. We filed for borrower's defense and haven't heard back, and it's almost been a year. I've been single-handedly supporting both of us for four years while he repays his debt so he can get rid of it faster. He just lost his job and has no permanent position. I'm now having to insure him. I'm constantly on edge and stressed. I used to cry every night in bed after he fell asleep. I'm tired of worrying about debt. I want my life back. I want my husband to feel like he can provide for me, his wife. He feels emasculated, and people in our lives sometimes point out that he should be contributing to our bills. He wants to. He wants to give me the world and take me on trips and take care of me like I've been doing for him. We thought the borrower's defense would help. But so far it is fruitless. I'm frustrated and have so many questions. It's a horrible feeling. It's crippling and makes me nauseous. It's no way to live.

Caroline, Arizona

I've paid over $140,000 on a $118,000 student loan. I still owe $101,000. My attempts to pay over these decades "in good faith" prevented me from having any savings or retirement. I'm now fifty-four years old, and I ended up in bankruptcy without the ability to discharge these loans. A week after filing bankruptcy, I got a breast cancer diagnosis followed by surgeries and radiation treatments. A ton of new medical debt. My bankruptcy filed for an adversarial proceeding in hopes of the lender showing compassion. No!! They are forcing us to proceed with litigation. No mediation or anything to spare me this stress! We need bankruptcy protection like other citizens. Student loan borrowers are not criminals.

Sharon, Pennsylvania

I'm stuck with paying almost $500 a month just in student and federal loans. We are living paycheck to paycheck. I am pregnant and scared because of money and if I don't pay this, my credit goes down and we will never be able to buy a house. We live in a one-bedroom trailer.

Kiana, California

I graduated from law school eight years ago with about $115,000 in student loan debt. I have been making consistent payments under the income-based repayment program, and I have been working mostly in the nonprofit sector after a series of internships. I now owe over $160,000 due to the interest that has accrued, even though I have been making all payments on time.

Shannon, New York

I decided to go to grad school to help increase my chances of finding a decent job. I finished my program in August and haven't been able to find full-time work. This has forced me to keep deferring my payments because I can't afford to start paying those off yet. When I can finally start, I'm going to owe between $80,000 and $100,000. I'm scared I'll never be able to afford to move out of my parents' house even when I do find full-time work.

Rachel, Virginia

I'm having to pay almost $450 a month. That's almost half of my paycheck, and I can't afford to eat, pay [my] mortgage, and care for my family.

Andrea, Maryland

I graduated in 1994. I owed $40,000. I taught for six years at community college level, then as a staff member at a nonprofit center from 2002 to 2017. I also taught at this university as a lecturer. I've been paying on my loans for over 22 years and have applied for forgiveness and was rejected, even though I've worked for a nonprofit public university and a nonprofit center at that same university. All of my payments have gone to the interest only . . . not a single penny to the principle. My balance owed now with 8¼ interest rate is $120,000!!! How the hell does this happen? I'm sixty-three years old and won't work or live long enough to pay this debt off. It's forcing me to put off retirement as long as pos-

sible . . . and my health isn't getting better. I need help! It's destroyed my ability to live a full life and to save money for retirement. HELP US, WE'RE DROWNING!!!

Cynthia, California

I am a 30-something married woman who thought I was doing everything right. I went to college to further my education to get a better job, but nowadays I regret going. I feel ashamed and disgusted with myself for getting in this position. Anytime I try to talk about it nobody ever believes me about the struggle that it is to live with this kind of burden. I took out around $70,000 worth of loans to attend college; I've been paying on those loans for nine years and I somehow now owe $157,000. I can barely afford to go to the dentist or the doctor. I sure can't afford to go on vacation. Anytime there's an emergency I have to rely on credit cards or retired parents. Not only am I mentally suffering with this debt on my shoulders, but I feel like no one understands the pressure that comes along with it. I feel alone, and I feel like I have no voice. I can never talk about student loans to friends or family because they just judge me. "Why did you take out so much?" "Don't you know how to do math?" "What do you expect the government to do?"

I'm so sick of hearing these kind[s] of questions and I'm sick of not being able to enjoy life. At this point, I feel like I am living at poverty level and would have been better off not going to college. I don't feel like I'm ever going to be able to buy a house or even save money. I feel so trapped under Navient's thumb, I don't know if I'll ever be able to enjoy life again.

Kristina, California

3

BETRAYED BY THE DREAM FACTORY

Samual Garner

My life and career have been scarred by the naïve exchange I made at college: an education of questionable value for a dangerous amount of debt. Every once in a while, when I'm feeling overwhelmed, I watch college commencement ceremonies on YouTube. These rituals remind me how perverse our higher-education system is—and of the empty idealism that colleges and universities sell us: *We are here today, donning our ceremonial robes and caps, to recite the traditional vacuous platitudes and wish you well in paying off high-interest student loans for which we are in no way held accountable. Let us now further romanticize our fair institution by singing the alma mater and conveniently forget that tuition has gone up 1,120 percent since 1978. Good luck out there, kids!*

I'm a consumer of those vacuous platitudes and a victim of this system. After finishing my master's degree in 2008, I found out—as in, I didn't already know—that I had $200,000 in student debt. Some well-paying professions might make this amount manageable, but for a bioethicist like me, it's been crushing. Many things had to go wrong for this to happen—or right if

This chapter by Samual Garner was first published by *Slate* on January 26, 2016, as "Betrayed by the Dream Factory," http://www.slate.com/articles/business/moneybox/2016/01/student _loan_crisis_at_its_ugliest_i_graduated_and_found_out_i_owe_200_000.single.html. Reprinted with permission from the author.

you're a school or a lender. Although the hefty amount I owe is unusual, my experience is not: Motivated by an idealistic view of education and career and vulnerable to predatory, disingenuous, or at least negligent institutions, young people and their families too often take on large amounts of student debt. No matter how much they owe, the consequences of that debt can be outsized. These young people may have to abandon their educations early; pay back far more, after interest, than they took out; manage exceptionally exploitative loan terms; shoulder serious, chronic mental distress; delay important life decisions; and participate less in the economy than they otherwise would.

I don't question the importance of higher education. But the detrimental effects of crushing debt shouldn't be the shared experience of millions of young people and their families. Currently, about 40 million Americans owe $1.2 trillion[1] in student loan debt, and it continues to grow. According to the Institute for College Access and Success,[2] students who borrow graduate with an average debt of $29,000 for a bachelor's degree. In 2014, 69 percent of graduates had student loan debt, and from 2004 to 2014, the average college debt grew at more than double the rate of inflation. Even with smaller amounts of debt than mine, starting a life quickly becomes very hard. So how do people get to this point? We've debated student debt for decades, but our understanding of how it shapes a young person's experience—from naïve teenager to indebted young adult—is still limited. Here's what happened to me.

* * *

When I was seventeen I was just starting to get the hang of school. My siblings and I had the privilege of expecting we would attend private colleges, which seemed reasonable—others in our family had done it, friends had done it, so we should be able to do it. My grades weren't good enough for Connecticut's Wesleyan University, so after getting rejected I quickly applied binding early decision to one of its conference rivals, Connecticut College, where my brother was a senior. I was very eager—and very fortunate—to get in. It was one of the most validating moments of seventeen-year-old Sam's life.

Despite its cost, Conn sold my family on its purportedly outstanding financial aid. When I was a freshman in 2003, the comprehensive fee, including tuition, room and board, and other fees, was about $40,000 a year; it climbed to about $46,000 by 2007, my senior year. A decade later, the comprehensive annual fee at Connecticut College (and many private colleges) is more than $60,000 per year. And about half the students pay full price. That must be because a bachelor's degree from a private college is $80,000 more valuable than it was ten years ago, right? No, that's crap. These days, I can't imagine any bachelor's degree that is worth $240,000. But my parents couldn't know tuition would rise so much, and my brother seemed to fare OK there—he got substantial grant funding that helped him leave with much less, and more manageable, federal debt.

I knew that my parents were financially stressed because of a fire that destroyed most of our home when I was 15 and because my dad had been struggling with his career for a few years. Given my brother's experience, we expected that Conn would help us make school affordable. Like many colleges' websites, Conn's website even says, "Don't let financial concerns discourage you from applying to Connecticut College. We offer generous financial aid." In my parents' attempt to protect me from the brunt of their financial hardship, they minimized my understanding of what it would take to pay for school.

When I began college I knew Conn had given us a fair amount of grant funding—money that didn't need to be paid back—and I believed my parents and small federal loans were covering the rest. I visited the financial aid office to sign for these federal loans each semester. Like so many students, I thought signing loan documents was just a routine. Having no appreciation of financial adulthood, I didn't really understand what these loans were or what repaying them would actually entail—and in a very different student loan terrain than their college days, my parents didn't either. But I *thought* I understood. I was in the right place, talking to the right people, doing what I was told was necessary. The college made no serious effort to explain my loans until an exit interview at the end of senior year.

Having followed the common advice to study what I loved, I had abandoned my initial plans to focus on biology and majored in music performance, but also minored in philosophy and was a few courses short of premed. By my senior year, however, I realized I was drawn to a subfield of applied ethics called bioethics, which deals with controversial ethical issues in science and medicine. Well-meaning faculty could only advise me on careers in academia. Academia was the setting I knew, so that became my plan: build an academic career in bioethics.

At my exit interview, the college reviewed only my federal loans with me. There was no mention of any private loans. And because student loans are deferred as long as you're in school, I hadn't received a bill. Everything they described to me was still an abstraction.

* * *

If only I had been friends with 2016 Sam in 2007, then maybe I would have done things differently. But I wasn't. So, still unaware of my total debt, I went on for a bioethics master's degree to bolster my chances of getting into a good PhD program. After starting courses at the University of Pennsylvania, I took out $70,000 in loans for tuition and living expenses, which I supplemented with income from part-time jobs. The associate director of the program suggested I work at Penn full-time and do the degree part-time for free. Looking back, that was obviously sage advice, but I thought the sooner I started on a PhD the better.

Save that one brief comment, no one, in five years of higher education, advised me differently or really broke down the cost of my education choices. Why would they? Schools benefit immensely from this ignorance. In fact, several students, faculty, and friends—many of whom had high-paying jobs—told me not to worry about my loans and that I'd pay them back without undue stress.

After completing my master's in 2008, I got a job working as a contractor science policy analyst at the National Institutes of Health in Bethesda, Maryland. I was lucky to land a good, bioethics-related job in a very bad economy. Like most people with loans, I started getting repayment letters within six months of leaving school.

I already knew that I had about $70,000 in federal loans from Penn and some federal loans from Conn—but I had no idea I *also* owed $100,000 in Sallie Mae-serviced private loans.

I was shocked. It turned out that my parents and Conn had had me ink them during my semesterly flurry of document-signing without discussing them with me. Now I was making $50,000 a year in an expensive region with close to $200,000 in loans. I was completely unfamiliar with the—at the time very limited—repayment options. It was a nightmare.

The decisions were unwise, certainly. But while I was in school, my parents were too stressed and embarrassed to take stock of my loans. They wanted me to focus on doing well and felt, as do many middle-class families, that they were in a financial Catch-22: They made too much to get enough aid but not enough to cover the cost of college. Financial aid awards come once per year, giving them little time to plan, and again, they expected similar aid and tuition rates as my brother. They'd lost much of their savings dealing with career challenges and the house fire. They didn't want to take me out of a school I was heavily invested in. Given the grant funding I received every year from Conn, even if they had pulled me out and sent me to our flagship state school—the University of Wisconsin—the full cost there still could have left me with a fair amount of debt.

I now saw what my trust and ignorance had cost. So I was angry. But I felt especially betrayed by the well-manicured dream factories that had educated me.

* * *

When I first started receiving loan statements, I was so distraught and confused that I missed a few months of payments and got a delinquency reported on my credit—not an uncommon occurrence for postgrads. After months of receiving inconsistent information from Sallie Mae, I got my payments in order. I made interest-only payments for my private loans because the interest rates were too high for me to make full payments. (Some of my loans had rates of 8 to 9 percent—compare that with the less than 4 percent for which one currently can get a mortgage.) I enrolled in the new income-based repayment program[3] for my federal loans, and for years I tried to refinance my private loans to lower my interest rates. I attempted to refinance about half a dozen times but was rejected each time for having a weak credit score, delinquency, and too low a salary.

According to my loan contract, when my grandmother dies all $100,000 of my private loans will go into default. Some relief came in 2011 when I started a new job as a contractor bioethicist in NIH's Division of AIDS. This was very fortunate, given the economy and the limited career options for someone with a master's in my field. My salary jumped to about $70,000, an increase of almost 50 percent. I was grateful but keenly aware that this meant something very different for me than it would have without the unrelenting scythe of my debt.

With every bump in salary comes a bump in payments. My current payment is about $1,500 a month—that's almost 40 percent of my take-home pay—and despite having paid more than $75,000 toward my loans, I still owe about $190,000. Remember, I started with $200,000 in debt. With more than eight years of some of my private loans at 8 and 9 percent interest, and my federal loans at more than 6 percent, Sallie Mae and the federal government have made it very hard to make progress.

My debt may take decades to pay off and ultimately cost more than twice my original balance. Depending on my income, my payments could peak at almost $2,000 a month. Without a substantial boost in salary, there's no way to get ahead of my debt. How do I get that salary? The surest way for me to move up in my field would be to get a funded PhD, but that would entail deferring my loans and allowing my interest rates to add almost $50,000 to my current balance.

Is it worth leaving the field that I've already invested so much in? What about jobs or programs that offer loan repayment? Unfortunately, many of these jobs (for example, some federal ones) are very difficult to get (I've tried and am still trying), and many programs (such as Peace Corps) aren't worth the cut in income. I also worked for a for-profit contractor for part of my time at NIH, so several years of my time there don't count toward the public service loan forgiveness program. Can I transition to a career that makes more money but is stable and reliable? How do I stay nimble in this economy when education is so expensive but so essential? Will I ever be able to afford a family?

Plagued by these questions and by years of significant and unrelenting stress over managing my debt, I hit a low point last year. In preparation for a speech I gave at one of Senator Elizabeth Warren's student debt press conferences,[4] I learned about "auto-default": Under Sallie Mae loan contracts, your loans are automatically placed into default and sent to collections if a co-signer dies. My grandmother—who is ninety-three and has Alzheimer's—is a co-signer on some of my private loans. According to my loan contract, when she dies all $100,000 of my private loans will go into default. This means that I could be required to pay the full loan amount immediately or risk being sued, having assets seized, wages garnished, and my credit wrecked. In most circumstances, student loans cannot be discharged in bankruptcy—and, under some contracts, if you start bankruptcy proceedings, your loans can be placed into default. My parents and I made poor financial choices, but they were ones that the system strongly encouraged.

After screwing over a lot of people, this insane policy got slammed with media coverage, forcing Sallie Mae to modify it, but it wasn't clear if these changes applied to me. So I spent several months trying to get out of this trap. I could barely focus on anything else. I had several Sallie Mae reps confirm that when my grandmother dies, I would auto-default and owe $100,000. I thought maybe I should get a lawyer, flee the country, or sell a kidney. I was finally put in touch with a rep from Sallie Mae who sent me an official letter stating that, essentially, because my grandmother had no assets I would continue to make my payments as I had been.

Fortunately, after that, I was also able to refinance some of these loans with a good, financially stable, and not-likely-to-die-soon friend (thanks, Steve) as a co-signer. After six years of attempts, I was actually able to start paying more of my principal balance.

My situation has finally stabilized, and I should be able to avoid default, though things haven't improved otherwise. My payments are still crushing, they will be around for decades, and they severely limit my life choices.

* * *

And all of this to go to school. Yes, I've been more fortunate than many: I was educated at elite schools, I live in a city with a strong economy, and I've had two good jobs. But I still struggle to find ways to retool myself for higher-paying careers that would help me dig out from my debt faster or to advance in my current path. My parents and I are working on ways to improve my situation. But, like many baby boomers, they are burdened with their own financial responsibilities, like taking care of my grandmother and their own health and saving for their retirement. It's true that my parents and I made poor financial choices, but they were ones that the system strongly encouraged. I've worked hard to take responsibility, make my monthly payments, advance in my career, and live modestly. While I've been lucky enough to avoid some of the most disastrous consequences of having student loans, like default, I will still spend the majority of my emotional and intellectual energy trying to find a way out of this, rather than trying to forge a career and a life.

The amount I owe is uncommon, but my story is not. The data show that millions are struggling with large amounts of student debt—debt that will result in some of the painful experiences I have gone through. So at a minimum, I hope this serves as a lesson to stay informed and temper your academic ambition with consideration of the financial costs and the investment you're making.

But that doesn't get to the heart of the systemic problem: Education is outrageously expensive and too risky; schools indoctrinate students and their families with lofty ideals and benefit from their ignorance without accountability; and students and their families can borrow at unprecedented rates, allowing schools to continue hiking tuition. Though its advent was surely well-intentioned, our loan system is confusing and exploitative. In a country we often think of as a meritocracy, it's appalling that we have an education system that frequently does more to punish students for getting educated than it does to reward them.

Ultimately, like many other enlightened countries that recognize education as a critical public good—foundational to the economy and a just society—we need to move toward free public education, including graduate school. Where will this money come from? Given the billions we spend on federal student loan programs and the disgusting amounts of money many college presidents and administrators make, I'm sure there's plenty of money that could put use in the right direction. To start, we need more substantial efforts to refinance and forgive student debt. There are millions of people like me who would like to get on with their lives.

4

COLLEGE AS AN INVESTMENT

Ken Ruggerio

IN 2018, THE FEDERAL RESERVE ANNOUNCED THAT AMERICANS OWE more than $1.5 trillion in student loans. It's a significant number, to say the least, and has become a central talking point for those looking to reform higher education and change the way Americans pay for college.

While the plight of students and college graduates struggling to meet their financial obligations is of great concern, there is little we can do about it at the level of the individual. Long-term reform of financial aid and how we pay for higher education in the United States is in the hands of Congress and the Department of Education, which have been unsuccessfully trying to solve the problem for over a decade.

The numbers we should be talking about today are $559 billion and $282 billion. In the 2015 academic year, postsecondary institutions in the United States spent $559 billion educating students, a number that is expected to increase 3 percent every year with no end in sight. Additionally, in 2018, American families will invest $282 billion in higher education from personal savings and loans.

While these numbers are significant, it's the word *invest* that is most important for students and families to remember. Too many students and families view college as an expense rather than a long-term investment that

Ken Ruggerio is a neighbor of the author and an expert in student loans. He serves as chairman and CEO of Goal Structured Solutions, the administrator of Ascent Student Loans.

should be carefully analyzed to minimize unnecessary costs and maximize returns. When the same families consider buying a car, they typically look at various models and compare prices and may consider future maintenance and even resale values. When they buy a house, they will probably engage a professional to analyze the market, compare prices, and examine maintenance and likely future operating costs and repairs, and they'll meet with financial institutions to compare and evaluate financing options. But when they borrow tens of thousands of dollars to finance an education, they typically don't analyze anything, and then they become upset when they realize their obligations may not align with the future income necessary to pay those obligations.

At a time when accurately determining return on investment for a college education can be difficult, it's important that students and families ask the right questions and have access to data and resources that can answer those questions and help them make informed decisions. For example, what are the graduation rates at a particular school for my major? How much can I expect to earn with this degree in my first year after graduation? How much is the total cost to attend this school for four years?

Choosing the right school can determine one's financial future. Some schools, often for-profit private schools, have a terrible record of graduating students, and students have a disproportionate rate of future loan defaults. Students who borrow money and then fail to graduate have the worst default rates.

Legislation has been put forward numerous times in attempts to build a national database of student-level outcome data (comparing the cost of education with the future income earned), but each time it has been shot down for a variety of reasons, including privacy and misuse of data. While progress is being made to give students and families the information they need to make smart investments, more must be done.

A recent nationwide study conducted by Ascent Student Loans revealed that while colleges often are doing a good job of communicating the cost of education, most are falling short when it comes to expected outcomes and return on investment.[1] The same study showed that more than half of students do not believe the value of a college education has kept up with the cost. This is likely because many students pick schools without comparing the schools' costs with the earning potential of their chosen majors.

Thankfully, there are a number of private loan companies, nonprofits, and state higher-education organizations that view student-level outcome data as critical to helping students and families make informed decisions about how much to pay for school. But the families and the students involved must reach out and access the information to make an informed decision. For example, someone borrowing money to attend a school that has a poor graduation rate or a poor record of grads finding good jobs will more likely lead to a bad financial outcome. Borrowing lots of money to take a future low-paying job does not usually work out well either. Borrowing $100,000 to obtain a degree in social work and then finding a job that pays $40,000 a year will result in many years of future loan payments—maybe forever—to retire that debt.

Private lenders pay to secure funds from depositors, other lenders, and investors. They pay interest on the money they obtain to lend to students. In turn, to make a profit, they charge interest on the student debt at a rate above the cost of their money. They also factor in the possibility of nonpayment from a portion of the borrowers. Because of this sourcing, the lender charges interest from the day a loan is delivered, and that interest compounds if not paid currently. Borrowers who defer payment or pay only a portion of what is needed to amortize their debt incur more and more interest, leading to increasing loan balances. This seems unfair to the borrower, but it reflects the realty faced by the lender. US government loans usually defer interest and compounding until six months after graduation and offer forgiveness for loans if the borrower works for certain nonprofit public interest jobs for a stipulated period (often ten years). The US taxpayer pays the interest in these cases.

Like some other lenders, Ascent Students Loans has built its own database to analyze how much a prospective borrower is expected to make after graduation based on the school and major. This database allows Ascent to help guide students toward more responsible financial decisions by approving only loan amounts that students can realistically afford after they graduate.

Additionally, recently the University of Texas released a first-of-its-kind public database of graduate earnings designed to help future students make informed investment decisions based on cost, campus, and selected major.[2] Hopefully other universities will follow this lead.

Limited information isn't the only issue. We also need to acknowledge and address the disparity in access to financial planning and financial literacy resources across the student population. Students who self-identify in more at-risk populations—first-generation students or those from lower socioeconomic backgrounds—often face barriers to accessing available funds and resources that other students do not. Ensuring more students are filling out the Free Application for Federal Aid (FAFSA) form is a key first step.

A college degree is undoubtedly still the best route to a well-paying, rewarding job and a high quality of life. Taking out a student loan doesn't need to be a burden. But it is only when students and families ask the right questions and gather the right information that they can turn college into worthwhile investment. Borrowing money to go to college with no realistic expectation of how the funds are to be paid back seems to happen too often with student loans.

While we wait for our legislators to act, private loan companies, universities, and nonprofits can work together to ensure outcomes-based data is available so students can make smart decisions when choosing colleges and majors and financing their education.

MY STORY

From Herding Goats to Graduating from College

Mohamed O. Mohamed

I VIVIDLY REMEMBER THE MOMENT I LANDED AT THE JOHN F. KEN-nedy Airport in New York City. It was a cold, crisp winter afternoon in December 2010. The beautiful landscape of America that I had so long heard of and imagined was covered by white snow, and three jackets weren't enough to prevent me from shivering. Everything was foreign. I remember trying to use a language I could barely speak to find the toilet. When I asked the airport workers, they pointed to the restrooms, but I kept looking elsewhere, thinking, "I don't need a place to rest! I just need a toilet to use."

The sterile toilets were a far cry from the makeshift huts I was so famil-iar with. I had been born into a nomadic pastoralist family in rural Somalia during the 1991 civil war. This war had devastated my country—killing hun-dreds of thousands and causing millions more to flee their homes. As pas-toralists, we moved frequently, but during the war we had to move around even more to avoid the conflicts between clan militias and to ensure that our animals always had fresh water and pasture. By the age of five, I could already herd goats and had begun to herd camels, which meant that I had

Mohammed was born in Somalia and came to the United States as a refugee in 2010. He was contacted through mutual acquaintances at Indiana University and agreed to share his story. In January 2017, President Trump by executive order banned further refugees from Muslim countries, including Somalia; the U.S. Department of State had vetted thousands of Somalian applicants in the Dadaad refugee camp in Kenya, but their visas were either never issued or cancelled as a result of the 2017 ban.

gained a man's responsibility. Camels determined everything for our men: a man's wealth was measured by how many camels he owned, his success by how generous he was in giving them away, and his work ethic by how well he cared for them. However, that simple life, measured by the number of healthy camels I owned, did not appeal to me, and I certainly couldn't picture myself repeating the cycle by raising children the same way.

All I knew were those camels and the people I grew up around; I actually thought that the world ended at the mountains behind our village, as if beyond them lay nothing but a vast blue sky. So you can imagine the jolt I felt the first time I sat in a car. I had burned my hand severely, and my grandmother's traditional medicine failed, so she decided to take me to the hospital. I remember sitting in her lap and asking why the trees were moving so fast toward us as we sped through the woods.

At the age of nine, I ran away from my camels and toward the city, thinking I was headed for the heart of abundance and the epitome of civilization. It didn't take long for reality to set in. The city was indeed the root of all evil. It was from there that all death and destruction flowed in angry waves. The clan militias battled for control, and thousands died, while many others fled to escape the horrors of the war. I saw dead people in the streets, homes burnt to ashes, stores looted, and families torn apart.

My own father was a victim of that carnage. At age thirteen, I became an orphan, having already lost my mother at age five. The moment I stood over my dad's grave and promised that I would never cry again was painful yet defining for me. I asked myself what else could happen for things to get worse. The answer was almost as simple as the life I had left behind: there was nothing worse. I reflected on all the people we had lost in the civil war—uncles, cousins, friends, family, and now my father. "This is it," I thought. "I have nothing left to lose."

But no matter the depth of pain and tragedy, life will continue, and people will move on with their lives. As is customary with orphans, my younger brother and I were sent off to live with other relatives. I moved to the capital city of Mogadishu with my aunt while my brother moved in with another aunt in a neighboring village. Unfortunately, the bigger the city, the bigger the problems. More wars, more death, more destruction. It was obvious that things were getting bad, but people tried to ignore the carnage raging around them. Many preferred to stay in their war-ravaged homes rather than resigning themselves to life in a refugee camp. But no one expected Ethiopia to invade Somalia and terrorist groups to gain a foothold in my country. In that ideological war, young men like me were the targets. If we survived the bullets, it was hard to avoid the opposing parties competing to recruit us as soldiers. That was when I finally decided to cross an international border and move to Dabaab, Kenya, to what was known as the world's largest refugee camp. The people who live there know it better as the world's biggest prison.

The camp is incomprehensibly massive. Close to half a million people lived there at that time, most of them destitute families who couldn't afford to live elsewhere. The United Nations and its supporting partners provide the minimum necessities, but life in the camp is harsh nonetheless. Dabaab is located in a semidesert area in the northeastern region of Kenya, where it's usually hot during the day and cold at night. People would sometimes walk for miles to get water, and electricity and sewage systems were unheard of. People made their homes using trees and grass, which caused further conflict. Nomads in the area warned refugees not to cut down trees since they provided nourishment for their animals. I saw my fellow refugees killed for cutting down trees, and the environmental degradation caused by the camp has had a terrible effect on the nomads and their animals, who have survived off that land for as long as they can remember.

At the camp, it's hard to get out without paying insurmountable bribes. People aren't allowed to go to other Kenyan cities even for health-related issues. There are few schools, and the highest level of education one can obtain in the camp is high school. After that, there's nothing: no job, no higher education. The refugee camp has been open since 1991, the beginning of Somalia's civil war, meaning that there are people in the camp who were born there and now have their own children who have never left the camp. I thought my life had been narrow and repetitive growing up as a nomad, but it was nothing compared to living in the camp.

Life in Dabaab was boring, and the days were very long. There was nothing to do from dawn to dusk. Few attended schools, and even fewer went to work. A typical day for most consisted of waking up in the morning and waiting around for the sun to set again. Day after day after day. People watched their lives slipping away before their eyes, watched their kids slip into the same numb awareness of perpetual nothingness. When there are no choices left for you, you lose the power to decide what your tomorrow will look like.

Life gets meaningless, but the people in the refugee camp have hopes. Some hope that their country will someday become peaceful again so they can return to their homes. Others hope that the world will stretch its arms open and accept them. Still others work hard day in and day out in hope that their children won't face the same fate that has stolen their lives. As the war continues in Somalia, and days stretch into weeks, months, and years, each passing moment dulls that hope, weakens it, and turns the whole world gray.

Very few lucky ones get the once-in-a-lifetime chance to resettle in another country, which helps people like me realize that the power to shape our future still rests in our hands. Getting the chance to live and study in another country, especially a country like the United States, is truly a second chance at life, a ray of sunlight in my gray world. For the first time in my life, I realized that I had the power to make a decision for myself. I could now go to school or work or choose between simple options like cooking or going to a restaurant if I wanted to. After living as a refugee, where no one decided what happened next, this was an alien feeling.

Two of my cousins and I were among the lucky ones chosen for that incredible second chance. We all went to Indiana as refugees in late 2010 with nothing in our possession. We left everyone behind, including my little brother. That was when I had my first encounter with Exodus Refugee Immigration. They welcomed me at the airport in my three coats and took me to a well-furnished apartment in the north side of Indianapolis. Compared to my makeshift house in the camp, the apartment we settled in first was like a castle with everything I ever wanted . . . like ice cream, TV, internet, and, of course, plenty of food. Exodus took great care of me for the next three months while I acquired my documents and found my first job. My existence evolved quickly from a life of quiet resignation to a life of freedom and choices. I felt like a prisoner who had finally been loosed from his chains.

Now that I was welcome in the land of opportunity, I wanted to do something for those who weren't as lucky as I was. I wanted to pay back and forward. I wanted to help the thousands who remained desperate—to make sure that my little cousins got the education they deserved, that my little brother, suffering from polio since birth, got the care he so desperately needed, and that my aunt got the medical attention she had sought for so long. I wanted to tell my friends that life doesn't have to be filled with long, meaningless days that fade away to nothing. I wanted to yell that there is a light at the end of the tunnel and that the power over their lives would one day be restored to them, and they, too, would become the chiefs of their own destinies.

When I got my first paycheck from my first warehouse job, I didn't know what to do with it. There were so many things I wanted to do and so little I could actually do. I had to rewind and reevaluate my situation. I realized that an opportunity for me didn't automatically become an opportunity for everyone else I cared about. I was told that my brother and our other family members would be able to join us, but after seven years I have yet to see that promise fulfilled.

I was in a position where I wanted to help others, but I needed to help myself first. After a long time contemplating my first big decision ever, I came to the conclusion that the best I could do was take full advantage of the opportunity I had been given. So I decided to go to college—something no one in my family had ever done. I decided to do whatever it would take to get an education, which I believed could end the intergenerational cycle of poverty. I took advantage of state and federal programs to take some English classes at a local community college and subsequently became a full-time student. I started without any plans of what I wanted to study and without an understanding of the meaning of having a major. I took classes that my advisor suggested and a few others that sounded interesting to me, like philosophy and sociology. School officials let me make my mistakes and change my mind as much as I wanted. At one point, I wanted to study computer science because it sounded complicated, then I changed to petroleum engineering in the hope of going back home one day and taking my place in making Somalia a petroleum-exporting country. But after many trials and errors, I ended up at Indiana University and majored in public financial management.

Although I was working throughout my college years, my income was barely enough to cover my rent and personal expenses. Government grants and merit-based scholarships covered the bulk of my education expenses. On top of being the first in my family to go to college—which meant having little understanding of the education system as well as its value—I am also a Muslim, and taking an interest-bearing loan is prohibited in my religion. Therefore, many students like me would simply go without a college education if there were no funds for it.

After years of trial and error, exploring uncharted territories, and learning a lot about myself along the way, I graduated from the School of

Public and Environmental Affairs at Indiana University in Bloomington with a degree in public financial management. This would not have been possible without generous financial aid.

Today, several years after my arrival in the United States from the world's largest refugee camp, I have my college degree, and I am very proud of it. I worked for the state government of Indiana as a budget analyst for a while and am now an investor relations and corporate responsibility analyst at one of the biggest corporations in the state of Indiana, Eli Lilly and Company. Indiana is the state that welcomed me to the land of opportunity and that opened my eyes to infinite possibilities. This state and this country helped me to reach beyond what I had imagined was possible.

Moving forward, I plan to get my master's in economic development; then, hopefully, I will take what I have learned here in my second home country and use it to influence change and contribute to poverty elimination programs and initiatives back in my first homeland. I think people like me are the best ambassadors for American values. I always challenge rumors about the values and principles that the people of this country and their government stand for, although some dismiss me as westernized.

My life has been transformed from the simple life of camel herding that I once knew. My perspective has widened, my views have evolved, and my endurance, confidence, and compassion have grown. Looking back, I can't think of anything I could have done better. What once seemed to be a risky choice turned out to be the best decision of my life. Resettling in the United States as a refugee not only made me the first in my family to graduate from college, but it also opened many doors for me. On my fifth anniversary of being in the United States, I became a US citizen. Just weeks after that, I won a scholarship to study in Washington, DC, and work as an intern for the US Treasury Department. A year later, I graduated with honors and was chosen as a commencement speaker for my graduating class. Then I won another scholarship to study at King's College in central London.

Sometimes I reflect on what my life might have looked like if I had never been given the opportunity to come to the United States. I quickly look to my cousins and my younger brother, who remain in the refugee camp to this day. I think of my friends and classmates who spent countless hours with me mapping our route out of the camp. It saddens me to see how dramatically different their lives are from mine. They still count the long, lifeless days. They still lose hope with every inching movement of the sun. The only difference between them and me is that I was lucky and they were not. While I live in the land of the free, they languish in the world's largest refugee camp.

My story is not meant to draw sympathy. Rather, I implore you to consider the power each of us has to change the world. We may not have the ability to change the whole world, but you can change the world of someone as hopeless as I once was. There are plenty of people—good people filled with hopes and dreams—who want to contribute to the greater good, people who could become the next innovators and astronomers, those who might never realize their potential because their lives are stolen from them. I know I have said several times that I am lucky, and to an extent I still believe that to be true. But I believe that we can do better. We have so much power to help more people, support them on their endeavors, change their world, and welcome them into the opportunities that we take for granted every day. Change the world by changing someone else's world for the better. It's possible.

PART 2
COLLEGE COSTS AND FINANCIAL AID

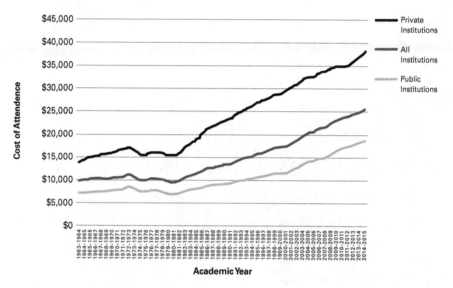

Figure 5.1. Overall cost increases at public and private institutions, 1963–2015.

5

WHY COLLEGE COSTS SO MUCH

TALK TO ALMOST ANY YOUNG PERSON FROM A MIDDLE-INCOME FAM-
ily and currently enrolled in or recently graduated from college, and
you will hear a common refrain: the cost is too high, and the resulting
student debt can be crippling. Data from the National Center for Education Statistics (NCES) supports what students know from their experience.
NCES information reveals dramatic increases in the cost of education in
recent years. For the 2017–18 academic year, the average cost for all four-
year public institutions in the United States, including tuition and room
and board, was $21,790 per year; for private institutions it was $49,260 per
year.[1] By comparison, in 1980, the average cost was $2,550 for public schools
and $5,590 for private schools. This translates to almost a 6 percent aver-
age annual increase across all institutions for almost four decades. Incomes
have not kept up with these rising costs: average wages increased on average 3.7 percent during the same time frame,[2] leading to an ever-increasing
affordability gap. The consumer price index increased only 2.96 percent per
year during this period, underscoring how much the increase in college
costs exceeded the increase in general consumer prices.[3] Figure 5.1 depicts
educational costs over a longer time frame: total costs began escalating significantly around 1980, and they have continued the upward trajectory in
the decades that have followed.[4]

Categorical Cost Breakdown

The costs of attending college can be broken down into two main components: tuition, and room and board. Tuition includes the academic costs of attendance and associated fees and is used to compensate faculty and staff and pay for a variety of student support services. Room and board include the costs of housing in institution-owned dormitories and the cost of meals for each student.

Across all institutions, the increases in tuition have been the most dramatic. In the 1980–81 school year, the average cost of tuition for public four-year colleges was only $800 per academic year. For private four-year institutions, the average was $3,620. In 2017–18, the average annual cost of tuition was $9,980 at public institutions and $34,700 at private institutions. Over thirty-seven years, this is a compound annual increase of over 7.0 percent at public institutions and 6.3 percent at comparable private schools. The increases in public school tuition, traditionally the most affordable option for students, were significantly greater than those in private school tuition. No other institutional revenues or expenses have kept pace with the rate of tuition increases. These increases are about twice the increase in the consumer price index during the same time frame.

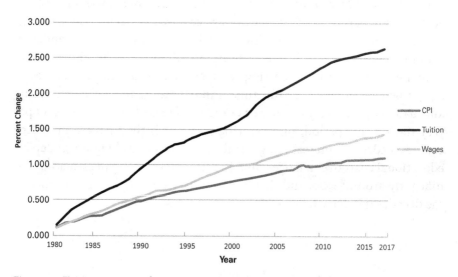

Figure 5.2. Tuition, wages, and Consumer Price Index (CPI) annual cumulative percent increases, 1980–2017.

The comparison of tuition increases with wage growth and consumer price index changes is depicted in figure 5.2.[5] The ever-widening gap between the cost of school tuition and wages or income is stark and demonstrates why college has become so unaffordable for so many.

The cost of room and board has also increased, although typically at a lower rate. In 1980–81, the overall cost of room and board was $1,750 at public schools and $1,970 at private schools. By 2017–18, this number had increased to $10,810 at public schools and $12,290 at private schools, an increase of about 5 percent per year.[6]

Why have tuition costs increased? There are five potential factors that could contribute to rising tuition costs at universities: (1) government funding per student is declining, (2) professors' salaries are not rising significantly and are largely offset by using others to teach, (3) administrative costs are rising significantly, (4) improvements in campus infrastructure are underway everywhere, and (5) more students need financial aid. Each is addressed below.

Government Funding Per Student Is Declining

While seemingly two separate issues, changes in government funding and enrollment numbers must be viewed together, as there is an inverse relationship between enrollment numbers and public funding per student. Increases in government funding generally have not kept up with increases in student enrollment, leading to declining levels of per-student funding.

State funding to universities varies greatly from state to state, but state funding overall has consistently declined as a percentage of university revenues. Total funding has increased and decreased with the economy and available tax revenues over time. From 2008 to 2013, states decreased funding for universities by an average of 28 percent.[7] Since 2013, state funding has increased but in minimal amounts. The statistics for 2017–18 indicate an average increase of 1.6 percent, with many states continuing to decrease funding.[8]

Across all four-year reporting public universities, state appropriations fell from about 24 percent of university revenues in 2007–8 to 16 percent in 2016–17.[9] University enrollment at comparable institutions increased during the same time frame by more than one million students,[10] resulting in a 24 percent decline in per-student state funding.[11] The decline in state funding appears to account for slightly less than half of the tuition increases incurred during the same period.

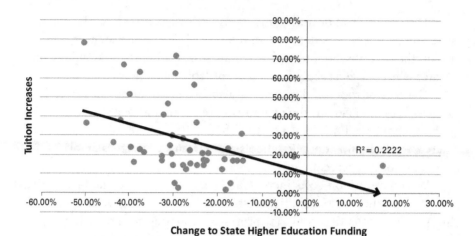

Figure 5.3. State cuts to per student higher education funding versus tuition increases, fiscal years 2008–13. *Data from Center on Budget Policy and Priorities.*

Traditionally, states provided much of the funding for public universities—especially university operating costs. This is no longer typical. Indiana University, for example, received less than 18 percent of its funds from state appropriations as of 2017.[12] The University of North Carolina reports that state sources provide less than 20 percent of their operating budget.[13] These levels are typical of current state university systems. State funding for universities was cut especially dramatically beginning in 2008, requiring increases in tuition to make up the shortfall.

The data in figure 5.3 from the Center on Budget Policy and Priorities and reprinted in the *Atlantic* demonstrates how state cuts in higher education spending closely correlate with tuition increases. As states reduce per-student funding, public universities increase tuition to make up the funding gap.

In the decades prior to 1980 especially, national policy supported increased enrollment and provided federal funding to match. In 1958, at the height of the Cold War, Congress passed the National Defense Education Act (NDEA) to "help ensure that highly trained individuals would be available to help America compete with the Soviet Union."[14] The NDEA included financial support for colleges and college students. Simultaneously, the federal government opened opportunities to the general public through what is known as the Federal Perkins Loan Program. More federal legislation, in the form of the Civil Rights Act of 1964,[15] the Higher Education Act of 1965,[16] and the Higher Education Amendments of 1972,[17] increased college access further, particularly for women and minorities. Not only were women and minorities no longer barred from enrollment, but special federal funds were allocated to support them. The greater availability of government funding likely reduced the need for universities to raise tuition.

College enrollment has increased substantially in recent decades, boosted first by the post–World War II influx, supportive government policies and financial assistance, college affordability, and then the baby boomer generation's coming of age. According to data from NCES, enrollment in four-year postgraduate institutions reached 10.0 million for the first time in 1974. By 1980, enrollment was about 12.1 million and rose steadily to approximately 13.8 million in 1990 and 15.3 million in 2000. Enrollment in 2019 was about 20.0 million, which is down from a peak of 21.0 million in 2010.[18]

While state funding for universities has fallen, federal funding has increased significantly, mostly in the form of student grants and loans as more need-eligible students attended colleges with ever-increasing tuition and attendance costs. Between 2007–8 and 2015–16, federal expenditures to students—primarily Pell Grants and veterans' educational benefits—increased by 11 percent in real terms. This level of increase exceeded the increase in the number of college students.[19] However, the average grant per student did not keep pace with the rise in college attendance cost. For example, the maximum Pell Grant amount increased about 2.8 percent per year since 1993–94.[20] As colleges have raised tuition, the government has increased the amount of total student aid but limited the maximum amount granted per person, contributing to an explosion of student debt.

Other sources of federal funding for universities have also declined, and often federal funds are tied to specific research grants or programs and are not available for university operations. This condition has contributed to increased tuition to fund operations.

With increasing student enrollment and fewer federal resources to support university operations, per-student funding (excluding financial aid to students) has especially declined. With more students enrolled in higher education institutions, federal and state funding has been increasingly stretched. According to an article in the *New York Times*, total state appropriations per student peaked in 1990.[21]

Since 2013–14, tuition at private universities has risen faster than at public institutions. Logically, private school funding should not be as affected by diminished state funds, but private schools may be affected by lagging private donations and federal funding constraints. Some believe that schools also increase tuition when competitors increase tuition because they fear a lower-price education may be perceived as a lower-quality education. Mitch Daniels, president of Purdue University, lamented that some people associate the sticker price with quality. They believe that if school A costs more than B, it must be a better school.[22] The same universities often discount the quoted tuition rates with generous scholarships and financial aid for need-based and merit students.

Professors' Salaries Are Not Rising Significantly and Are Largely Offset by Using Others to Teach

Some believe the increase in the cost of higher education is due to rising salaries for faculty. This explanation suggests that in a competitive market, measured in part by the ratings system published by *US News & World Report* and others, schools compete for the best-known and best-regarded professors to enhance their ratings and relative attractiveness to top students.

Research reported in the *Chronicle of Higher Education* highlights changes in full-time faculty salaries across all four-year institutions from 2003 to 2015.[23] According to this data, a full-time professor at a public institution made an average of $110,213 in 2003, with numbers adjusted for inflation. This same professor, working at the same institution, made $111,053 in 2015, an increase of only 0.8 percent. An associate professor at a four-year public institution made an average of $81,033 in 2003 and $80,012 in 2015, a decrease of approximately 1.0 percent.

Despite a common belief that faculty salaries increase steadily along with the cost of living, this appears to be inaccurate. According to California State University (CSU) system data, rising student tuition and fees do not correlate with increases in faculty pay. In fact, in a release by the California Faculty Association (CFA), it was noted, "From 2005 to 2015, faculty salaries have remained flat, yet tuition and fees have been steadily increasing. Tuition and fees for CSU students have increased by a whopping 283% since 2000."[24] A secondary report states, "Over the past decade—in good times and bad, whether state funding was up or down, when tuition was raised and when it wasn't—CSU expenditures on faculty salaries have remained essentially flat."[25]

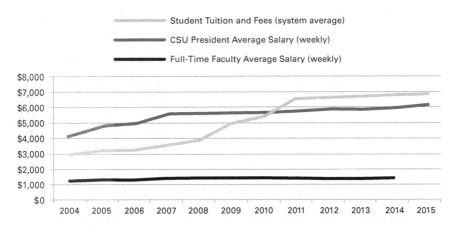

Figure 5.4. CSU student costs versus weekly salary for executives and faculty, 2004–15.

It appears more likely that total professor compensation per student is actually declining. The data points to a change in teaching philosophy at many universities to reduce faculty costs. In general, over the past decades, there has been a dramatic shift from using full-time tenured or tenure-track professors to using part-time or "contingent" (also known as "adjunct") professors to minimize costs of compensation for academic faculty. In recent years, full-time faculty represent only slightly more than 50 percent of total faculty at universities.[26]

A 2015 report published by CNBC suggests "teaching salaries, one of the biggest single line items, have remained relatively flat";[27] similarly, a report from the American Institute of Research (AIR) emphasizes the frequent use of contingent faculty as a cost-saving factor:

Over the past several decades, colleges and universities have increasingly turned to contingent faculty (i.e., non-tenure-track faculty)—and, in particular, part-time faculty—to meet their instructional demands. Since 1975, the number of contingent faculty has nearly doubled as a proportion of all instructional staff, while the proportion of tenured and tenure-track faculty accounted for at least half of all instructional faculty across all types of institutions of higher education. The growing reliance on contingent faculty is commonly viewed as a cost-savings measure. Full-time contingent instructors earn 26 percent less per hour, and part-time contingent workers earn 64 percent less per hour than their tenured or tenure-track counterparts. Furthermore, contingent faculty typically receive fewer or no benefits. Salaries of tenure and tenure-track faculty combined range from $60,000 to $100,000 per year, whereas the average annual salary of full-time contingent faculty is

$47,500. Part-time faculty, who frequently are compensated per class or semester, earn an average of only $2,700 per course, without benefits.[28]

It is unclear how switching to untenured faculty for teaching affects the quality of course instruction. It probably depends on the specific individuals and the nature of the course. But it is clear that using adjunct staff reduces costs, and faculty compensation does not appear to explain why university attendance costs have risen so much, as further depicted in figure 5.4.[29]

Administrative Costs Are Rising Significantly

As already noted, studies indicate that the increased use of part-time faculty has decreased compensation costs for teachers. However, instead of reallocating those savings to reduce tuition, monies saved on faculty compensation are used to cover other expenses, including increased costs in administration and student services. In fact, according to data released by the Department of Education, "administrative positions at colleges and universities grew by 60 percent between 1993 and 2009."[30] This growth was ten times the rate of growth of tenured faculty positions. Additionally, research conducted at Cal Poly Pomona indicates a 221 percent increase in the total number of administrators in the CSU system, from 3,800 in 1975 to 12,183 in 2008, or 4 percent a year.[31]

During the academic year 2015–16, only 28.5 percent of a public university's expenditures were for instruction, including faculty salaries. The proportion of university expenditures for instruction and research has declined in recent years while the proportion spent on academic support and student services has increased.[32]

Administrative functions that require more staff and greater expense and contribute to tuition increases cover a wide variety of people and jobs. Virtually all university students arrive on campus with computers, smartphones, and other technology devices, for example. In response, universities have greatly increased their technology systems and administrative support.

Student services, including funding for student-led activities, student support, tutoring, disability services, and psychological support services, received increased investment across all types of institutions. Public four-year colleges and universities boosted student services by 18 to 21 percent, and private four-year institutions increased such services by 23 to 26 percent.[33]

The increases in student enrollment and financial aid have also contributed to the need for a new professional class of university administrators. Trained professionals are needed to manage the amount of federal money designated for higher education grants and loans. Institutions must find ways to sort students into eligible programs, and government rules, regulations, and compliance paperwork and reports can be extensive.

A typical complaint, especially by elected officials, is the higher salaries for executives and upper-level management at universities. Universities seeking qualified administrative staff must compete with private industry for such staff and offer competitive compensation. Ironically, for nonadministrative staff (i.e., faculty) the university needs to compete only with other universities, which typically pay less than corporations.

Universities are also beginning to use part-time administrative staff to save money, which appears to have slowed the rate of increase in costs but is not likely to reverse the trend. An *Inside Higher Education* article explains that public institutions are employing "substantially more part-time faculty and professional staff, such as employees who work in admission, human resources, information technology and athletic departments."[34]

Some believe university executives have done a poor job controlling administrative cost increases. There is no compelling data to support or reject the notion that such costs have increased unnecessarily. In private business, unless costs are controlled or offset by profit and earnings gains, the executives likely would be terminated for poor performance. Universities are not measured in terms of profit and earnings, so the necessity of administrative cost increases likely will be debated without resolution.

Another complaint often expressed is the increased cost of athletic programs, especially higher salaries for coaches at major institutions. In some cases, sports facilities and even salary supplements for coaches are paid by alumni and related sports foundations that operate outside the university budgets. However, salaries for major college coaches in the primary revenue-generating sports—men's football and basketball—have escalated greatly. Jim Harbaugh signed a seven-year contract to coach University of Michigan football in December 2014. He earns approximately $7.5 million per year. His compensation package was eclipsed by Nick Saban's contract at the University of Alabama.[35] In basketball, Duke's Mike Krzyzewski makes around $9 million, and Kentucky's John Calipari makes about $7.5 million per year.[36]

Despite financial support from alumni and foundations, costly athletic facilities and salaries are also paid for in part by added student fees. In 2014, students at thirty-two schools paid approximately $125 million in athletic fees, according to a survey by the *Washington Post*.[37] Increasing student fees to pay for athletics is a common practice. Florida State University charges students a $237 fee but permits free student admittance to football games. The University of Virginia's $657 student fee for athletics generates over $13 million annually to pay for part of the increase in athletics spending. The University of Maryland charges $406, and Rutgers charges its students $326.

University administrators generally believe a competitive sports program is important for generating sports-related revenues, attracting students, and securing donors to contribute to all areas of the university. The schools referenced above all generate tens of millions of dollars in sports-related revenues.[38] Successful sports teams also seem to trigger more donations from alumni and more applications from qualified prospective students.[39] And successful college sports teams add to the enjoyment of attending college for many. But the significant funding required for high-profile teams, coaches, and facilities also adds to the cost of a college education.

Administrative costs associated with increased scope and services appear to drive some higher tuition costs. What is unclear is how such costs may be reduced or constrained in light of student demands and competitive educational environments.

Improvements in Campus Infrastructure Are Underway Almost Everywhere

If one visits nearly any higher education institution in the country, one can see recent improvements made to the campus infrastructure. Point Loma Nazarene University, in San Diego, California, for example, recently constructed a new science and technology building. Claremont McKenna College, in Claremont, California, recently opened a state-of-the-art athletics facility. Institutions across the country are making improvements in the quality of their campuses, from improving technology in classrooms to improving the state of dormitories and campus aesthetics in general. In fact, in some states, state legislation requires that higher education capital improvements will be funded. For example, New Jersey's 1999 Higher

Education Capital Improvement Fund Act states, "In order for New Jersey students and businesses to be competitive with their peers in today's global and technological society, the public and private sectors must continually take steps to preserve and enhance the facilities and technology at our colleges and universities. To do otherwise would result in the loss of potential students to more technologically advanced and well-developed and maintained institutions in other states."[40] Improved infrastructure has become a necessity in today's competitive higher education market.

A report from *Inside Higher Ed* indicates that "spending on auxiliary developments, such as dormitories, rose $524 per student at non-research colleges" between 2001 and 2011.[41] College students typically expect better housing conditions than prior generations of students. In response, universities across the country are constructing new or remodeling older dorms. Smaller apartment clusters with common facilities are replacing massive, impersonal dorms. Healthier and more varied food service options are being developed, as are convenient services in residential living areas.

Many campus buildings are old, having been built in the 1950s in response to the post–World War II boom in student enrollment. These outdated facilities are being replaced at significant cost, although often part of the cost is offset with donor contributions. It appears to be easier, according to some university officials I have interviewed, to raise private donations to build facilities rather than to fund operating costs or student aid.

Conditions, teaching methods, and academic knowledge have all evolved, also requiring new facilities. Davidson College recently constructed a new science building to replace single-purpose buildings housing science departments such as chemistry and biology. The new building allows scientists from different disciplines to work in close proximity to solve multidisciplinary problems.

In response to dramatic industry changes brought about by the internet and digital media, in 2014 Indiana University combined the school of journalism, the telecommunications department, and the film studies program into a new media school. This necessitated redeveloping a building to accommodate journalism classes as well as a TV studio and advanced technology.

Indiana University also started a new School of Global and International Studies, bringing together faculty and students from many disciplines that are not limited to a single geographic region. This necessitated a new building in 2015 serving five hundred students, faculty, and support staff with interactive classrooms, breakout rooms, and well-equipped conference rooms with advanced audiovisual capabilities, facilitating a high degree of collaboration not possible in older buildings with traditional classroom configurations.

A recent trend in university construction is development of innovative facilities responding to contemporary trends in business, research, and science. Such facilities include innovation centers, entrepreneurial centers, business incubators, and science-related collaborative facilities. They frequently rely on common-use spaces instead of classrooms and offices. According to architect Jay Silverberg, "The single-purpose building is now a thing of the past."[42]

In recent years, for example, Clemson University opened a seventy-thousand-square-foot innovation center; the University of Pennsylvania opened its fifty-eight-thousand-square-foot Pennovation Works, which includes a business incubator facility; and Virginia Commonwealth University opened its eighty-thousand-square-foot Cabell Learning Commons. Wayne State University developed its $93 million Integrative Biosciences Center to facilitate collaboration among science disciplines. Almost every university is designing and developing new facilities in response to changes in social, academic, and workforce requirements.

More Students Need Financial Aid

Many schools have embraced a need-blind admissions policy, leading to the admission of more students who need financial aid to attend. Top schools, including both public and private universities, are significantly increasing the number of need-eligible students.[43] To the extent that government aid does not fill the need, the schools frequently offer school-based scholarships, effectively discounting their listed tuition prices for some and raising prices for others.

Other schools may lack the financial resources to offer need-blind admissions policies. By potentially admitting fewer need-eligible students and more full-tuition students, schools could reduce financial requirements, although such action would clearly discriminate against students from poor families. Similarly, there has been a significant rise in the number of foreign students admitted to US universities; China is the largest source. Foreign students from all countries typically pay full out-of-state tuition, and many schools also charge extra fees. Recently, the number of foreign students has dropped for the first time in many years as US relations with China and other countries have declined.[44] If this continues, tuition for US students may need to increase further to make up for the shortfall of full-paying foreign students.

Conclusion

The forces behind the rising costs of higher education in the United States are varied and complex and—despite great concern from students, their families, and the general public—show no signs of abating. Major contributing factors are greater administrative costs associated with increased student services, declining government support on a per-student basis for operations and research funding, more students who require financial assistance, competitive athletic programs, better facilities and improved infrastructure in response to technological advancements, student expectations, competitive posture, and the need to update aging facilities. These cost increases are only partly offset by the increased use of less expensive contingent or adjunct professors and admittance of more full-tuition students, including foreign and out-of-state students.

6

THE HISTORY OF FINANCIAL AID FOR
COLLEGE STUDENTS

O N NOVEMBER 8, 1965, PRESIDENT LYNDON B. JOHNSON WALKED into the gymnasium of Southwest Texas State College, now Texas State University, in San Marcos, Texas, and signed the Higher Education Act (HEA) of 1965. This law designated federal funds to provide financial assistance for students who otherwise would not be able to afford higher education. In doing so, President Johnson signaled the United States' commitment to the importance of higher education: "For the individual, education is the path to achievement and fulfillment," he declared. "For the nation, it is a path to a society that is not only free but civilized; and for the world, it is the path to peace—for it is education that places reason over force."[1]

History of Financial Aid in America

Historically, education has been an important path to upward class mobility. In the middle ages, the most common models of financial support for education were apprenticeship, in which students worked for their teachers in exchange for instruction and patronage, and patronage or charity from wealthy families, who paid for poor students' education as a form of religious penance. By the seventeenth century, the patronage model spread to colonial America.[2] Alexander Hamilton, America's first treasury secretary,

The author thanks Indiana University student Samantha Young for assistance with research and the preparation of drafts of this chapter.

was a beneficiary of this type of financial aid. In the fall of 1772, a hurricane swept through St. Croix in the British West Indies. Hamilton published a letter describing the destruction to the island and, in doing so, gained the attention of many prominent members of his society. Local businessmen started a fund that was used to send Hamilton to attend university in New York.[3]

For centuries, the patronage model held sway, meaning that students with the desire for an education but no funds with which to pursue it sought wealthy members of society willing to support their studies. However, some colleges and universities also became the recipients of endowments from wealthy citizens. In the post–Revolutionary War era of the United States, the idea of a philanthropic scholarship was fairly new but quickly became popular. Universities began to open lending agencies providing early variations on student loans. Financial aid in the United States continued to expand and change.

Until the post–World War II period, financial aid was still very much based on a philanthropic or patronage model. The return of American soldiers from World War II, and the social adjustments that followed, including significantly more students, changed the model. The G.I. Bill—formally known as the Servicemen's Readjustment Act of 1944—provided benefits to servicemen regarding unemployment, low-interest housing loans, and education. In 1944, 1.15 million students were enrolled in higher education. By 1954, only ten years after the Servicemen's Readjustment Act was implemented, 2.45 million students were enrolled in higher education.[4]

In 1954, the College Board opened the College Scholarship service, which matched low-income and minority students with colleges. Their method of having students fill out a profile form and then matching them with a college and aid package is considered an early precursor to the Free Application for Federal Student Aid, or FAFSA, which is the current primary method of determining student financial need.[5]

The Servicemen's Readjustment Act paved the way for more students to receive higher education, and it also changed the structure of the institutions providing it. The socioeconomic makeup of higher education became more diverse, and hundreds of thousands of Americans who would previously have been barred from entering higher education due to lack of funds returned from military service to form a newly educated citizenry. When Lyndon B. Johnson signed the HEA into law, he effectively committed the US government to an ongoing investment in the education of its citizens, an investment that was tightly connected to issues of national defense and security: education, after all, according to President Johnson, "is the path to peace." For a century that had seen warfare on a level previously unimaginable, this was a heady promise.

It cannot be overstated how significant the Higher Education Act of 1965 was for the evolution of student financial aid. The HEA has been reauthorized nine times since its establishment, and still regulates how federal aid is allocated.[6] Title IV of the HEA delineates the terms of financial need and the grants that will be provided to students whose situations fall under those terms;[7] Title IV also requires universities receiving federal funding for students to maintain certain accreditation standards as well as to report data on their operations. With this act, the allocation of federal aid became a method by which the US government assured that universities maintain standards and remain accountable for the quality of education they provide, but added new administrative burdens.

Contemporary Financial Aid

The face of financial aid in the United States has changed significantly over the years, but the underlying principle is still the same. In short, it is money that has been provided to a student in order to assist in payment of his or her education. Today, there are many different types of financial aid. Student aid can come from federal, state, individual school, or private sources. It can be provided as a grant, which is typically not repaid, or as a loan, which requires repayment.[8]

In the fall of 2015, undergraduate students accounted for 85 percent of the approximate 21 million postsecondary students. Overall, students are receiving more aid today than students received several years ago. Between the 1998–99 school years and the 2018–19 school years, total federal, state, institutional, and private aid increased from $103.5 billion to $260.6 billion. In the same time frame, the average amount of aid per full-time equivalent (FTE) undergraduate student increased from $8,680 to $15,210.[9] This increase in aid was necessary because while the cost of college was increasing, family incomes were not rising at a comparable rate, creating an affordability gap.

The process of applying for aid varies depending on the type of aid. Eligibility is determined by the organization administering the aid. For federal aid, students must submit the FAFSA, which is administered by the office of Federal Student Aid within the US Department of Education. The FAFSA determines a student's expected contribution to the cost of attendance based on reported income. This amount is subtracted from the cost of attendance, and the remainder determines how much need-based aid the student qualifies for. Non-need-based aid is determined by subtracting the financial aid already awarded to the student, including need-based aid and private aid, from the total cost of attendance. While a student may be offered multiple types of aid, all federal aid is offered in one financial aid package typically administered by the school of attendance.[10]

Federal aid is also affected by a student's eligibility. For the majority of federal aid programs, a student must demonstrate need. A student must also be a US citizen or an eligible noncitizen, such as a US permanent resident, and maintain satisfactory academic progress. The aid must be used only for educational purposes, and the student cannot be in default on a federal student loan. The student must also demonstrate that he or she is qualified to obtain a college or career school education by having a high school diploma or a general educational development certificate.[11] Federal aid comes in two primary forms: grants and loans.

Federal Grants

Grants are financial aid that does not have to be repaid and is typically need-based. Different grants have varying award amounts and criteria.[12] One of the largest federal grant programs is the Federal Pell Grant, first established in the 1980 reauthorization of the HEA and named after Senator Claiborne Pell.[13] This grant is awarded to undergraduate students who have not obtained a bachelor's or professional degree. The amount awarded changes on a case-to-case basis, depending on financial need, cost of attendance, status as a full- or part-time student, and length of attendance during the academic year. Other student aid does not affect the award amount of Federal Pell Grants.[14]

Federal Pell Grants are paid through the school of attendance, and a student cannot receive a Federal Pell Grant for more than twelve semesters. In order to pay for the Federal Pell Grants, the US Department of Education will send enough money to each school to cover all eligible students at that school. While the amount varies from year to year, during the 2016–17 award year the maximum award value was $5,920.[15] In 2015–16, 44 percent of undergraduates were receiving Federal Pell Grants, with an average award amount of $3,820. This was up from 2008 to 2009, when only 28.5 percent of undergraduates were receiving grants, with an average award amount of $3,310.[16]

Another part of federal aid is the Federal Supplemental Educational Opportunity Grant, or FSEOG. The award amount for this grant varies based on financial need, time of application, amount of other aid received, and availability of funds. The FSEOG is campus-based aid. This means participating schools receive a set amount of funds. It is up to the school's financial aid office to award students, and once the funds for the year have been allocated to students, no more awards can be made. As such, if a student applies too late in the year, he or she may not be able to receive FSEOG funds. The award amount for an FSEOG can range between $100 and $4,000.[17] The FSEOG is one of the smaller grant programs. In 2015–16, the Federal Work-Study Program and FSEOG accounted for 1 percent of all undergraduate student aid, compared to the Federal Pell Grants, which accounted for 15 percent.[18]

There are additional grants that have more specific requirements such as the Teacher Education Assistance for College and Higher Education Grant. This grant provides up to $4,000 per year for students studying education who agree to teach in a high-need field at either the elementary or secondary level, or at an educational service agency that assists low-income families. If this service obligation is not fulfilled, the funds received become a direct unsubsidized loan that must be repaid.[19]

Iraq and Afghanistan Service Grants are available to students who were under twenty-four years old or enrolled in college when their parent or guardian died as a result of military service in Iraq or Afghanistan after 9/11; they must also be ineligible for Federal Pell Grants based on the Expected Family Contribution criteria but meet the remaining requirements. This award amount is equal to the maximum amount for the Federal Pell Grant. However, due to budget constraints, award amounts for both the Teacher Education Assistance for College and Higher Education Grant and the Iraq and Afghanistan Service Grants were reduced between October 1, 2015, and October 1, 2017.[20]

Nationally, the amount of federal grants available has changed significantly in the last two decades. In 1996–97, $25.3 billion in grants were awarded. By 2006–7, that amount had increased to $61.1 billion, representing a 9 percent annual compound growth rate. By 2016–17, the amount of federal grants issued increased again to a whopping $123.8 billion.[21] Despite the significant increases in federal grant spending, levels of student debt continue to increase dramatically.

Federal Loans

The largest source of aid for students comes from federal loans, accounting for 33 percent of total undergraduate student aid and 63 percent of all graduate student aid in 2015–16. Unlike grants, loans must be repaid.[22] The largest of the federal student loan programs is the William D. Ford Federal Direct Loan Program, under which the US Department of Education is the lender. The Federal Perkins Loan Program is school-based, with the school as the lender.[23]

The William D. Ford Federal Direct Loan Program offers four types of loans. The first type, Direct Subsidized Loans, are available only to undergraduate students who have demonstrated financial need. When a student is enrolled at least half-time in a participating school, there is a grace period for the first six months once he or she leaves school. During deferment, the US Department of Education will pay the interest on Direct Subsidized Loans. This eliminates the compounding of interest and higher future indebtedness of unsubsidized loans.

The school determines the amount the student can borrow. For students borrowing on July 1, 2013, and later, these loans can be received for 150 percent of the time of one's published program. For example, a student enrolled in a bachelor's degree program with a typical length of four years can receive Direct Subsidized Loans for six years.[24]

The second type, Direct Unsubsidized Loans, are similar but with a few major differences. Just like Direct Subsidized Loans, they are available to undergraduate students enrolled at least half-time in a participating school. That school determines the amount the student can borrow. However, graduate students enrolled at least half-time can also receive Direct Unsubsidized Loans. The student is responsible for paying all accumulated interest. No financial need must be demonstrated, and there are no time limits on eligibility.[25]

Direct PLUS Loans are the third type of loan under the William D. Ford Federal Direct Loan Program. They are available only to graduate or professional students and the guardians of dependent undergraduate students enrolled at least half-time at an eligible school. The borrowers must have a good credit history or have a guarantor who does. Exceptions can be made with documentation of extenuating circumstances. These loans require an application in addition to the FAFSA.[26]

The final type of loan under the William D. Ford Federal Direct Loan Program is the Direct Consolidation Loan, which consolidates all federal loans into one loan, resulting in one monthly payment as opposed to multiple payments. While this can simplify payment, it can also increase the length of repayment, resulting in higher interest rates. In addition, this method can also result in the loss of borrower benefits associated with the original loan.[27]

Perkins Loans are federal loans administered through participating schools. Instead of the US Department of Education acting as lender, the school is the lender. Funds depend on financial need and availability of funds at the school. Perkins Loans are available to undergraduate, graduate, and professional students who demonstrate financial need, are enrolled full- or part-time, and are attending a participating school.[28]

The amount that can be borrowed depends on the type of student and the type of loan. As of 2017, undergraduate students can borrow up to $5,500 per year and graduate students up to $8,000 per year in Perkins Loans, dependent on financial need, year in school, and availability of funds at the school. Undergraduate students can borrow between $5,500 and $12,500 per year in Direct Subsidized Loans and Direct Unsubsidized Loans, and graduate students can borrow up to $20,500 in Direct Unsubsidized Loans. Both graduate students and parents of dependent undergraduate students can cover the remainder of college costs not covered by other financial aid in Direct PLUS loans.[29] Like with federal grants, the amount of money available for federal loans has increased in recent years but not as rapidly as grants. In 2006–7, there was $73.6 billion available to students. The amount peaked in 2010–11, reaching $119.2 billion, and in 2016–17 the amount was $96.3 billion.[30] Federal loans to undergraduates declined in recent years while graduate students, who are ineligible for most federal grants, relied more heavily on loans.

When a graduate who has government-sourced student debt is unable to repay that debt, the borrower may be eligible for income-based payments. The borrower would commit to pay a maximum of 40 percent of their future income, for example, for up to twenty years in lieu of having to pay the loan balance. For graduates working in qualifying public service jobs, any loan balance can be extinguished after ten years. Forgiveness or extinguishment of a loan balance may be taxable as income by the federal government.

The government subsidizes student loans in multiple ways, but even with subsidies and relaxed payment terms, about 6 percent of loans to students who graduated are classified as in default. For those borrowers who did not graduate, the default rate is about 18 percent; all default rates are increasing.[31]

Other Forms of Aid

Students receive more than just federal aid. Students can also receive financial aid from states and from their schools. The amount of state grants has been fairly steady, fluctuating from $10 to $11 billion per year since 2010–11. In the same time frame, enrollment has increased and tuition has risen, making the states less able to make education affordable.

Part of the gap in student affordability has been covered by private grants. Institutional grants to undergraduate students increased from $22 billion in 2006–7 to $47 billion ten years later. Private and employer grants likewise increased from $8 billion to $12 billion in the same ten-year period.[32] Private and employer grants now exceed the total financial aid from states.

Private Loans

Private loans are also available. Generally, when a student receives the maximum amount available from public grants and loans, he or she (and potentially his or her parents) seeks a private loan to cover any remaining gap. On average, the gap is about $10,000 per year. Private loans for education are typically funded by lenders including banks, credit unions, and Sallie Mae, a financial services company originally formed by the US government to provide student loans. Private loans are widely used, especially by students in graduate school, where federal loans are less widely available and expenses are typically higher.

A loan amount is determined by the lender based on the borrower's perceived ability to repay the loan, their credit score, and the default history of the school they attend. Because students typically have little income, often parents or others are asked to cosign and guarantee private student loans. At year-end 2017, public loans typically charged 3.5 percent interest and waived interest accumulation until six months after graduation, with the government paying the shortfall. Private lenders do not have the same government subsidies, so private loans were typically at 6 percent interest for a good credit applicant by comparison, and the interest started accumulating and compounding from the date the loan was given. The interest may not be tax deductible, and student loans (public and private) may not be discharged in bankruptcy. The private lender industry provided about $11 billion in student loans in 2017, filling a need gap but creating significant future expenses for student borrowers.

Throughout history, Americans have relied on financial aid to attend college and secure a path to a better life. Former president Barack Obama and his wife, Michelle, both received financial aid and loans so they could attend college and receive an education that otherwise was unaffordable: "Michelle and I, we're only where we are today because scholarships and student loans gave us a shot at a great education. And we know a little bit about trying to pay back student loans too because we didn't come from a wealthy family. So, we each graduated from college and law school with a mountain of debt. And even though we got good jobs, we barely finished paying it off just before I was elected to the US Senate."[33]

Texas Senator Ted Cruz also credits the availability of financial aid with providing him the opportunity to receive an education and realizing the "promise of America." He received over $100,000 in student loans while pursuing his education.[34]

Florida Senator Marco Rubio is another politician who attributes his success to the availability of financial aid: "College affordability is an issue that is very personal to me. The only reason why I was able to go to college was because of federal grants and loans. But when I graduated from law school, I had close to $100,000 in student debt."[35]

MY STORY

I've Got Angels All around Me

Austin Galy

You can chain me, you can torture me, you can even destroy this body, but you will never imprison my mind.

—Mahatma Gandhi

EDUCATION—AGENCY WITHIN ONE'S SELF AND WITHIN ONE'S MIND— is an escape from it all. Here's the funny thing about life: No matter how hard we try to compare ourselves to others, no two stories will ever be the same. Each of us is born with a particular set of life circumstances that is unique to us and only us—circumstances that are predetermined by systems and mechanisms well beyond our power and control. A number of life chances predicated on not one but an array of factors: our social location, our identities, societal norms and expectations, the stories of our parents and their parents before them. Factors that we succumb to, both consciously and subconsciously, well before we're ever granted the agency to explore and make decisions for ourselves as individual beings.

Austin Galy is Assistant Director of the University of San Diego's Karen and Tom Mulvaney Center for Community Awareness and Social Action. Among his many responsibilities and activities, he directs the MacDonald Scholars program at the University of San Diego. The program provides students the opportunity to pay it forward through programs to help those in need.

One of my favorite quotes of all time—I'm not sure who said it or if it's just something I made up in my head one day (chances are the latter)—is "Learning is all about unlearning. We must unlearn everything to learn everything. And once you see it, you can't unsee it." If there's one thing and one thing only that I've learned through education, it's that everything we do and know and think and say came from somewhere. It's epistemology— the theory of knowledge and how we know what we know. So I say to unto you, question everything. Take nothing at face value and interrogate the systems responsible for producing the knowledge we know.

So often we hear that education is empowerment, and with that I don't disagree. However (and this is a big however), miseducation of any sort is not education at all. Miseducation is enslavement. Miseducation is a world without hope for a better tomorrow and a way of keeping people locked within their circumstances and life chances. Education, on the other hand, is like our stories. It is unique to each one of us. And no two people should ever have the same relationship with it. Because *how* one sees the world is and will always be unique to us as individuals—a way to honor individual- ism and liberation from predetermination; the freedom to explore. Again, agency within one's self and within one's mind. Educational empowerment moves us beyond acceptance and into a realm of challenging that which we're born into. A transformative space where people can envision a better life for themselves and where circumstances are barriers, not barricades.

In hindsight, it would've been nice to know these things as a child. It certainly would've saved me a lot of trouble. Perhaps then I wouldn't have been so hard on myself. Perhaps then I wouldn't have blamed myself for so much, and instead I would've realized that being a victim of circumstances makes me, well . . . normal. Again, these are the measures I speak of that are beyond our control.

It's important to note that education was, and still is in many ways, my medicine. It cloaks me and heals me, protecting me from my past and of- fering healing powers through new hope and vision. Through education I found the power of forgiveness, and I learned that letting go requires more strength than holding on. Again, unlearning in order to learn.

My life circumstances were far from ideal as a child, and yet they were chosen for me nonetheless. This is my sorrow that I must learn to embrace and accept anger—to forgive, or else it will forever conquer me. Education can indeed be used as a tool for many things, one of which is the ability to transcend anger and relinquish control—to *let go*. When you allow yourself to be consumed by anger and rage, they narrow the scope through which you see the world. They cloud your judgment, and the world can seem like a very lonely and unforgiving place.

Education, on the other hand, casts vision to recognize the boundlessness of our hearts and the understanding that our minds shall forever remain free from imprisonment. The only thing holding us back from ourselves is, well . . . us. Education teaches us that. Attaining liberation from one's self is the process of unlearning. And like a mason, we must learn to deconstruct, brick by brick, the various border walls that exist within us. Walls that limit our vision and feel like boxes and categories into which we must place little bits of ourselves. Education has taught me that I don't have to subscribe to constructs or boxes, and that's okay. I subscribe to boundlessness. With the removal of every brick comes a more expansive way of seeing and being in the world. Once you see it, you simply can't unsee it.

I've got angels all around me, and education saved my life. Three months before my twenty-fourth birthday, I nearly died after being struck by an improvised explosive device (IED) while on my final deployment to the Middle East. Apart from losing my closest friends that day and nearly leaving behind a widowed wife, I also lost the one career I had given my entire life to—my service to this country. As I lay in a hospital bed fighting for my life, I knew that my time to depart from this earth had not yet come. Nothing else seemed to make sense at the time, but the core of who I was as a human remained. In that moment, I made the decision to end my chapter with war, and from that day forward that's exactly what I set out to do. Out of my tribulations I was reborn, and through the horror of war I came to understand the necessity for peace and love.

I sit here today, four years removed from my accident, as the assistant director at a university and nine months away from completing graduate school. None of which would ever have been possible without access to schooling. Education has transformed my life, and there simply are no words powerful enough to describe the emotions I feel because of that. Like many thousands of soldiers before me, my educational benefits became a mechanism for change. A refusal to accept what was predetermined and a drive to defy the odds of my story. Education also allowed me to realize that my story was mine alone to hold and that only I held its authorship. And the only person standing between me and the next chapter was myself. Why my life was spared on that day in 2014, I still don't fully comprehend. Nevertheless, I know in my heart that I am called to do something with this opportunity I have been given. If not for me then for others like me—others whose stories tell of similar circumstances but who perhaps never had the opportunities that I've been given. The opportunity to learn and unlearn and see the world in all of its infinite beauty and vastness. My hope is that one day each and every person may have that opportunity. And until then, it's a matter of paying it forward, plain and simple.

> If you have been brutally broken and still have the courage to be gentle to others then you deserve a love deeper than the ocean.
> —Nikita Gill, writer

Education is a journey toward love and self-discovery—learning to love myself as myself and all of my infinite imperfections. Unbeknownst to me at the time, education, for me, was all about rediscovery—something I knew very little about when I chose to leave the military and return to school. Once again, I reestablished purpose in my life, but this time it wasn't through violence; it was through compassion, newfound understanding, and newly obtained knowledge. College has been more than just a home for me; it's been a place where I've grown, a place where I've learned to redefine love, and a place that's transformed how I see the world, including my role in it.

Since moving to attend and now work at the University of San Diego, my educational journey has taken me on a path full of twists and turns, leading me to what I now understand to be my life's calling—the reason why my life was spared that day and on many others before that. Through education, I discovered that my purpose is to examine and understand, to the best degree possible, my story. My life has been a tale of resilience, and yet, somehow, I have been given the opportunity to find redemption. My story is mine, yes, but it is no longer mine alone to hold. I realize I have been charged, given a duty if you will, to share my journey and what I have learned from it—the hard mistakes and lessons learned along the way. Many of the twists and turns I encountered along my path are indeed reminiscent of what other young men and women are experiencing right here, right now. And through the power of self-discovery, I have found my place as a wounded warrior, healing and learning among and alongside others whose stories parallel mine.

For a number of reasons, it's difficult to talk about the earlier chapters of my life. I am twenty-eight years old today, and yet I feel as though I've just barely scratched the surface of confronting my past. Eighteen years ago, at age ten, I fled what was an incredibly abusive household, never to look back. Had I stayed, I would've died—simple as that. To this day, I have never seen my family. It is what I had to do in order to survive, yet I still carry the burden of that pain with me every step of my life. As a family-less child, scared, lonely, and afraid, I had to fend for myself on the outer fringes of society. I was confused and unaware of how to seek help. Desperate only to feel love and belong anywhere, I sought the approval of a local gang at the age of twelve. Not knowing how or what family was supposed to look like, I was desperate to fit in, and that meant I would do anything to be accepted. By age thirteen I had been charged and sentenced to juvenile hall and, ultimately, jail, where I spent the remainder of my teenage years. Not just because I was a criminal but because I was the aftermath of miseducation and poverty. I was the physical manifestation, the by-product, of unjust ignorance. I embodied the world that I had grown up in, and for me, that world was only as big as the south side of Atlanta.

Yet despite all of that, here I am. Some might say I'm an accident. Maybe I'm poetic justice. Or perhaps my justice is a small glimpse of the what ifs. What if households were never broken, and what if home was indeed where the heart was? (Home has no heart for some of us.) What if we dissolved systems that lock away children who are crying out for help and love? What if discipline were rooted in love and understanding rather than black-and-white facts? What if context mattered, and what if encouragement became the new form of capital punishment? What if we paid attention to people's stories and asked questions rather than assumed or judged? What if we took into account privilege and the differing circumstances of others? Acknowledging that some of us aren't always dealt a winning hand in life and that bootstraps are only a lifeline as long as you're born with boots. Perhaps then there would be more accidents like me. More stories of redemption—education unchained. A mind unleashed is a force unlike any other.

Along with the principle of unlearning, I also believe in the power of intimacy and compassion. I believe that intimacy is shared weakness and that there is a profound understanding of the need for peaceful and just reconciliation when the struggle is lived, not just studied. We must learn to clothe ourselves not just with our stories but with the stories of others. For it is in that moment that we are all capable of offering warmth, love, and compassion to others.

Through my educational journey, I have come to learn where my strengths lie and where they do not. Life experience, trials and tribulations, failures—these are the elements that have allowed me to excel in recent years as a student. Not because I was any smarter than anyone; I can assure you that was the furthest thing from the truth. Sociology and my other coursework only ever came easily to me because it never felt like schooling at all; rather, I was recounting and unpacking my life from the inside out. Things just started to click.

Many of the social phenomena I studied in my coursework weren't at all phenomenal to me. They were just my past. They were my story. But framing my own experiences through a social justice lens humbled me and taught me things. It brought me to a whole new level of appreciation and understanding. I had never even heard the words *social justice* growing up. But then again, the words are irrelevant; it's the feeling that counts—the hairs on the back on your neck standing up and the lump in your throat when you witness something that you know deep within you is immoral or unjust. And that understanding is something I now crave. Education has allowed me to see the added value in my life's work. It has provided me with a sense of clarity unlike anything else.

Thanks to my education, I know wholeheartedly where I stand and who I am today. Schooling has taught me that careers ought not be limited to choices nor lifestyles; rather, we must strive to have them reflect our identities as human beings, however they take shape. Furthermore, no matter how certain I am or anyone else is, we must never stop challenging ourselves to grow. And the pursuit of my education and development represents just that—an opportunity to challenge myself so that every day I can become a slightly better version of who I was the day prior. They don't call it *lifelong learning* for nothing.

Thanks to the education provided to me through the University of San Diego and the financial assistance that made it possible for me to go there, I have found myself—including my place in the world. I stand here today certain of who I am and of where I am needed. My labor of love has become understanding the associations between gender (specifically hypermasculinity) and mental health, in particular how they manifest in deeply traumatized settings. Here in San Diego, I have the opportunity to work alongside various groups including incarcerated teens and adults affected by our justice system, active duty and combat veterans, and various gangs and extremist groups throughout the region. Given my own personal experiences and life story, working with these different groups is important for me. When you find something that you truly love and are passionate about, personal and professional development are no longer separate thoughts or expressions. It's a feeling of being whole. And that's exactly how I feel about my professional career. It's no more work than it is a chance to look deep into my soul and understand my own story.

I thank the powers that be every day for having given me the opportunity to discover my life's calling. I know that without access to a quality education, there would be no intersection between passion and calling. And the odds of me surviving my past would have been nil. Education gives each of us the agency to discover what we're passionate about and subsequently find ways to embody those elements in our everyday actions, lives, and careers. It's a labor of love, where the quality of one's life is measured by how deeply one has touched the lives of others. Again, paying it forward.

PART 3
UNIVERSITIES TAKING THE INITIATIVE

7

WHAT SCHOOLS ARE DOING TO REDUCE
STUDENT DEBT

THE RISING COSTS OF COLLEGE ARE OUTPACING STUDENTS' AND their families' ability to pay for them with their own resources. This means students and their families must look elsewhere to find the funds necessary to cover the costs of securing a university education. In evaluating whether a student can afford to go to college, several factors need to be considered, including the cost of attending a school, personal and family financial resources, eligibility for public grants and loans, and availability of private or school-controlled scholarships and aid. Each school has different resources, different policies to address need-eligible students and applicants, and different objectives to achieving a balanced class. However, it is instructive to review what some exemplary universities are doing to support their students financially and reduce the amount of debt their students need to assume while funding their education.

One extraordinary concept to support students with financial need is "no loan" policies where a school guarantees every eligible student will graduate with no student-related debt. This is a significant and expensive policy at a time when the average student loan debt amounts to around $37,000.[1] The significant need for financial aid has not gone unnoticed by universities, and many have prioritized raising scholarship funds to help students in financial need, including no-loan commitments.

The author thanks University of North Carolina at Chapel Hill graduate student Lacey Lumpkin for assistance with research and the preparation of drafts of this chapter.

The Need for Loans

The average student debt of $37,000 is a high figure for someone just starting out in his or her career. While $37,000 is an average, many students graduate or leave college with significantly more debt. The numbers increase when debt for graduate school is included in the calculations.

The rising cost of college and the limited amount of gift aid (scholarships and grants that do not have to be repaid) leaves a gap that students often have to pay, at least in part, with loans. While the average cost of attending a four-year college (this includes tuition, fees, room and board, books, supplies, and other miscellaneous costs) for the 2017–18 academic year was $24,300 at public institutions and $50,300 at private nonprofit institutions,[2] the average amount of nonloan aid given fell short at $9,380 for public institutions and $22,010 for private institutions.[3] This gap is a widespread problem, as demonstrated by the fact that 69 percent of 2015–16 college seniors took out student loans.[4]

Most students at four-year schools seek some form of financial aid to fund their education. During the 2015–16 school year, 86 percent of undergraduate students were awarded financial aid. This figure has been rising over the years, indicating that the need for financial aid is increasing.[5] So how are schools responding to this increase in need? Is there adequate funding at schools for all eligible students? The answers vary by school because each has different resources and a different set of students with specific-need profiles.

Generally, however, schools with lots of donors and large endowments are able to have bigger scholarship programs and help more students. Schools that lack the big endowments necessary to fund more robust scholarship programs typically are less able to meet student financial needs. Students at institutions with modest endowment and scholarship funding will generally have a hard time filling the gap between college cost and available resources without taking on significant amounts of debt.

No-Loan Policies

There has been a recent trend among schools with more resources to implement "no-loan policies." Many schools—like Pomona College,[6] Columbia University,[7] and Vanderbilt University[8]—offer no-loan financial aid packages to their students. Most limit these awards to their low-income students, but several offer the option to their entire student population. These schools generally have several things in common: they are often private schools with large endowments, often have smaller student bodies, and generally have selective admissions requiring demonstrated high academic performance. These schools need to have relatively large amounts of money to transfer into gift aid and smaller student populations, which limit demand. High academic admissions standards may lead to enrolling students who had greater access to college preparatory classes and/or private schools and who come from wealthier families who do not require aid, reducing total financial aid requirements at selective schools. Schools offering financial aid packages made entirely of gift aid sounds like a dream among the nightmarish stories of Americans drowning in student loan debt.

Davidson College

Davidson, North Carolina, is a small suburb outside Charlotte that is home to award-winning restaurants, a national arboretum, and a top college according to virtually all college surveys. Many have heard of Davidson in the context of the school's most prominent alumni, NBA MVP Steph Curry. But Davidson is also well known for its academics and more recently the Davidson Trust.

Davidson College is one of the schools committed to excluding loans from financial aid packages through the Davidson Trust, which was established in 2007 by unanimous vote of the college trustees, led by then-president Bobby Vagt. The trust meets 100 percent of a student's financial need by providing them with grants and work opportunities on campus, which range from eight to ten hours a week.[9]

Davidson was the first liberal arts university to implement a no-loan program like this. The school has had a tradition since its inception to keep the cost of attendance as low as possible so that a Davidson education is financially accessible to many.[10] According to economics professor Clark Ross, "Davidson was founded as a work college to ensure accessibility for those of talent who sought higher education, regardless of ability to pay."[11]

To a school with an endowment of just $500 million at the time the Davidson Trust was approved, which was significantly less than the typical endowments of other elite liberal arts schools, eliminating loans from financial aid packages seemed daunting and was estimated to cost the school an additional $3.5 million annually. The trustees were faced with raising

$70 million to augment the endowment right away. The initial fundraising came from sources including the Duke Endowment.

Subsequently, Ted Baker, a Davidson alum and CEO and chairman of Florida Rock Industries until it was sold to Vulcan Materials, joined Bobby Vagt to set up the Baker-Vagt Scholarship "to provide assistance to students for whom a Davidson education would not otherwise be financially feasible." In 2004, Baker donated another $25 million for scholarships. He said, "Davidson has always been important to our family, and I am pleased to offer this additional scholarship support as an investment in the future."[12]

The Davidson Trust is an expensive program that requires considerable funding. Like most schools, Davidson is always searching for more funding for its trust, as the number of admitted students demonstrating financial need increases every year. For example, in the class of 2011, 33 percent of students qualified for need-based aid. That figure rose to 44 percent for the class of 2015. During that same period, Davidson witnessed a 93 percent increase in the number of students who qualified for Pell Grants.[13]

Before Davidson's decision to eliminate student loans, about 20 percent of the school's budget was spent on financial aid. That figure has increased to approximately 30 percent. Over 50 percent of Davidson's class of 2022 received need-based financial aid including merit and athletic scholarships. About 62 percent of new Davidson students receive financial aid.

The effects of the trust transcend economics and contribute to the sociodemographic diversity of the student body. The percentage of minority students increased from 19 percent in 2003 to almost 30 percent in 2011.

Lifting the financial burden of student debt has allowed Davidson students more freedom to pursue their interests. In 2016, more Davidson graduates went into education than any other field, and community service organizations were the fourth most popular field, both of which are typically lower-paying professions. According to Helen Duffy, class of 2020, "Now I am leaning toward becoming a social worker. I am able to take on this much lower-paying job because I do not have to worry about student loans."[14] Zoe Hall, also class of 2020, plans to go to graduate school and notes, "If I had lots of loans from Davidson I would have had to work before I went to graduate school."[15]

The effects of the Davidson Trust are also shown through the academic and professional success of its recipients, including students from underrepresented groups, first-generation college students, and Pell Grant recipients. Davidson's high academic standards and student achievements (e.g., retention, graduation, and postgrad employment rates) have remained consistent after the implementation of the trust and the subsequent change in student demographics.[16] President Carol Quillen has described the Davidson Trust as "a community project" focused on "creating a society where equal opportunity is actually real."[17]

University of North Carolina

In 2004, University of North Carolina's (UNC's) director of scholarships and student aid, Shirley Ort, had a vision: the school should guarantee that any student who is good enough to be admitted should be able to earn a degree and graduate without student debt. This was unheard of for a public university. With support from the chancellor and the board of trustees and permission to use some of the general tuition proceeds to fund the concept, the Carolina Covenant was created.

The covenant is a promise to admitted students who are low-income (at or below 200 percent of the poverty line) that they will receive a debt-free education unless they elect to take out discretionary loans (e.g., to cover an unpaid internship or semester abroad). The covenant covers 100 percent of a student's demonstrated need. All eligible students who complete the required financial aid application are automatically considered. There is no cap on the number of covenant scholars.

The Carolina Covenant offers more than just money. There are other barriers that hinder low-income students from being successful in college, and the covenant aims to help students overcome those barriers by providing services and mentorship as well as academic and personal support.[18] These extra resources include workshops on topics such as business etiquette, academic skills, and financial management. Scholars even receive perks like vouchers to performing arts events. The goal is to create well-rounded, well-adjusted students who have the tools to succeed in the real and professional world.[19] Each scholar is assigned a faculty or professional staff mentor. Scholars also have access to peer mentors who are upper-class Covenant Scholars who help the new students navigate UNC. While the focus of most financial aid is on the financial aspect of attending college, universities like UNC recognize that money is not the only key to a student's success. It is important that these students are also given access to a variety of resources that provide support.

Promise Program

What does the success of the Covenant Scholars program look like? More than eight thousand students have progressed through the program since its inception in 2004.[20] Currently, 14 percent of new UNC students are Covenant Scholars.[21] As of the 2015–16 academic year, Covenant Scholars had an average cumulative GPA of 3.15 by their fourth year.[22] This is in comparison to the 3.31 cumulative, four-year GPA of all students at UNC. The four-year graduation rate of Covenant Scholars has increased by 23.7 percentage points since the creation of the program and is now 80.4 percent.[23] By 2015, the four-year graduation gap between Covenant Scholars and non-covenant students had nearly closed. It went from being a 17.7 percentage point gap before the creation of the covenant to a 3.6 percentage point gap. More recently, employees of the financial aid office indicated that the gap is now down to 2 percentage points.[24]

How can a public university afford such a program? One reason is that UNC maintains an 82/18 ratio of in-state versus out-of-state students. Many other schools of similar caliber have far more students who are considered out-of-state. For example, the University of Virginia and the University of Michigan have around 30 percent and 40 percent students from out of state, respectively. It can cost more to fund the higher cost of out-of-state need-eligible students, although there are social and financial benefits to having the diversity provided by out-of-state students, who also typically pay higher tuition.

Another reason UNC offers such a program, according to staff in the financial aid office, is the culture of the school. UNC views itself as "The University of the People." The university has made it a priority to fully meet a student's financial need. They want to recruit the best students and having this financial aid package helps.

At the time the Carolina Covenant was established, the university was able to use general tuition revenue toward financial aid without limitation. Subsequently, there has been a shift of the political environment of North Carolina, and the State Board of Governors instituted a 15 percent cap on the amount of tuition revenue that can go toward need-based aid.[25] Previously, the culture was to help as many students as possible; now a consideration is, "Why are students who are paying tuition subsidizing tuition for low-income students?" This puts considerable strain on providing funding for the covenant and other need-based scholarships while retaining the promise to meet all financial need. The university is trying to make up for the lost money by fundraising. UNC's major fundraising campaign, Carolina Edge, has a goal of raising $4.25 billion and hopes to provide $1 billion funding for scholarships and grants.[26]

Extensive private donations allow for scholarships like the covenant to exist. There is a culture and history at UNC of providing funding for less-fortunate students, and donors have supported the university's mission in this regard for many years.

The Covenant isn't the only way UNC is helping its students with financial assistance. There are also a variety of other need-based scholarships that are used by 40 percent of UNC's students. The Office of Scholarships and Financial Aid administers over 1,200 scholarships, and most are need-based.

UNC meets 100 percent of the financial needs of all students; it is one of the only public institutions to do that. Part of the financial aid for non-covenant students can be loans. However, 65 to 70 percent of a student's financial package is gift aid (grants or scholarships). According to Terri Hegeman, the director of development for scholarships, as a result of this high amount of gift aid, "UNC has some of the lowest borrowing of any public flagship, and most students don't borrow at all. The most common amount of debt for a graduating student at Carolina is none."[27] UNC wants to make that percentage of gift aid even higher; they are working toward having fewer loans as part of the aid.

Josh Wilkes moved from Dallas to the small town of Clarkton, North Carolina, with his mother after her divorce when he was twelve years old. His mother worked full-time, raised a family, and cared for their extended family. There was not much money to pay bills, much less college tuition. Josh was accepted at UNC and became a Covenant Scholar. After graduating, he joined Wells Fargo as an investment banker.[28]

Marquis Peacock grew up in Goldsboro, North Carolina. He wanted to go to UNC but did not think he could afford it. His parents had modest jobs, and he had two siblings. When he was awarded a Covenant scholarship, he knew he could attend UNC; he would be one of the few from his high school to go to college. He graduated from UNC and is now in medical school, well on his way to becoming a doctor.[29]

Without the Carolina Covenant and other donor-funded scholarships, students like Josh and Marquis would never have had the opportunity to excel and achieve at university.

Princeton University

While Davidson was the first liberal arts college to offer such a program, Princeton was the first university in the United States to provide a no-loan financial aid package starting in 2001.[30] They are able to offer this type of aid because of a large endowment, valued at $22.8 billion at the end of March 2017 (compared to Davidson's $780 million),[31] and a comparatively small student population—currently 5,251 undergraduates.[32] The endowment provides about 80 percent of the school's budget for scholarships.[33]

Princeton uses a need-blind admissions process for all of its applicants including international students, which is not as common.[34] All financial aid is based on need only; the school does not award merit-based scholarships, as a student's merit is evaluated during the admissions process, not the aid process. Education costs (tuition, fees, room and board) are fully covered for students who have a gross family income of $65,000 or lower.[35] As a family's gross income increases, the amount that is covered decreases because the student is expected to be able to contribute more. Regardless, students either do not incur debt or graduate with very little debt, which happens when the student decides not to use all the financial resources available to pay for his or her education. For example, a student may take an unpaid internship instead of working to gain career experience one year and replace the work-related income with a loan. With these types of exceptions, every student's need is met through grants (95 percent of aid) and campus employment (5 percent of aid).[36]

Princeton uses a comprehensive method to determine a family's financial situation, not just their income. According Robin Moscato, director of financial aid, "The university has excluded home value and most retirement funds when calculating a family's ability to contribute and has increased grants to help students pay for dining options and study abroad programs."[37]

Princeton notes that it is often more affordable to low- and middle-income students than state universities despite the listed higher tuition and attendance costs.[38] During the 2014–15 academic year, around 60 percent of undergraduate students were awarded financial aid. According to Princeton's records, "83 percent of recent seniors graduated debt free."[39] While some students chose to take out student loans for extra expenses, their debt remained low at about $6,600 for four years.[40] This is the lowest student debt amount of any university in the United States.[41]

This absence or low quantity of debt among Princeton graduates has a profound effect on their careers and life trajectories, as debt often dictates the paths students must take after graduation. For example, two-thirds of the first class to graduate with no or minimal debt agreed in a survey that "the benefits of graduating with little or no debt have had a significant impact on their postgraduate plans."[42] When graduates are not burdened by student debt, they can experience more freedom to pursue avenues such as continuing their education in graduate school or taking a fulfilling but lower-paying job like being a teacher or working at a nonprofit organization.

Harvard University

Harvard's first scholarship was awarded in 1643. Since then, the school has committed substantial funds, energy, and staffing support to make Harvard affordable to students from lower-income families. The amount of scholarship funding has increased from about $80 million in 2005 to approximately $190 million in 2018.[43]

In 2004, then-president Lawrence Summers announced Harvard's Financial Aid Initiative (HFAI) to provide access to a Harvard education for exceptional students regardless of their economic background or ability to pay. According to Harvard's director of financial aid, Sally Donahue, "We wanted to deliver a clear message that Harvard's doors are open to all talented students, so what we said when we launched HFAI in 2004 was that if your family makes less than $40,000 a year, we will not ask them to contribute to the cost of your education."[44]

The income ceiling for families paying nothing was increased over time to $65,000. Families with incomes between $65,000 and $150,000 contribute no more than 10 percent of their income.[45]

According to Donahue, since the start of the HFAI, the number of low-income students at the university has increased 30 percent. She says, "Over 16 percent of the Class of 2022 are first-generation students. These changes are largely the result of our enhanced financial aid program and have changed the face of the college."[46]

Brandon Buell grew up in a small town in upstate New York with fewer than five thousand people. He was one of twenty-eight students in his graduating high school class. His parents were factory workers, and his grandparents were dairy farmers. He was admitted to Harvard but did not have the financial resources to attend without extensive financial aid. Thanks to

HFAI, Buell was able to enroll at Harvard. He said, "One of the primary reasons I came here was because the aid I received."[47]

Ahilya Khadka emigrated from Nepal to Iowa when she was sixteen to seek a better education than was available to her in Kathmandu. She knew about Harvard but felt it would be unaffordable. However, she was admitted and given a full scholarship. "It felt unreal," she said. "You hear things about how expensive college is all the time, but to get into my dream school, and then to see the financial aid offer, I said to myself, 'Oh my God, is this real?'"[48]

According to Harvard president Drew Faust, when HFAI was expanded in 2011, "access and affordability, enabled by generous financial aid, are fundamental to Harvard's identity and excellence. We admit students without regard to their financial need, and we make sure that they are given the means to attend and take advantage of the Harvard College experience."[49]

Harvard can afford to provide generous financial aid because their endowment is large—$37 billion. In 2014, Kenneth Griffin, founder and CEO of Citadel LLC, donated $125 million to Harvard for student financial aid. This is the largest donation in the history of Harvard. Griffin indicated, in regard to his donation, "The greatest legacy I can leave behind is for Harvard to open its doors to everyone who's qualified to go there. Simply put, my Harvard experience changed my life. My hope is that this gift will make it possible for the best and brightest in our nation and in our world to have the same experience I had at Harvard."[50]

Brown University

Brown University is also increasing access for lower- and moderate-income students by eliminating loans starting with the 2018–19 academic year.[51] No-loan aid is offered to incoming and current students including international students. Brown has been on a path to no-loan aid since 2003, when they implemented a need-blind admission policy. Their aid package provides grant-only aid to families who have incomes below $100,000 and eliminates family contributions for those who earn less than $60,000.[52] All admitted students will have the opportunity to finance their education solely through gift aid and campus employment.

Even though Brown has a smaller endowment—$3.5 billion at the end of June 2017[53]—than many of the other schools that have offered no-loan packages to their students, they have procured the funds to expand this offer to all students through their initiative, The Brown Promise. During the 2017 fiscal year, 35 percent of the endowment spending went toward financial aid.[54]

Brown students will have the ability to take out loans if they choose to, as sometimes they are necessary to fund extra expenses such as study abroad, summer classes, and unpaid internships.[55] As with other schools, a major goal of this no-loan policy is to diversify the school's student population. But another goal is to fill the gap for moderate-income families that are often left out (and don't even apply to Brown) because their incomes were too great to meet the previous aid-eligibility requirement. These families, who are not too poor but not at all wealthy, lacked the financial resources to pay for school.

Brown's goal of reaching these "stranded" families developed when the school admissions staff realized applications from moderate-income families failed to keep pace with other income brackets.[56] As with other schools, Brown wants to provide the opportunity for students to have more freedom in choosing their futures by not having their aspirations limited by the obligation to repay loans.[57] In a video campaign about the new initiatives, students spoke about what it would mean to them to not have student debt. They all expressed that the impact would be positive and that a weight would be lifted off of their shoulders.[58]

University of Michigan

While the total cost of attending the University of Michigan (UM) at Ann Arbor can seem overwhelming, the university has a long history of supporting need-based students. University president Mark Schlissel said, "We want all of Michigan's talented children and their families to know that if they work hard and study, a UM education will be within financial reach."[59]

About 70 percent of Michigan resident undergraduates and 53 percent of nonresident students receive financial aid. In 2016–17, almost $525 million in financial aid was awarded to UM students.

Michigan's Go Blue Guarantee promises to pay full undergraduate tuition and mandatory university fees for up to four years for eligible in-state students who have family incomes of $65,000 or less and limited assets not to exceed $50,000. The university is the only one in Michigan to cover 100 percent of demonstrated financial need for in-state students. With generous support from private donors, the university offers a variety of scholarship programs and promises partial tuition support for families earning up to $150,000.

Krystal Johnson would not have been able to attend UM without considerable financial aid. She received work-study, grants, and scholarships that covered her entire tuition and room and board. Krystal had grown up in Detroit in a low-income working-class family; her parents had not attended college. She eventually received a master's in social work and is now working in Detroit providing psychotherapy and case management for emotionally disturbed children and their families.

Reducing Aid

While some schools are moving to eliminate student loans, others are going in the opposite direction because the expense of no-loan policies is too great. Motivation for reducing the amount of gift aid could be poor performance of the school's endowment, less support from the state and federal governments, the cost of other campus needs, or just a small endowment.

One example is Cornell University, a prestigious East Coast college in Ithaca, New York, which in 2013 reduced its financial aid packages by lowering the income cutoff from $75,000 to $60,000 for eligibility of no-loan aid.[60] They also restrict no-loan aid to families with less than $100,000 in assets, including home equity.

Another high-profile example was the reduction in aid offered by University of Virginia through their Access UVA financial aid program, which guarantees to meet 100 percent of a student's demonstrated need.[61] It previously met this need with grant aid and work-study only; however, in 2013 the board of visitors voted to include loans in the aid package to meet the students' needs. The university cited rising demands and costs of the program in conjunction with decreased funding from the federal government as reasons for this change. The news was met by much protest, because the absence of loans was a significant draw for low-income students, and lower-income students would likely be adversely impacted by the new policy.

Schools that cannot afford to meet 100 percent of financial need for all students may still have programs that help a portion of students graduate debt-free. These schools have the same goals as Princeton and Brown but don't necessarily have the resources. They implement these programs on a smaller scale and offer aid to a smaller pool of students.

At Virginia Tech, this type of scholarship is the Virginia Tech Presidential Scholarship Initiative (VTPSI). The basic eligibility requirements for this scholarship include being an incoming student who resides in Virginia and being Pell Grant-eligible while also demonstrating "significant" financial need. The scholarship package includes tuition, fees, and room and board for four years. Other benefits include academic support and faculty/student mentoring. While this is an attractive option, only a maximum of fifty students will receive this aid each year; the incoming class of 2021 had almost seven thousand students.[62]

The Centennial Scholars Program at James Madison University (JMU) awards students grant aid that covers tuition, room and board, and meals for a maximum of four years.[63] Unlike many other schools, this aid is offered to both undergraduate and graduate students accepted into the program. The program is also limited with regard to the number of scholarships awarded.

Conclusion

A number of colleges and universities in the United States have some form of no-loan policies for either students whose families have low incomes (e.g., Harvard and Stanford) or, in some cases like Davidson and the University of Pennsylvania, the whole eligible student population. All of these schools have a common goal of increasing access to higher education to those of lesser means. They want their student populations to be financially diverse, which they see as an advantage in allowing students to meet and interact with other students from different backgrounds and financial status.

These schools typically have a need-blind admissions process. This means that a student's financial need is not considered in the application process. Being need-blind also contributes to having a student population that is financially diverse because having need does not disqualify students from being admitted, which can be the case for need-aware schools, which do look at a student's financial situation and consider it in the admissions process. They can reserve spots for students who have the ability to pay while rejecting students who do not.

The schools that are need-blind and are able to meet 100 percent of their students' need (with or without a loan component) usually benefit from large endowments and generous donors who make these scholarship programs possible and smaller class sizes (with the exception of UNC). While these schools have progressive financial aid policies, they are the minority. Most schools cannot afford such scholarship programs, especially no-loan policies.

Many no-loan programs serve the poorest students, typically from families earning less than $65,000 per year and with limited assets. There are many students from families that make more but still cannot afford the cost of a college education.

So what is available for the average students who don't gain admission to the limited number of institutions that have no-loan policies or who come from families making more than the allowed maximum income? Unfortunately, the answer usually requires significant loans. As more students qualify for financial aid and increased government aid does not keep pace, there will be less grant money per student, necessitating more student debt. The ability of schools to close the gap and limit the amount of student debt will depend more and more on private donors. The key question for college affordability may be "will there be enough private donors and scholarship money to offset the increases in the cost of attending college, the increasing number of need-eligible students, and the lack of sufficient government funds?"

MY STORY

Tattooed Tales

Hannah Locklear

ONE OF THE FIRST THINGS MOST PEOPLE NOTICE ABOUT ME IS NOT my smile, my eyes, or even my presence in a room; they notice my tattoos. I don't have as many as some people, but my tattoos are distinct enough to make an impression on anyone who sees them. My tattoos aren't just pretty works of art or forms of expression; they tell a story—of heartbreak, love, and everything in between. They tell my story, and this is how it starts.

On December 15, 1997, my mother gave birth to me in a fit of sweat, swearing, and cursing my father for causing it all. I don't remember it, but I know that from the moment I came into this world, I changed both of their lives forever.

My dad was twenty years old at the time. He had dropped out of high school in the tenth grade and started selling drugs and working construction to support his family. My mother was thirty years old and hadn't grown up yet. She'd already had two kids by two other men and thought she had found her soul mate in my young dad. I think they were both still just lost kids.

I was born at Scotland Memorial Hospital in Laurinburg, North Carolina. Laurinburg is part of Robeson County, which is where I grew up. The

Hannah Locklear is a student at the University of North Carolina at Chapel Hill. She was contacted through a mutual acquaintance and agreed to share her story.

county seat, Lumberton, is the center of the Lumbee Native American tribe; both my parents and I are members of the tribe.

Robeson is a mostly rural county with farmlands covering the low-lying terrain, which once was covered by swamps. Food processing and other factories provide blue-collar work at such places as chicken and turkey processors and Smithfield's hog farms.

Lumberton and Robeson County are among the poorest communities in the United States. Like most families around me, I grew up in poverty. We moved around a lot, especially when Mom could not afford the rent. Sometimes we moved in with my grandmother—my mom's mom—until we could find another place. There we all shared a bed—me, Grandmother, Mom, my sister. The first place I ever considered home, where I knew I had the same place to go every night, was my college dorm room.

As a youngster, all of my extended family and friends were Lumbee tribe members. We stayed close to other tribal members; we did not typically associate with whites, who also lived nearby.

Like many Native Americans, the Lumbees often suffered from drug and alcohol addiction. My father and mother were both addicts, and my father was a dealer. The life of a drug dealer isn't glamorous, especially if he is Native American. My grandparents were not able to help financially or emotionally because of being on drugs, in prison, or sick. For the first seven years of my life, I lived in a trap house. Not the fun place in rap songs where people have fun and get "lit," but a sad place where broken people go to numb themselves. We had some good times, but mostly it felt like I could be stuck there forever.

One outlet from my problems at home were powwows, which drew Native Americans together from local and more distant areas. The powwows featured lots of dancing, drums, and singing. We had powwows typically every season and even occasionally traveled out of state for bigger gatherings. Often, we would dress in regalia and ceremonial dress with feathers and long dresses. The powwows featured Native Americans selling cultural goods including native jewelry, special quilts, and clothing items. They also offered lots of food, unfortunately including fried bread and other fried foods that tasted great but in hindsight were not very healthy. Powwows took my mind off of the troubles at home.

My dad went missing when I was seven, and it was almost certainly drug-related. My family fell apart after that. My grandma fell deeper into drugs, both my grandfathers were in prison, and my mom was working multiple jobs to provide for my siblings and me. The only place I felt safe was at school. There I could read stories about people with different lives. I could excel and be noticed and feel proud. I never felt proud of myself at home, but when I was at school I did.

It was in school that I first realized I had been raped for years. From the time I was around five until I was a preteen, I had been sexually assaulted, and I'd never known that was what it was. I read a book called *Speak*; that novel changed my life. I learned then that the power of knowledge can change your life, not just by making you more employable but because it can change your view on the world and teach you to protect yourself. I learned to protect myself mentally, and that was one of the best lessons school taught me.

I attended the local elementary school for Native Americans. I don't remember any whites at the school. I met Native American teachers who had graduated from college. I never realized before that there was life and education beyond the tribe and Robeson County.

These teachers inspired and encouraged me. They found books for me to read; there were few books at the school, but these teachers bought or borrowed books and lent them to me and others. After I finished reading all the books available to my class, the teachers borrowed books from more advanced classes for me to read. I owe so much to those teachers; they showed me the path out of poverty, stimulated my imagination, and gave me hope.

Some of the teachers who inspired and encouraged me were also named Locklear, which is a common name in the Lumbee tribe. I am especially thankful to Ms. Katrina Locklear and Ms. Jacqueline Locklear, and to Ms. Shanna Roberts, Ms. Everette, and Ms. McGirt.

I attended an integrated middle school that included Native Americans and white Americans. I was smart and read constantly, which resulted in my middle school placing me into higher-performing classes. Soon I was in classes with mostly whites, while other tribal members and friends from elementary school were in other classes. This continued through high school and put me in a strange position of not being part of either culture. I was suspended between white culture and Native American culture.

When I was in middle school I was able to disassociate from my life at home and focus on doing well in my classes. I did well in middle school; I had the highest grade-point average in both seventh and eighth grades. In high school, my native culture and tribal friends and family made things more difficult. The pressures to drink and smoke to forget I didn't have a happy home were very inviting, but I still chose to focus on school. I played sports, joined clubs, and worked to help pay the bills. I was busy all the time and never rested. Being so busy allowed me not to think about family, drugs, violence, and my terrible surrounding environment. I stayed up late most nights to do homework after extracurriculars and my various jobs. I had a goal through all of this—to get far away from home and go somewhere nobody knew my name or story. I wanted to go somewhere that didn't hurt, somewhere I could make new memories and a better life.

I found salvation in reading. I devoured books, especially books about other people's lives who lived far away. One book stands out in my memory: *The Absolutely True Diary of a Part-Time Indian* by Sherman Alexie, about a Native American boy who grew up on a reservation and was transferred to a white school off the reservation. The boy had trouble fitting in, especially at home, after experiencing a different culture. He was of two worlds. I completely identified with him.

High school challenged me. Again I was living in a white-dominated culture by day and in a Native American culture at night. I was not accepted in either. At home, other kids called me a token Native American. I spoke differently; I used bigger and more complex words. I became an outsider.

I began to distance myself from my Native American culture. Native Americans fight a lot, for example. Fist fights occur all the time for many different reasons like money disputes, disrespect toward someone, relationship dramas, family conflicts, or just perceived offenses. I stayed away from fighting, and this made me different.

Native Americans also embrace and accept a culture of drug and alcohol addiction. Drinking and doing drugs prevent people from advancing, but the culture is permissive and accepting.

When I turned eighteen during my senior year of high school, I got a dramatic tattoo on my arm. It is a half-sleeve in memory of my father. I suffered from depression and hurt myself early in high school, and this tattoo was a testament to my growth and to the journey I faced after my father's disappearance. It's bold and, like I said, the first thing most people notice about me. My tattoos are also the first thing they misunderstand about me. Since then I have gotten several more tattoos for the losses of other family members and to celebrate stories of love. But to an outsider, especially a white person, I probably look like another thug.

I suffered from anxiety and depression but did not seek treatment. I buried my bad memories and stayed too busy to think about all that was bad in my life. I focused on school and school-related activities. It was only when I was in college that I met a psychologist and began professional treatment. This led to a better understanding of some long ago acquired personal problems and medical conditions.

The therapy, coupled with a program I had attended earlier about drug culture, ultimately let me forgive those around me—including my mother and grandparents. I realized their actions and drug dependency were part of a circumstantial structure that surrounded them and not evidence of personal weakness and failure. I plan someday to help those who remain trapped in this unforgiving and damaging culture.

In high school, I knew I wanted an escape from my surroundings. There were two possible options: college and the military. I could join the army, and I even talked to recruiters from nearby Fort Bragg. When they realized I wanted to go to college, they pushed me to apply for a military scholarship that would pay for school but require service later. However, I wanted to be a teacher and help others.

I didn't have money for college, but my mother always encouraged me to be the best I could be. No one in my family had attended college, but if I wanted to go, it was with my mom's encouragement and support. She just did not have any money.

Frank Cooper, an uncle on my mother's side, also encouraged me. Frank is a teacher and knows a lot about Lumbee culture and history. He taught me about traditions where Lumbee tribesmen stood up for rights and fought injustice against the odds, like when they chased away the Ku Klux Klan in the Battle of Hayes Pond. I learned about Henry Barry Lowry, who took from the rich and gave to the poor, much like Robin Hood did for poor whites in England many years before. I realized my culture was more than alcohol and drugs and included a proud history of achievement against considerable odds.

I became determined to go to college despite the complete lack of financial resources. I also decided I wanted to go to the University of North Carolina (UNC) at Chapel Hill, which was an excellent school and not too far from my family and culture. I took college entrance exams including the ACT and did well. My grades and test scores were good enough to gain admission, but how could I pay for school? Without substantial financial aid, I could not go to college no matter how hard I worked or how smart I was.

I did some research, found out about the Gates Foundation scholarships, and applied. Eventually, I received a Gates Foundation scholarship and a couple of other scholarships and then was admitted to UNC as a Carolina Covenant recipient. That meant I could go to UNC without financial worries. This Native American girl, who had grown up surrounded by drugs and alcohol, who had moved from place to place, never having a regular home, whose friends and neighbors had rarely made it beyond high school or had dropped out even earlier, was going to the University of North Carolina. I still pinch myself sometimes to make sure it is really true.

I am at UNC now with a double major—education and sociology. I am on the dean's list and live in the Honors College. I am getting good medical treatment and live in a safe, secure, and intellectually challenging space where my fellow students relate to people like me who read books.

I will always be a member of the Lumbee tribe and value my history, culture, and traditions. I hope to help those who are still trapped and unable to find a way out of poverty and substance addiction.

Because I suffered all my life but still excelled in school, key people along the way felt I deserved help. My teachers, Frank, my mom, college counselors, and financial aid staff made my journey possible. But I feel there are a lot more people like me who don't get so lucky and are still trapped. There aren't enough caring people to save everyone. If there were, I would still have my dad, and maybe my family would have nice reunions.

I like to think that if people knew how bad others hurt and still tried to do well, maybe they would help more. My mom thinks I'm crazy because we have always been taught that the world owes us nothing. However, I think that as people who know better, we owe something to everyone else. I tattoo myself and continue my education because I owe it to myself and everyone else like me to make a way for others to follow. Just the same, people with more fortune owe it to others so they become more fortunate. It's the price of the human condition to be empathetic and help.

PART 4
GIVING BACK

8

THE IMPORTANCE OF PHILANTHROPY

The Start of Philanthropy in Higher Education

Philanthropy is defined as "an act or gift done or made for humanitarian purposes."[1] Philanthropy is the American way. It is so American that in 1998, the United States Postal Service created a stamp titled "Giving and Sharing: An American Tradition."[2] The motivation behind this stamp was to celebrate the fact that charitable donations in the United States that year had exceeded $150 billion.[3] Institutions of higher education in this country have taken part in that tradition by being recipients of such philanthropy. In 2012, 10 percent of the $316 billion (i.e., $31 billion) in charitable donations went to higher education.[4]

The connection between philanthropy and higher education has been prevalent since the inception of these educational institutions. Many colleges and universities were created with funding from private donors. Some of the country's most prominent universities were founded by rich magnates who provided the initial capital. For example, Leland Stanford was instrumental in creating Stanford University; James Buchanan Duke had a large role in funding Duke University; and the University of Chicago was founded using funds from John D. Rockefeller. Without humanitarian acts or gifts, many of these institutions would not exist or would have been unable to survive.

The author thanks University of North Carolina at Chapel Hill graduate student Lacey Lumpkin for assistance with research and the preparation of drafts of this chapter.

Harvard University was the first institution of higher education established in the American colonies. Its founding was partly the result of its first benefactor, John Harvard, who left the school half of his estate. In an effort to promote additional donations, Harvard issued a pamphlet in 1643 titled "New England's First Fruits," an argument for the need for such an institution and how it was made possible through donors.[5] This was an early fundraising effort. Harvard was successful at getting the public to understand the importance of their donations, and this support led to it becoming one of the world's best-funded and premier universities. Other universities followed suit, successfully soliciting private donations and contributing to an American higher education system that would not have been possible otherwise.

Philanthropy for educational institutions became increasingly important following the Revolutionary War, as ties were cut between the United States and England—and subsequently funding from England for education ceased. Further, states were not obligated to appropriate any funding toward colleges.[6] This meant that colleges often had to rely on private donors for financial support, which effectively reduced dependence on government funding for schools. The United States wanted to ensure that the government was not the sole source of funding for universities. This was done by encouraging private institutions to develop and grow. As a result, the donations of wealthy individuals and formal associations to these private institutions was critical throughout the early to mid-1800s.[7]

The type of support garnered from these fundraising efforts has changed over time. During colonial times, in-kind gifts were necessary to start a school, often because of a lack of hard currency. These gifts could include everything from land on which to construct buildings to animals, books for the students, or even a sugar dish.[8] Today, financial funding is necessary for expanding and sustaining a school. Private funding supports scholarships, new buildings, new academic and development programs, and athletic programs and facilities. According to author Ann Blackman, "while past major donors largely built institutions, current major donors are transforming them."[9] While physical gifts like land were helpful in the past, in modern times monetary donations are of the greatest importance to help both students and the institutions themselves: "These gifts are sometimes used to fund current operations through annual giving campaigns. However, many gifts are given specifically to an institution's endowment fund so that they will support specific purposes or activities—such as student scholarships or medical research—for many years to come."[10]

The sources of philanthropy have shifted somewhat from individuals to an organized and institutional giving base. The sources of organized giving are typically foundations and endowments. These organizations often have greater resources and can make larger grants. Recipient universities are also often given greater flexibility than is available from public funds. This is important for universities, as it also allows for broader, less specifically defined research efforts, general campus development, new investments, and investments in businesses that may produce future profits that will go toward the college or university.

Endowments are typically larger donations given for the ongoing support and sustainability of the university. Endowment gifts are generally invested, and the interest earned and any profits realized support educational activities annually and over the long term. The principal gift is retained and does not expire. According to researchers and writers John R. Thelin and Richard W. Trollinger, the rule of thumb for many universities is to spend 5 percent or less of an endowment in one year,[11] but the return on investment varies.

Because public universities typically receive less in donations than private universities, the overall endowment funds for public universities are usually smaller; the top public school endowment fund value of $18.2 billion in 2012 was held by the University of Texas, whereas in the same year the top private endowment fund was around $30.2 billion at Harvard.[12]

Philanthropy and access to higher education go together. There are insufficient public funds to cover the financial needs of university students. Historically, underserved communities have lacked access to higher education for a variety of reasons including the cost of attendance. According to Thelin and Trollinger, there is extensive evidence of philanthropy in higher education working to provide access to students who may not have access to college or resources for an adequate education; providing these resources and support improves the economic outcomes for individuals. Philanthropy strengthens the country's economy and provides greater social access and mobility.

Why Is Philanthropy Important Today?

Philanthropic gifts are critical to funding many essential activities, including research budgets at many of the United States' top universities. A key part of the funding for research budgets comes from donations to fund important research opportunities that are more extensive, longer term, and often ideal for younger or less-experienced researchers who have greater difficulty competing with more-experienced researchers for government or large institutional funds.[13]

Philanthropic efforts also cover eligible student financial aid costs, subsidizing tuition and/or room and board, and as a result provide opportunities and access to college for first-generation students, individuals from underserved populations, and individuals from poor families who otherwise could not afford a college education. Donations to support the hiring of well-respected professors, expand or modernize lab and classroom facilities, and fund or expand new programs improve the overall quality of education for all students.

To foster strong relationships with donors, universities usually focus on developing specific initiatives targeted to gain philanthropic support. They usually define and then implement a vision of the university's future and list specific targets and objectives. The University of North Carolina's $4.2 billion For All Kind: Campaign for Carolina is one such campaign, but most universities initiate similar funding campaigns periodically. For All: The Indiana University's Bicentennial Campaign is another example.

According to the Council for Aid to Education (CAE), universities received approximately $40.3 billion in private donations in 2015; this is the highest amount donated since the CAE started to record the information in 1957.[14] Data also indicates that in 2015, more than half of donations came from foundations (28.8 percent) and alumni (26.9 percent). Additional donation sources are as follows: nonalumni individuals (19.9 percent), corporations (14.3 percent), and other (10.2 percent).[15] Donations from individuals, usually alumni, have been the root of philanthropic culture for years, and many bigger donors have a history of giving. "Cultivating a Culture of Philanthropy: New Approaches to New Realities," an article by former vice president for advancement at Georgetown University James Michael Langley, states that many donors who gift $1 million or more to a university or college on average have a fifteen- to twenty-year history of previous giving; "further, when an alum makes his or her 15th annual gift, the probability of him or her leaving a large portion of his or her estate to an alma mater, according to our analyses, increases by 80 percent."[16] Attracting and retaining two or more decades of giving is often a defining characteristic of loyal alumni donors.

Despite the importance of private donations to fund higher education, there is evidence that education is not receiving a fair share of private giving. In 2013, educator and author Judith R. Fox wrote an article published in *Philanthropy NYU*, a publication of the George H. Heyman, Jr. Center for Philanthropy and Fundraising at New York University, titled "The Importance of Philanthropy to Education."[17] It discussed how it is generally believed that successful and wealthy people have a duty to help others and improve the condition of the world, but it is less obvious that this perceived obligation includes supporting education. Whether that support is directly for schools, funding research, libraries, museums, or curriculum development, many ignore and often overlook the importance of education and how heavily reliant schools are on contributions from donors and philanthropists: "Perhaps because talk about education is 'in our faces' regularly, often the object of criticism rather than celebration, educational programs and institutions may not command the serious attention from donors they deserve."[18]

A study by the Center on Budget and Policy Priorities (CBPP) emphasizes the importance of philanthropy in higher education—state funding at public colleges and universities has decreased over time by almost 28 percent while tuition costs have increased by approximately 27 percent.[19] This has made access to college even more challenging, as financial aid is harder to obtain.

In today's society, to obtain desired professional and well-paying jobs, education is even more important than in previous times. Many jobs and professions now require college degrees regardless of their skill level and worth ethic; a job-seeking candidate with a degree is often chosen over one without, despite the specific requirements of the work. As the CBPP describes it, these trends and effects of degree inflation contribute to less economic opportunity, growth, wages, and productivity and weaker societies. This cycle will never be broken, and desired growth may never be achieved without providing assistance to the areas that really need it.[20]

In Olivier Zunz's book *Philanthropy in America: A History*, he concludes that American philanthropy is not just an activity for the well-to-do.[21] The University of Virginia history professor states that even people with average incomes in the United States donate money to fund research and the common good. Zunz believes that this inclination stemmed from the creation of community chests that aimed to fundraise for community projects and charity organizations; many more people became involved in investing money to support the enhancement of various community and global efforts: "American philanthropy is not a matter of the rich helping people in need, but of people, rich or not, providing for their own future."[22] Philanthropy is becoming more of a self-interested task as donors realize that they are contributing to their own welfare by bettering society, as Rockefeller, Harvard, Carnegie, and Sage set the precedent and foundation for. "Charity had been for the needy; philanthropy was to be for mankind," Zunz writes.[23] Anyone can contribute to the needs of higher education. This concept of self-interest in giving should contribute to the motivation for all to consider donating whatever they can for higher education.

Examples of Philanthropy in Higher Education

A good example of modern philanthropy in higher education is the case of Charles and Shirley Weiss and their support of students in North Carolina. Their involvement in educational philanthropy started when Shirley, a former professor of mine, asked her husband, "Charles. How can we give back to our University and community?"[24] This question was answered with the creation of the Weiss Urban Livability Program in 1992. The program is geared toward graduate students who display an interest in urban affairs (regardless of their area of study). It provides a supplemental fellowship to graduate students who are nominated by their departments and then chosen by the faculty advisory board.[25] Part of the motivation behind creating this program was the Weisses' very clear understanding of students' needs in today's higher institutions: "Graduate students need the money—it's that simple," Shirley said.[26] Another motivation was the fact that they cared about the school where they had spent a good portion of their lives teaching, and they wanted it to succeed. Part of a school's success depends on the quality of the students it attracts, and scholarships can help attract top-quality students who need money. Lastly, they wanted to promote one of their special interests, urban livability: "We want to encourage the best students to come to this university and see how, in their specialized field, they can create a higher level of urban livability."[27] This idea continues to support graduate students at UNC Chapel Hill.

Another way philanthropy plays an active role in higher education is through funding assistantships and associateship programs. These positions are often key to many graduate students' ability to further their education. Having tuition covered, receiving an additional stipend for living expenses, and gaining teaching experience is an opportunity made possible because of generous donors. At Ohio State University, the Office Associate-ship Program offers many positions to students in need, especially within the Knowlton School of Architecture, considering that studying architec-ture is expensive and demanding, which makes it difficult to work consis-tently while still in school.[28] Ohio State professor and architecture section head Robert Livesey states that having the partnerships to make these pro-grams possible benefits the entire college as a whole.

"Because of this support, we can afford to have more graduate assistants and teaching assistants, and that helps us with our student-to-faculty ratio in our large lecture courses," he said. "The program is hugely important to us in terms of maintaining the idea of education by discourse."[29]

Philanthropy at Pennsylvania State University also shows how donor support can have a great impact on a school and its students. Penn State's College of Education states that their priority is to offer an exceptional edu-cation to students taught by some of the top educators and supported by innovative methods and technologies. Penn State declares that the college is able to pursue and carry out this goal through many philanthropic invest-ments—"Gifts to the College of Education make tangible differences in the lives of students and faculty. Philanthropy enables us to catalyze important advances in learning and provides the financial support our students need to realize their dream of a Penn State degree. We continue to have ambi-tious goals for the future and your donation is an important part of our path forward."[30]

Penn State takes pride in the many accomplishments their college has achieved with the help of generous giving and philanthropy. Many of the philanthropic efforts that benefit Penn State involve programs established by alumni in hopes of reducing barriers for students pursuing an education, typically through scholarships.

In 2003, John Gilmartin, a Class of 1965 Penn State alum, created the John Gilmartin Trustee Scholarship to assist students, including future teachers, who suffered from the dwindling state support for public colleges and universities such as Penn State. Gilmartin has made many contribu-tions to the school, including other scholarships and opportunities that en-gage individuals from varying background and communities. Donors such as Gilmartin are why many students—like Dana Mitchell—go on to excel. In return, Dana plans to give the same encouragement and support to her students after she becomes a teacher.

Another initiative taken by Penn State's College of Education is their Summer College Opportunity Program in Education (SCOPE), a rigorous program that provides academic enrichment and preparation to low-income, first-generation college attendees or underrepresented students.[31]

Conclusion

Fulton Blackman and his coauthors in their book *A New Way of Giving* claim that "America's intellectual infrastructure was donated by philanthropists."[32] American colleges and universities would not be what they are today without private donors. They also will not flourish in the future without continued support. When donations flow into colleges and universities, buildings and facilities are constructed, making schools more attractive and user-friendly to students. New majors are created, and current ones become more robust and better targeted to student interests and changing technology. Resources are made available to create innovative programs that add to student development. Students who otherwise wouldn't be able to afford the cost of a school are provided scholarships and, therefore, access to an education. In short, philanthropic donations allow flexibility to support the projects and transformations that government funding does not finance; they enhance student experiences and establish partnerships and networks between like-minded individuals who will contribute to the longevity of universities. To achieve their goals, universities require more funding than the government can provide: "Complementary and alternative funding is needed, and philanthropy is making an increasingly important contribution."[33] Over time, when universities thrive, society thrives. Education contributes to greater economic growth and stability; with the proper resources, many more people will have access to education that, in turn, can lead to further development on both personal and global levels.

9

GIVING BACK

Milt Stewart

M Y NAME IS MILT STEWART. I AM A RETIRED INTERNATIONAL LAW-
yer, having practiced for forty-six years in an international law firm
with 550 lawyers in eleven offices. I am also vice chair of the Indiana University Foundation board of directors and volunteer chair of IU's $3 billion
capital campaign.

Everything I have achieved, everything I am, and everything I have are,
in large part, due to the extraordinary public education I received in primary and secondary school as well as at the college and postgraduate level.

I have said in the past that I was a poor kid. This is not entirely fair
to my parents. Like millions of couples at the end of World War II and at
my father's discharge from the Army Air Corps, my parents found themselves with few possessions or financial resources. My father had been a
blacksmith and a farmer before he had entered the armed services in World
War II. When he was discharged, he promised my mother that they would
have a better life and that he would have a better job and career.

I was born in December 1945, at the very end of World War II. Along
with my brother, I was the beneficiary of my father's commitment. He obtained a clerical job with a large insurance company and was transferred to
Lincoln, Nebraska, a town with an excellent school system. Although the
family resources were meager, my brother and I never knew we were poor.

Milt Stewart has been active, successful, and generous in donating his time and energy to
raising funds to support Indiana University's initiatives, including scholarship funding. He
was introduced to the author by a mutual acquaintance at IU.

We lived in an abandoned air force barracks for the first five years of my life and in a rooming house for the next five years. Although our economic circumstances were limited, we were loved, well nourished, and well educated.

My first seminal moment in public education was in the sixth grade. I was lucky enough to be placed in what now would be called a gifted-and-talented program. My teacher, whom I will never forget, was Mildred Bartos. A kind, gray-haired, lifelong teacher, Mrs. Bartos was also a task master. From day one she demanded rigor, focused attention, and showing up with your homework—which was considerable—done. She taught us that in order to excel, we had to work hard, be diligent, and be prepared.

The next critical step in my public education was our family's move to West Lafayette, Indiana, where my father had been transferred to because of a job promotion. West Lafayette High School (WLHS) was ranked among the top ten high schools in the nation. It was essentially a laboratory school for Purdue University. The high school campus was adjacent to the Purdue campus. Enrollment at WLHS was approximately six hundred students. Every year, consistently 100 percent of the graduating class attended a two- or four-year college. Over 98 percent graduated from the college of their choice. Although WLHS offered the usual athletic and extracurricular activities, its primary focus was academic.

Early in my sophomore year, the guidance counselor, Mr. Evans, called me into his office. He asked, and I quote, "Where are we going to college, young man?" Being a bit of a smart ass, my answer was, "I don't think that is in the cards for me. No one in my family has ever attended college." Mr. Evans answered, "That is not a satisfactory reply. If you really want to attend college, and you should, we can help you find a way."

I discussed the issue at dinner that evening with my parents. After reflection and discussion, they indicated that if I really wanted to attend college, I could do so essentially for free at Purdue University because my mother was on staff. Both because I did not want to attend college and live at home and because Purdue focused on agriculture, engineering, and pharmacy (none of which interested me), I told my parents that I would not attend Purdue.

With my guidance counselor's help I began to interview and visit colleges in and around Indiana. I swam, ran track, and played football competitively in high school. Several small colleges offered me athletic scholarships, but I knew I was not good enough at any of those sports to successfully compete at the collegiate level.

In the process of interviewing and visiting schools, I was invited to Indiana University. A friend and I went for a long weekend. Both of us fell in love with the campus and the prospect of attending a Big Ten university, but cost was a major obstacle.

I arranged a meeting with the financial aid office and was fortunate enough to be offered a fee-remission scholarship for my first year, which paid my tuition. My parents were able to give me $100 a month, and that, along with my meager savings from summer jobs, got me through the first year.

I did extremely well academically in my first year and received a sizable scholarship in my sophomore year. I also worked one and sometimes two jobs on campus each semester. Thereafter, based on a combination of my grades and need, scholarships saw me all the way through my undergraduate political science degree at Indiana University. I graduated in 1968 with honors and, in the same month, also married and received my commission in the US Army. I was also debt-free, having successfully avoided student loans.

I was often told that I liked to argue and debate and should consider becoming a lawyer. I had never met or known a lawyer and, frankly, didn't understand what the profession was about. However, I met with the dean and admissions officer of the IU law school and was encouraged to apply. I visited practicing lawyers to learn more about the profession. When I applied to law school at IU, I was admitted.

In law school, I again received scholarships all the way through, including winning two prestigious fellowships: the competitive State Farm fellowship and the Edwards fellowship, which is the largest single scholarship awarded by Indiana University. I graduated from the Indiana University Maurer School of Law in 1971, summa cum laude, and to my great good fortune was given a deferment from my initial active duty obligation with the US Army. The legal market was extremely strong in 1971, and I was able to interview in all the cities where I thought my wife and I might want to live. We picked Portland, Oregon. I practiced mergers and acquisitions law initially, first in Portland and thereafter around the world. My firm had grown to be an international player in both the mergers and acquisitions and corporate transactional markets.

And now a few words about philanthropy. It would have been impossible for me to attend Indiana University, either as an undergraduate or in law school, without the incredible generosity of alumni and other donors who consistently give scholarship funds to the university. Scholarships for students with a combination of need and academic excellence were, and are, especially important.

As I indicated at the beginning of this chapter, everything I have achieved is attributable, in large part, to my quality public education. My education at the university level occurred because of the philanthropy of those who had preceded me at Indiana University. It is hard to imagine Indiana University without philanthropy. From countless buildings, fellowships, professorships, and scholarships to the funding of athletics and extracurricular activities, Indiana University, and hundreds of institutions like it, would be shells of their current forms without philanthropy.

Education is the great leveler of American society. Public education is critical to that mission. At the higher-education level, philanthropy is the fuel that enables the scholarships, loans, and financial assistance that are critical for students of modest means to obtain higher education degrees. These students can then pursue careers and have life achievements that they could not have dreamed of without financial assistance.

Unfortunately, many alumni of institutions of higher learning, even if they are motivated to support scholarships for students, are not aware of the ways to do so. Many of these ways of supporting students are win-win.

1. Make a quick and easy gift of cash. The benefit to the donor is an income tax deduction, and for the school there is an immediate benefit to student scholarships.
2. Secure a fixed income while avoiding market risk by establishing a charitable gift annuity. The donor receives substantial tax benefits and a higher rate of income from his or her assets in the form of an annuity.
3. Maximize heirs' inheritance while still benefiting the school. You name the school as beneficiary of your retirement plan and leave other assets to your family. This can substantially reduce estate and income taxes.
4. Avoid taxes on capital gains by giving appreciated stock or bonds that have been held for over one year. This can result in a substantial income tax reduction and avoidance of capital gains tax.
5. Share your enjoyment of a collection or other personal items of value by donating tangible personal property related to the school's educational mission. This, too, can result in a substantial charitable tax deduction based on the full market value of the collection.
6. Make a large gift with little cost by giving the institution a life insurance policy you no longer need. This can result in a current and possible future income tax deduction.

7. Give all or a percentage of your real property to the institution. If you like, you can make the gift subject to a retained life estate, which means that you, or you and your spouse, will continue to live in and enjoy the property for the rest of your lives. You will still obtain a significant tax deduction.

8. You may make an outright gift of your property to the institution and receive, in return, a charitable remainder trust that will pay you an income for the rest of your life or the lives of you and your spouse.

9. Alternatively, you can leave your property to the institution by making a gift in your will or living trust. These gifts remain amendable and even revocable and leave you in control of the assets for your lifetime.

These foregoing examples are not meant to be exhaustive. There are many variations on them. They are not offered as legal or accounting advice. If you are interested in making a gift pursuant to any of these mechanisms, please consult your lawyer and accountant. In addition, the gift officer of any institution you might wish to benefit through a gift should be happy to meet with you and explain these and other options further. If you decide to make a gift, remember that it's not the size of the gift that matters; it's the difference it makes in the lives of the students.

10

JOHN KUYKENDALL AND
DAVIDSON COLLEGE

D AVIDSON COLLEGE IS FULL OF STUDENTS RECEIVING FINANCIAL
aid, and it's also full of success stories. These things are not mere coin-
cidences; scholarships allow a diverse group of students to attend Davidson,
and then Davidson is able to give those students the tools they need to succeed and have a "disproportionate impact for good" in their communities.[1]

Davidson's recent history has seen a lot of upward mobility, made possible by its financial aid services. John Kuykendall has both benefited from
and initiated these changes during his time as a student and then as the
college's president.

John grew up on a dairy farm outside of Charlotte, North Carolina.
Both of his parents worked in the city, so John went to public schools there
and spent the afternoons studying in his parents' offices until it was time
to go home. When it was time for John and his brother to attend college in
1955, the family found the cost of college to be an unaffordable barrier. His
mom worked for the local school system, but his dad was just beginning a
new job. "There was a gap in time in which our family really didn't have the
resources for the full freight of my older brother and me to go to Davidson,"
says John. But his father, a Davidson alumnus himself, was insistent and
encouraged both of his sons to seek scholarship aid.

The author thanks Davidson College student Alivia McAtee for assistance with research and
the preparation of drafts of this chapter.

At that time, the financial aid program at Davidson wasn't as clearly divided between merit-based and need-based aid as it is today. There were a few named scholarships given out by individuals or corporations, most of which were unrelated to financial need. Fortunately, both John and his brother were able to secure scholarships. John received coverage of his tuition, room, fees, and books from the Union Carbide Corporation, and his brother received comparable funds through a program called the Baker Scholarship. John was able to cover the rest of his expenses through summer jobs, a small allowance from his family, and a stipend from the ROTC Advanced Cadet program.

Even in 1955, the importance of scholarships at Davidson was clearly evident, according to John: "A number of the people who went to Davidson on [The Union Carbide and the Baker] scholarships in particular wound up having remarkable careers later on in all kinds of areas: Rhodes scholars, the editor of *Time* magazine, the head of the Guggenheim Foundation. It's quite an array of things that these people did, and it was probably a result of the selection process at the beginning because some of these people never would have come to Davidson had it not been for financial aid."

As a student, John supplemented a diverse course load (he tried majoring in chemistry, then economics, before deciding on English) with a comparatively diverse set of extracurricular activities. He served as the student government president, was a member of a social fraternity, volunteered with a nondenominational religious group through the YMCA, played soccer, and was an ROTC Advanced Cadet. After graduating, John became an ordained minister. He later received his PhD from Princeton University and served as a professor of religion and campus pastor for Auburn University before being asked to be Davidson's president in 1984. Reluctant to leave his passion for teaching behind, John continued to teach one class a semester at Davidson during his presidency.

In addition to being a professor, as president, John was able to make great strides in Davidson's financial and humanitarian endeavors. During his tenure, a financial campaign larger than anything previously begun at a liberal arts college was completed and brought in over $160 million. Many of those funds went toward creating more scholarships. John's inaugural address, called "Scholarship and Servanthood," emphasized how Davidson seems to be a preparatory experience for people who would eventually give back to the community in great ways: "I was talking about the trajectory of the lives of the people who graduate from Davidson and how they wind up being the people who were really counted on in their communities to be the folks who can get things done and be sensitive to the needs of other people." He invested in that belief by opening an office of community service and bringing the Bonner Scholars program to campus.

John also oversaw the first-ever Project Life bone marrow donor recruitment drive in 1990. Now, nearly one hundred colleges have followed suit, and thousands of Davidson students have joined the registry. That achievement is just a small mark on his lifetime of commitment to service. When asked what sort of community service projects he's been involved in since graduating, John let out a laugh and said, "Oh gosh, you know I graduated over sixty years ago!" To name a few of his endeavors: he's served on the board of nonprofits such as the Red Cross and the Bonner Foundation, volunteered for the Head Start Program with the Alabama Council on Human Relations, and helped with the Crisis Assistance Ministry.

When asked about his current ties to Davidson, John humbly says that he's "not involved, but present" on campus. Although his time as a student, teacher, and president at Davidson is over, John still visits every day and has his own library carrel. John also has both a scholarship and an award in his name. The Kuykendall Scholarship, funded by John and his wife, was established for students who've had high school careers distinguished by service and/or come from underrepresented groups in the larger society, whether that is due to racial, ethnic, or physical differences.

According to Davidson's website, the John W. Kuykendall Award for Community Service "recognizes alumni who have provided extraordinary service to their community, demonstrating leadership in the spirit of John W. Kuykendall, our 15th president." John says that he was honored, gratified, and just a little bit embarrassed when the award was announced: "If you look at the list of [recipients], my goodness what a wonderful array of people who have done all kinds of different things. It's an honor to have my name associated with them over the years."

John's story reminds us of how far the financial aid programs at schools like Davidson have come. He is also a testament to the great things someone who is empowered by a scholarship can accomplish.

Eli Kahn

Eli Kahn attended Davidson almost fifty years after John Kuykendall enrolled. Eli is a more contemporary testament to just how much a scholarship can affect one's course in life. As a MacDonald Scholar, Eli was required to complete 280 hours of service annually in exchange for his scholarship. For him, though, servitude was a way of life, not a chore.[2]

Eli had grown up in Baltimore, Maryland, and had been diagnosed with leukemia as a toddler. He'd survived thanks to the care he'd received at Johns Hopkins Hospital. When Eli was twelve, he decided to show his thanks. He started a fundraising project called Cartridges for a Cure, which recycled used inkjet cartridges. All of the proceeds went to Johns Hopkins to support childhood cancer research, and Eli was able to raise nearly $100,000 by the time he graduated high school.

When he arrived at Davidson, he dove right into service. He volunteered at the Ada Jenkins Center, which provides health and educational services to those living in poverty to increase their social mobility, and The First Tee, which provides educational programs for children through golf.

"The Bonner and MacDonald scholarship program[s] were such an integral part of my Davidson experience and helped foster a community with other students who shared similar interests. It also afforded me the opportunity to work directly with great organizations across Davidson and Charlotte during my time at Davidson and helped spark my interest in pursuing a career in the nonprofit sector after graduation," says Eli.

During the summer after their sophomore year, Eli and his friend Colin Ristig '13, embarked on the service trip of a lifetime. With the help of grants from both the Dean Rusk International Studies Program and the Center for Civic Engagement at Davidson, the two participated in a two-week auto rickshaw rally across India, improving the lives of the villagers they met along the way. The pair heard about the Rickshaw Challenge through their mutual love of *Amazing Race*–style adventures. The organization provides a couple of options for tours through India on traditional rickshaws. Eli and Colin chose the Deccan Odyssey trip, which covers almost seven hundred miles on India's southwestern coast, starting in Panaji and ending in Mumbai.

For Eli and Colin, an awesome, immersive, and adventurous vacation to India wasn't enough. "We wanted to connect this amazing opportunity to explore India with a larger cause," says Eli. Through a family connection, they were able to partner with the charity Unite to Light, which produces solar reading lights to distribute to third-world countries. The lights improve the education, health, and prosperity of the people who receive them by providing a clean and free source of light. Eli and his friend decided to bulk order some lights and distribute them to villages they passed through on their rickshaws: "Unite to Light and the Rickshaw challenge provided us with the opportunity to fulfill a dream of participating in this amazing race while also helping out a great organization."

The two were able to distribute lights to several different schools and community centers during their trip, supplying one hundred lights to the villagers. Eli says the villagers were "extremely friendly and welcoming. I think that most people we passed were so shocked to see a caravan of foreigners driving brightly painted rickshaws to begin with."

After graduating from Davidson, Eli was selected as a Davidson Impact Fellow and worked for the Foundation for the Carolinas in Charlotte. The fellowship allows students to get their foot in the door at nonprofits while working with direct supervision from high-level leaders. The Foundation for the Carolinas works to connect donors and nonprofits and is one of the largest community foundations in the country. After Eli's fellowship ended, he joined the foundation's team as a program associate and spent four years working there. For Eli, service started as a way to give back to a personal cause: cancer research. It ended up providing him with a scholarship, a career, and countless other opportunities.

Many students who come to Davidson on scholarship become successful. Then, many successful Davidson graduates give back to their alma mater by endowing scholarships. It's unknown whether Davidson's alumni are successful because of the school's strong scholarship program or Davidson's strong scholarship program is due to the successful alumni. One thing is certain, though: if one stops, the other will surely fall in succession. It is so imperative that scholarships continue to be endowed, not just at Davidson but at all schools. That way, individuals will have a fair chance to attend the institution that can catalyze the potential for success already within them.

MY STORY

Getting an Education and Giving Back in Africa

Edward Kabaka

I WAS BORN IN THE LITTLE VILLAGE OF MIKEI IN NYATIKE SUBCOUNTY, Migori County, in Kenya. I lost both my parents at the age of nine. My early years were marred with pain and agony. I became the head of a household of four siblings when I was twelve years old. I had to go and work in the gold mines to raise money to buy food for our family. Life was horrible. Every day started with complete uncertainty; I was not sure whether there would be food on the table. When I wasn't working in the mines, I often walked for up to five hours to sell cassava roots or sometimes exchanged them for other goods in a barter system in an open-air market called Ayego.

My village of Mikei was underdeveloped, with no access roads and no high school. The existing elementary school was completely dilapidated. The community had a single source of water from the river Migori, which was three hours away by foot. The walk was dirty. There was no electricity in the entire community and no health facility within ten kilometers. The living conditions in the village was exacerbated by the high HIV/AIDS prevalence, which resulted in many children left behind as orphans.

Edward Kabaka shared his story from a small village in Kenya, a country where he is active in many initiatives and community-enhancing projects. He was introduced to the author by a mutual friend who worked with him on projects sponsored by Kids for Peace, including development of medical facilities in a village in Kenya and an initiative to provide shoes for children. The gift of financial aid to allow someone from a poor family to obtain an education transforms lives, not only in the United States but around the world.

I was a child laborer from an early age. I had no option but to work for people to ensure that our family had food on the table. I worked everywhere I could. I did weeding, manual work, and gold mining; I worked on tobacco farms, burned wood to create charcoal for fuel, and many other hard jobs in order to make ends meet. I was beaten and whipped by rod or rope during plowing with oxen. The scars and marks are still evident on most parts of my body. The trauma that I went through cannot be quantified. Life for me was scary and painful, and I grew hardened in the process of trying to cope with the reality of the unkind and unfavorable environment.

The situation became even more unbearable when I attended high school (Kanyawanga). It was hard to go in tattered clothes, yes I could not afford the uniforms the school required. I had to take a break from school periodically to work in the gold mines to raise money for school fees. Then I resumed my studies in subsequent months. I still managed to pass with good grades and met the college entry requirement in Kenya.

I attended Meru Teachers Training College to pursue a certificate for teaching in elementary schools. At that time, I could not afford even the fare for transport to college. I had no usable shoes, but, after talking to a friend, I received a donation of slippers to put on my feet. Slippers ordinarily are used at home or for bathing, but the donated slippers were still in good condition, so I used them as shoes. I attended the Teachers Training College, which is about 750 kilometers from my home village, with the donated slippers on my feet. Some other people donated just enough money to pay my bus fare. I had nothing left for any level of shopping.

When I reached college, everyone stared at me; I looked strange in that environment. I did not have a big box with my personal possessions like everyone else. I lacked the money to pay any college fees. When I arrived, the security guard at the gate thought that I wanted some manual work. One important thing that I had was the admissions letter that identified me and distinguished me from the casual workers. When I was allowed to go to the admissions department, I could not produce any of the items on their four-page list of requirements for attendees. The admissions officer laughed at me. She asked if I was really coming to attend the college without any of their requirements. She then told me to go back home. It was already approaching 4:00 p.m., and I had only two dollars left. I could not afford my transport back home. I didn't even have enough money to afford a late lunch or supper.

I managed to make a collect call to Reverend Nicholas Oenga from a public telephone booth at the college gate. He agreed to send me fare to go back home the next day. I spent that night in the cold at the gate next to the security house.

Later, with well-wishers and more manual work, I was able to raise some money to pay for my college fees. I also received a scholarship from World Vision Kenya. Adding that to my work savings, and with help from others, I was able to return to Teachers College. Without this financial help, I would not have been able to attend college and might still be working in the gold mines or doing other manual labor.

After completing my two-year program, I was employed by the teacher service commission to teach in elementary school. I became one of the best science and math teachers in the area. My students performed better than students from other schools in the region. Even with this rewarding work as a teacher, my heart, mind, and soul were not fully satisfied. I wanted to work with and improve local communities, build their capabilities, and enhance their potential support for the people.

Following my passion, I founded a not-for-profit organization called Rieko Kenya in 2007. The vision of Rieko Kenya is to aspire to have a world free from poverty, hunger, and social injustice. Its mission is to alleviate poverty and give a voice to the disadvantaged and poor communities in Kenya. I wanted to use Rieko Kenya as an instrument of delivering opportunity and prosperity, ensuring sustainable development, actively engaging the communities to participate in decision-making and local initiatives, and enhancing capacities for locals to determine their own destiny. Rieko Kenya was started to inspire local people to start with what they know and build with what they have to secure what they want.

In 2009, which was a great turning point in my life and career, I secured a scholarship from the Canadian International Development Agency (CIDA) to pursue my study of community development leadership at Coady International Institute within St. Francis Xavier University in Canada. My time at this transforming college shaped my thinking about development. I learned community development approaches. This is a strength-based development practice that is based on people's assets rather than their problems, strengths rather than weaknesses, and community potential rather than shortcomings.

After returning to Kenya and working with Rieko Kenya, I managed to build people networks and links, inspire active community participation, and gradually transform the plague of poverty in Mikei village and its environs to a more productive attitude. The community initiatives also led to multiplier effects and the emergence of both anticipated and unexpected improvements in people's lives. As a result, we now have better roads, a good secondary school, electricity, women-owned small-scale businesses, and local saving and lending communities (SILC). With a partnership involving Kids for Peace and the American people, we now have a wonderful and life-transforming school for orphans and vulnerable children aged three to eight. The school provides quality education, day care, meals, uniforms, and scholastic materials. We now have a more enlightened community, people actively participating in their own development agenda, human and children rights being upheld, and heightened HIV/AIDS education both in schools and at the community level. Even though the community still lacks clean water, exposing villagers to major health threats, many in the community are boiling the water collected from the river. Life has been transformed and significantly improved (compared to ten years ago) through our community strategies and initiatives.

My happiness and our achievements resonate with the number of people in the community whose living standards have positively changed. I am not finished yet, but I am happy inside and out to see meaningful and impactful positive transformation realized. It has been a life journey that started painfully but ended in realizing magnificent positive change for poor, disadvantaged, and marginalized communities—including my own village. Without support including financial aid from others, I never would have been able to achieve this, and my village would still be poor and without hope.

PART 5
STORIES FROM SCHOLARSHIP DONORS

11

BARNARD SCHOLARSHIP

Not Just about the Money

David Barnard

MY DAD, GEORGE BARNARD, GREW UP IN IN CRAMERTON, A SMALL town in North Carolina. He was the fourth of four children. Unfortunately, his dad had tuberculosis and died when Dad was nine. This forced his mother to work in the mills to support the family. The money, however, was not enough, so the family, at times, had to rely on the support of their neighbors—many of whom were also poor.

The Allens Believed in Dad

When Dad was a teenager, a couple in his church (The Cramer Memorial United Methodist Church) believed in him. They were Dr. and Mrs. Allen. They thought that Dad should not only graduate from high school but also go to college. They spearheaded a "love offering" at the church that Dad says raised $500. Dad used these funds as the seed money to go to Duke, where he met Mom—Pat Croom, who also was a student at Duke. Dad graduated from Duke and then went to the University of North Carolina for his MD and the Menninger Clinic for his psychiatry residency.

David Barnard was introduced to the author by a mutual acquaintance at Davidson College and agreed to share his experience in giving. He is a member of Davidson's Board of Trustees and retired as a partner and portfolio manager with Wellington Management Company in Boston.

Passing On the Gift—Returning to Cramerton

Dad worked many years at Shands Hospital at the University of Florida. When he retired, Mom and Dad reflected on the importance of the gift that they had received many years earlier from his neighbors at Cramerton. They wanted to pass on that gift and returned to Cramerton in search of a way to do so. They met Jennie Stultz, who was the mayor of Gastonia and also the head of the local education foundation. They agreed it would be best to set up a scholarship for Gaston county as a whole and look for students like Dad who had "done well with a head wind but could benefit from a tail wind."

With Consistent Donations to the Endowment, the Scholarship Increased to $5,000 per Person per Year

We initially started the scholarship with a $100,000 gift to its endowment. This was enough to sponsor two students at the $2,000 per year level. By making consistent gifts to the endowment over the years, however, we are now able to have a Barnard Scholar each year and award them each $5,000 per year. It is now among the larger scholarships for Gaston county.

Not Just about the Money; Includes Receiving the Love and Support from Our Family

The Barnard scholarship, however, is not just about the money. It is also about receiving the love and support of our entire family. The vast majority of the winners come from families with multiple problems—not the least being financial. Many of these students have faced substantial hardships in their lives but somehow remained successful. They need not only money but also love and support. We offer it—if they want it. This can range from Mom sending them "care packages" at college or birthday presents, to members on the selection committee helping them solve legal issues, to having lunch or dinner with them to discuss their life plans. This support is critical for this group of students. One past candidate offered to turn down the Myers scholarship (the most prestigious one in the county) if it would allow her to win the Barnard. "I don't just need the money," she said. "I need the support, too." Fortunately, she won both!

How Do Families Stay Together? A "Shared Property" and Family Charity

A colleague of mine at my former firm was an estate attorney. I asked him what keeps families together. He said two things: a shared property and a family charity. He explained that everyone is so busy that we will not get together to play, but we will gather to help others. This is why a family charity is so important. All eleven public high schools in Gaston county are eligible each year to nominate one person for the scholarship. The Community Foundation of Gaston County, the administrator of the Barnard scholarship, sends Mom and Dad, all five of their children, their spouses, and each member of the selection committee those applications. Receiving those files is one of the highlights of my year because these are truly remarkable students, and we know that we will be able to help one in a material and life-changing way. The buzz flows through our family as we all vote and narrow the list to four finalists. The selection committee, which is composed equally of Barnards and non-Barnards, then meets at Dad's childhood church to pick the winner. Those interviews are extremely powerful, moving, and almost religious in nature. By the end of the day, we have picked the winner, grown closer as a family and committee, and started building the next strong relationship with the winner.

Why Do We Give?

The real reason is not just because we want to help others. We understand the power and importance of the gifts that our family received years ago and feel an obligation to pass on those blessings, but it is much more. Awarding the scholarship is one of the highlights of my year each year regardless of whether I am serving on the selection committee. We have changed someone's life—someone who is special—in a powerful and positive way. We did something important, something that mattered. What can feel better than that?

12

ROBERT J. LAKE SCHOLARSHIP

In Memory of My Father

Gilmour Lake

I WENT THERE. . . . MY DAD WENT THERE. . . . I LOVE DAVIDSON AND all it represents. Two of my best friends came to visit me one day—E. Craig Wall Jr. '59, board of trustees' chairman; and John Kuykendall '59, president of the college. They asked me about starting a scholarship for children of Presbyterian ministers, and that was meaningful to me because I am the child of a Presbyterian minister and understood the financial challenges a minister faces when sending a child to college. What really sold me was the respect I had for those two men and the mission behind helping outstanding children of Presbyterian ministers to attend Davidson.

When I think back to my time at Davidson, one of the most meaningful values of my college experience was the friends I made. Many of those same people are my closest friends today. I just stayed with one of them recently so we could go hear John Kuykendall preach.

The genesis of my giving is my dad. He believed in being generous, and that probably has as much to do with my philanthropy as anything else. I learned at his knee how important it was.

The Lake Scholars Program has been a blessing to my family. We have a Lake Scholar dinner every year, and my children and grandchildren come

Gilmour Lake graduated from Davidson College in 1958. He founded and supports the Julian and Robert J. Lake Scholarship Program, which memorializes Gilmour's father, Julian '28, and brother, Robert '66, both Presbyterian ministers. Gilmour and his wife, Nancy Ball Lake, live in Winston-Salem, North Carolina. He serves on the college's board of visitors.

to that event and meet the scholars. It is wonderful that my grandchildren, especially, get to be around outstanding young people, and hopefully they will become those kinds of folks as they grow up. It's a mission I really believe in, and the real beauty is getting to know the students. What a blessing it has been to us.

Sarah Boyce '07 was a Lake Scholar. Thus far, her law career has included a clerkship with US Supreme Court Justices Sandra Day O'Connor and Stephen Breyer and a stint with the Hillary Clinton presidential campaign. She practices law in Washington, DC. She said, "I believe I would've gone to Davidson regardless of the circumstances, but the Lake Scholarship was a blessing financially, and even more so because it has led to a lasting relationship. When I got married, there was no question Gilmour and Nancy would be on the guest list."

13

CHANGING A LIFE TO CHANGE
THE WORLD

Dwight Worden

S HE CAUGHT MY EYE IN THE LOCAL PAPER. A STORY AND PHOTO OF A talented young high school senior graduating number one in her class. She was full of hope and promise; her goal was medical school. But as I read on, I found that seemed an impossible dream. Veronica (not her real name) was undocumented, having been brought to the United States from central Mexico at age three by her parents. Both parents were also undocumented and very poor. Dad worked two different jobs as a baker, and mom took in day care kids at home to make ends meet for the family of five kids. Veronica, her older sister, and one younger sister—all born in Mexico— were undocumented. Her youngest sister and younger brother, born in the United States, were citizens. Sadly, this kind of fractured family is common.

Veronica desperately wanted to attend college and become a pediatrician. Her hope was to return eventually to her community to provide medical services to the poor. But college seemed a distant reach. This was a time when anti-immigrant sentiment was prevalent in California. Scholarships were not available for Veronica, nor were a driver's license, a bank account, student work-study eligibility, the ability to get a job, or many of the other college aids available to most students. Reading all this in the article and

Dwight Worden is a lawyer, city council member, and former mayor of Del Mar, California. He is also a neighbor and friend of the author and so agreed to share his story.

reading Veronica's simple expression that she hoped things would work out somehow, I decided I would help. This young woman was a star and should be allowed to shine.

I wrote to the author of the news article, asking him to send my contact information to Veronica: "Tell her I want to help fund her college career. She not only should go to college, she should be a senator!" Weeks went by with no response. Finally, I called the reporter and said, "I guess there are people in this world who aren't interested in free money, but probably not too many. Why haven't I heard from Veronica?" The reporter responded, "Oh, did you send me an email about Veronica? I got so many hate emails about that article on Veronica that I stopped reading them. People were so angry that I would paint an 'illegal alien' in a favorable light." My determination to help grew.

Eventually, with the reporter's help, I made contact. Seeing no options, Veronica was headed to the local junior college. I offered to pay her tuition and college expenses if she went to a four-year university, for which she was well qualified. We redirected her to the University of California, San Diego (UCSD) as a biology premed student, and she was promptly accepted. I thought she should go to Harvard, Stanford, or Yale, but Veronica insisted on a college where she could live at home and help her family.

The next obstacle was that UCSD insisted on charging out-of-state tuition because Veronica was not documented, even though she had lived in San Diego since age three. At the time, the state government was pressuring the UC system to crack down on the undocumented. After much haggling on my part and Veronica's, her tuition was eventually lowered to the in-state rate.

Other obstacles remained. Although her grades and test scores were tops and clearly scholarship worthy, her undocumented status made her ineligible for any financial aid. Likewise, she was not eligible for student work-study as a way to pay bills. She had to ride the bus to and from UCSD, two hours each way, every day, so she could live at home with her parents. In-campus housing costs were completely unaffordable, and she wanted to help her family. Driving to college was not an option either, as Veronica was not eligible for a driver's license. Sometimes her uncle was able to drive her, but usually it was the bus.

Veronica was not only brilliant, determined, and extremely hard working, she was also ethical to a fault. She refused to use a false ID, to misrepresent her status, or to pursue any other shortcuts. When not studying or in class, she did volunteer work in her community or helped her mother with the childcare. She took every obstacle in her stride, with grace. We cried together when her father lost his job (twice), and we talked through her paralyzing fear when her father's ability to work was jeopardized by the loss of his driver's license (eventually he got it back). She lived with the constant threat of deportation and with overpowering poverty. She was and is a bit shy, but, amazingly, remains an optimistic and endearing person harboring no bitterness.

Veronica excelled at UCSD, graduating with honors. Her graduation picture adorns my desk. It was a proud moment for her family, for her, and for me. Veronica was the first in her family to go to college. But medical school was, we learned, out of reach. Not for academic reasons—Veronica easily made the grade—but because of her undocumented status. Medical school requires students to complete related work assignments as part of their studies and internship. Unfortunately for Veronica, hospital work requires having documented status. She could never complete required assignments at the medical school and related hospital to obtain her degree.

We debated the options. Veronica thought she might go to Mexico to go to medical school, even though she had never set foot in that country since she was three years old and knew no one there. I urged her to stay and hope for a change in the immigration law that would allow her to go to medical school in the United States. I cautioned that once she stepped across the border into Mexico, she might never be able to come back even if the immigration law were to change during the Obama years, when immigration reform seemed at least a possibility.

Veronica decided to stay in the United States. With her UCSD honors degree in hand, she signed up to go to that local community college. Likely, she was the first junior college freshman with an honors BS in hand. But she still couldn't work because of her status, and her ethics would not let her do nothing, so community college—where her learning would continue—was her only option. Of course, she excelled, just as she had in high school and at UCSD. But medical school, or even a menial job like flipping burgers, was no closer.

Then, a bit of good fortune came her way. President Obama's DACA program was enacted by presidential executive order, granting temporary legal status to "dreamers" like Veronica. Veronica quickly applied for DACA status and was approved. For the first time, Veronica had legal status, albeit temporary. This changed her life dramatically.

Veronica had never been out of San Diego, as that would have required passing the border checkpoints north of San Diego on I-5 or I-15. She'd never been on an airplane, never seen snow, and never had the experiences most of us take for granted. So my partner, Betty, and I offered to take her on a trip anywhere she wanted to go—we suggested Yosemite, the Grand Canyon, wherever. She picked Washington, DC—she wanted to see the nation's capital. She took her first plane ride, and we spent a week in DC. On the way back she stopped by the marine base in North Carolina to visit her younger sister (the US citizen sister) who had enlisted. While there she met Alejandro (not his real name), who was also a marine and would eventually become her husband.

Back in San Diego with her new legal status, Veronica decided she would forgo medical school and go to nursing school instead. She found a program at California State University in San Marcos that she could complete in about two years, going full time and living at home. Medical school would take too long, there were still questions on ultimate eligibility, and Veronica felt she needed to start helping her family financially sooner rather than later. Nursing school would have to do. Nursing is a great profession, but I still hope that someday she may get to medical school—she would be a great doctor and would have likely become one in any other country.

I covered most of her nursing school tuition, and Veronica continued to live with her parents to help out with her mother's childcare work and save money. She got a driver's license when California changed the law to allow undocumented residents to obtain licenses. Veronica was able to buy an inexpensive well-used car and got her first paying job—working at Panera Bread. For the first time, Veronica was out of the shadows, driving, working, helping her family with expenses, and living a fairly normal life. She was immensely proud, as were we. Who would have thought a job cleaning tables at Panera Bread would be such a big deal?

To nobody's surprise, Veronica excelled in nursing school and graduated with honors and multiple awards. After graduation she secured a job at a top San Diego hospital as a nurse. She quickly distinguished herself, moving up in the system and earning good money, which she used to help her family. She and Alejandro had stayed in touch while Veronica attended nursing school and were dating. Marriage was planned. Things looked good for a change. Then, a setback happened. Veronica's two-year DACA permit expired, and her pending application for extension was delayed "in processing." The hospital that employed her as a nurse laid her off—they could not have an undocumented person working at the hospital. But eventually, when her DACA extension was renewed, Veronica was quickly hired back to her old job.

Marriage to Alejandro followed. He had been born a US citizen, so Veronica can be on track for citizenship if she wants it. She has permanent legal residency status as the spouse of a US citizen and no longer fears living in the shadows or being deported as immigration policies and practices change.

As Veronica prepared to graduate from nursing school, I met with her and her parents. I wanted to explain to them why I had sponsored Veronica through college and nursing school and why I had paid for lawyers to help her and her family obtain legal status. My Spanish is pretty good, but I asked Veronica to translate this particular discussion so that I could be sure the words came out right. I told her parents that I assumed they must have wondered why this gringo stranger had been willing to spend so much money on their daughter. What was my angle? What did I want? These were logical questions, and I wanted them to have my answer.

Two reasons, I said. First, I had two daughters and had always planned to put them both through college. But one died at age eighteen. So, while I knew Veronica was not my daughter, it felt right to me to spend that college money on a worthwhile student, and my pick was Veronica. I haven't regretted that decision for a moment. To the contrary, it is one of the proudest undertakings of my seventy-one years.

Second, I explained to Veronica and her parents that immigration policies often put obstacles in the way of good people who only want to work hard and make a good life, even people who came here as young children. I wanted Veronica's parents to know that not all Americans are anti-immigrant despite some of the rhetoric that is now commonly heard—and that my assistance to Veronica and to them was, in my own small way, my effort to make a difference. I wanted Veronica and her parents to know I was proud of what they had accomplished, that I admired their work ethic, and that I knew the extra hurdles they all had to overcome to get the things I took for granted. When I told them I admired the beautiful job they had done raising five kids, all of whom were quality students and people, we all cried and exchanged hugs, and that was the last time I saw her parents. I'm in regular contact with Veronica, though, and hope to retain that relationship indefinitely.

My support helped Veronica and her family, but I also benefited from the knowledge and feeling of satisfaction that I was improving the world a bit by helping and enabling a young woman to realize her ability and dreams—and that she would go on to help others. I am only sorry our rules prevented Veronica from becoming the doctor she wanted to be and allowing her to have a possibly even greater impact.

14

ON REFLECTION

Judy Benson

I HAVE HAD SOME TIME TO REFLECT ON THE JOYS I HAVE REAPED FROM the many scholarships that my late husband, Roger, and I have offered over the years. They run the gamut from personal friends and family who, without our help, simply could not have garnered the funds necessary to further their education to the many unknown students from the University of San Diego School of Entrepreneurial Studies to the University of California, Los Angeles (UCLA) School of Nursing and the Anderson School of Business, to name a few.

The thank-you letters we have received over the years described the incredible gratitude of the students for the opportunity to achieve their dreams. Our scholarships are gifts that keep giving forever.

There is just nothing more satisfying than knowing you have played a part in someone else achieving their life goals.

Judy and Roger Benson have been generous donors to multiple scholarship programs. Judy was introduced to the author by a mutual acquaintance, an alumnus of the University of Michigan. She lives in Southern California.

MY STORY

Searching for Financial Aid

Anya Thompson

I AM ONLY EIGHTEEN YEARS OLD, BUT I HAVE ALREADY LEARNED THAT nothing is what it seems, and the future is completely unpredictable. My first ten years of life were relatively uneventful. I lived near San Francisco, California, with my mom and dad. My father owned a business, and Mom was a stay-at-home mom who enjoyed caring for me, blogging, writing, and social media. Life was pretty good, but it was about to change.

I think I was eleven years old, in fifth grade, when the changes happened. A traumatic experience triggered uncontrollable anxiety. Everything became a challenge, daily tasks were more difficult than they should be, and I worried constantly about everything. I was different and became subject to bullying at school; I frequently did not have the strength to go to school and stayed home. I was an emotional mess. Finally, I was diagnosed with anxiety disorder and started therapy and medications. The medications helped, and my life eventually stabilized, at least for a while.

My life has been kind of a roller coaster but with more lows than highs. My family provided essential support, but even that changed. I was insulated from so many things. Then my father's sales and training business collapsed in the global recession that started in 2008. We moved into a smaller home to save money, and I was moved from a private school, where the

Anya has won awards and additional scholarships for her art. She continues at college at California State University while working part time for an art gallery. The author knows Anya's mother, who introduced Anya and her story.

143

staff was aware of my medical issues and had resources to help me, to a less-regarded large and underresourced public school; we didn't have the financial resources to continue my education and treatment. My mother also got a job to help pay the bills and was no longer as available to provide emotional support to me.

In my first day at the big public school, I suffered a panic attack. I could not handle the bigger school and so many changes in my routine. I could not return to private school because we had no money, and I could not be homeschooled because my mother needed to work. So much was changing in my life, and I could not deal with it all. I knew I could not go back to that public school, so I looked for options and found an alternative. I enrolled in an online school so I would not have to deal with others.

My father questioned why I needed to do my work online instead of going to "normal" school. My grandparents were critical of me for not attending a regular school. No one made it easy on me, but my mother and eventually my father were supportive, and I was able to proceed.

Within a couple of months of enrolling in my online school, my life changed again. My mother was supporting the family by then and decided to move us to Southern California, where living costs were lower and opportunities were better for her. I did not handle the move from Northern California very well and developed extreme habits I could not control. I knew my bad thoughts and various compulsions were wrong but could not stop. I was diagnosed with obsessive compulsive disorder (OCD) when I was thirteen years old, but things only got worse. I withdrew and watched television compulsively.

My parents were not getting along. My father was always angry; he had lost his business and had to rely on my mother to pay the bills. He resented moving from his home in Northern California. I perceived he was angry at me for presenting so many challenges and burdens. Eventually my parents divorced, ripping apart my sheltered homelife.

I did pretty well at school during these troubled times. I seem to be naturally smart, and I think I applied myself to my schoolwork to avoid dealing with other issues. At some point, I also realized good grades and college could lead to a better life. In my family, it had always been assumed I would go to college someday and that my parents would pay most of the costs. But with the economic setbacks and then the divorce, it became clear there was no money to pay for college.

In high school, I experimented with different classes and courses of study. I liked to sketch and draw, and at one time I was convinced I wanted to be an art major. I took art classes at a local studio. Another time I planned to be a fashion designer, using my design and artistic skills and interest in movies and television. I was focused on whatever interest I had at any particular time, but my interests changed frequently.

I eagerly sought information on colleges—where and how to apply and what financial aid may be available. But I had to put aside college plans when I had a major relapse in my OCD. Maybe it was my parents' divorce, or perhaps it was the lack of friends and shared activities; regardless, I was emotionally overwhelmed. I began an extensive treatment program and set aside any other thoughts about college and my future. I needed to focus on the present and dealing with issues related to my illness.

My OCD treatment was helping, and as time progressed, I was able to go places on my own and without having a panic attack. I was able to continue with my schoolwork and make good grades despite the distractions. My artwork also helped.

I had grown up with the close support of my parents, but after the divorce, my father was not present and was often critical when we were together. He began a relationship with another woman, whom I resented—I probably felt he had replaced my mom and me in his life. The custody agreement that was part of the divorce required me to spend six weeks with my dad and his new girlfriend in their one-bedroom apartment. I suffered a psychological breakdown on one of my visits.

Eventually, my dad and his girlfriend moved far away, and we did not see each other. At first there were weekly phone calls, but after a few months, my dad stopped calling, and our connection was severed. I resented his disappearance, but I also felt a sense of relief. It was one more thing I did not need to be anxious about.

I resumed my interest in going to college, but I was far behind in the normal college application process. I had missed the deadlines for taking the SAT and ACT exams. I guess in a normal school, someone would have told me what I needed to do. But nothing in my life was normal, and I needed to find out everything for myself, although my mom was a big help, too.

I decided to go to a local community college instead of a four-year university. The community college did not require as much in the application process and was much less expensive. It was an easy decision.

I focused on my art, finding relief and solace in artistic expression. Through the art studio, I made friends with others with similar interests. My life was looking up with art and the expectation of attending college soon. I also began a new exposure therapy to combat OCD, which was scary but offered promising results.

To attend college, even community college, I needed financial aid. Any financial aid, I learned, starts with completion and submission of the Free Application for Federal Student Aid (FAFSA). When I asked a guidance counselor about the application, I was informed the completed application was due the following week, or I would not qualify for financial aid during the coming school year. I was also told it should take only thirty minutes to complete the form, which is available online. Not true.

My mother and I worked furiously to fill in all the required information, including the last two years of Mom's tax information. It took several hours to secure the right information and complete the form. I wish I had known much earlier how important this form is and about the required deadlines.

The form requires applicants to list at least one school to have their information sent to. No problem. I listed the community college. I assumed they would handle the details of my financial aid. I learned it is wrong to assume anything.

I went online the summer before I was to start school and tried to register for classes. Because I had not formally graduated from high school, I was required to take a placement exam to determine what level classes I was allowed to take in college. I was able to take the placement exam shortly thereafter, but I was still not allowed to register for classes. Just when I thought everything was arranged, I realized there was more to do.

Next I was required to attend a new student orientation and have a counseling appointment before I could register. I received a personal college email account. I should have paid more attention because the school communicated with students only through this email account, even though my regular email address was listed in my application and records. The person conducting the orientation recommended all students check their school account every day, which I thought was a bit much. Finally, I was able to register for classes.

About six weeks before classes were to begin, the school sent me an email indicating my financial aid had not been arranged. Unfortunately, I had neglected to check my school email account regularly and found the notice just a few weeks before I was to start school. Without financial aid, I had no way of paying for school, and the semester was almost ready to start. I felt panicked.

I contacted the college's financial aid office and was told to complete various financial forms and bring them to the office in person. There were multiple forms, and I had already provided some of the information requested on the FAFSA. It was frustrating. To complicate matters, I needed to produce a driver's license, but I did not have one. However, I was scheduled to obtain my license a few weeks before school started, so I thought I would be okay. Unfortunately, I failed the driver's test and was unable to obtain a license when I had expected I would. More complications and more hurdles. In the midst of the uncertainty of obtaining the necessary financial aid, my father stopped paying support, including medical costs related to my therapy sessions. My dream of attending college seemed to be in jeopardy.

Then the college rejected my application for financial aid. My mother is a single mom but by then had a new boyfriend, and I had mistakenly listed the boyfriend as a stepdad. This was not smart; the financial aid office now wanted to know my "stepdad's" income. My mom had to send documents indicating that she had not remarried, and there was no other financial support. Finally, my application for aid was accepted, just before school was about to start.

I was awarded about $9,000 in total for the year. I was told that this was about the most someone could receive in financial aid. My mother and I were amazed I received so much, but it should not have been surprising. Mom was a single mother running her own business, with two dependents and no support from her ex-husband. This was the only time having no money actually came in handy, and it even paid off to have a deadbeat father for once.

So, excited to have my financial aid money and for this long, drawn-out process to be over, I immediately started the process to receive the money. To receive financial aid, a recipient must choose a dispersal method. At my college, there were three options: check, direct deposit into a bank account, or a financial aid account with a bank that is partnered with the school. The financial aid account seemed like the best option because it gave rewards to students for their achievements. After choosing this dispersal method, I opened an account with a bank to receive the money.

However, two days after choosing my dispersal method, the bank put an "identification hold" on the account; I had to prove my identification before the bank would release the funds. This happened two days before school started. I had to provide at least two forms of identification: a valid form of photo identification (e.g., a state ID or driver's license) and a Social Security card.

This presented two problems. Number one, because I had failed my driver's test, I did not have a driver's license, and I didn't know then that a state ID was an option. Number two, my father had taken all of my important documents with him when he'd left town and claimed to have lost them when I'd asked him to provide them. With only two days before school started, I made an appointment at the local DMV to take my second behind-the-wheel test. Of course, as luck would have it, I failed the second test, too. Completely hitting rock bottom, I took comfort in the only place I knew I could—in my own head. With my mental defenses down, my previously quiet OCD attacked in full force right in time for my first day of school.

To sum it up, my first week of college was a mental hell. While I made it to class physically and everything went fine, I felt completely out of control. I didn't have my financial aid problem fixed, I was in a brand-new environment, which was something I hadn't experienced since seventh grade, I had no friends, and I had just been cut off financially by my father. I felt so helpless because I couldn't fix any of these problems, at least not immediately. So I just kept asking myself, "Why me?" After more tears and moments of complete catatonia, I was snapped out of it by my mother, who told me to stop being a victim, solve the problem, and change my paradigm.

After researching what I needed to do to get my Social Security card and a state ID, I got to work. I went to the DMV after school with my mom and got my state ID and then went the next week to the Social Security office to get my replacement card. Unfortunately, the wait felt like an eternity. In reality, it was about two and a half hours, and during that time I was notified by email that if I did not prove my ID to the bank within the next thirty days, my account would be closed. That was a serious problem because receiving an ID card would take one to two weeks and getting a replacement Social Security card would take another one to two weeks minimum. I called the bank and talked to two technicians, but they just repeated the same thing: my account would be closed in thirty days if I did not verify my identity. At that point it was mid-September; I would be cutting it incredibly close to the deadline. But all I could do was wait, albeit impatiently.

As the days went by and the month progressed, things started to get better little by little. After being in school for a couple of weeks, I established a routine of driving to school with my mom; I made friends, and

I even started enjoying school. But while things were improving, the expenses of going to college were accumulating, and my mom couldn't cover all the bills forever. The Uber trips from the college to home were adding up, and I had to buy supplies for school. I really needed that financial aid. Finally, after almost four weeks, both the state ID and the Social Security card came. I quickly scanned both into the computer and submitted the documents online to the bank. Finally, I was correctly ID'd and approved to access the aid money in the account.

I was able to pay my mom back for all the expenses she had paid, including supplies and transportation. I felt liberated for the first time since my school odyssey had begun. My newfound financial security let me feel like my life was starting to rise from the rock bottom I had experienced earlier.

There is a constant myriad of problems that arise throughout life that are easy to wish away, but sadly, that is just not how life works. You must jump into the thick of the problems and wade through the mud until you come out on the other side. In the area of financial aid, I had come out clean and with new lessons: Start the financial aid process six months in advance. Do not wait until the last minute. And keep on top of all communications, even ones you don't know about (which makes no sense, but there it is).

Looking back on my story, it encompasses miscommunication and human error. When high school or college representatives talk to prospective students about financial aid, they talk about it in extremely nonchalant terms, implying the process is quick and easy—no big deal. This could not be further from reality. For someone who has been through the process before and has all their government documents in order, the process should take only a week to complete. But first-time college students like me may not be that lucky. For me, the financial aid process took three months from start to finish. I learned that I could rely only on myself to achieve what I wanted and needed (with maybe just a little kick in the pants from Mom). I learned from counselors and advisors, but in the end, it was up to me to get it right.

I believe the importance of self-reliance applies to literally all aspects of life, especially dealing with the government and institutions like colleges. If they say to provide five documents, bring more. And be patient. Even when someone demands what you have already given them, just comply. If someone wants it once, they'll be sure to ask for it three more times. Always be overprepared, and don't panic. Persistence is the key to securing needed financial aid.

PART 6
PAYING IT FORWARD

15

UNMET SOCIAL NEEDS AND
INADEQUATE FUNDING

COMMUNITY-BASED SCHOLARSHIP PROGRAMS LIKE MACDONALD Scholars provide funds for students who qualify for financial aid but require the recipients to undertake community service projects to help others in need. There seems to be an infinite number of social needs that are not being fulfilled by regular governmental and charitable efforts, and students who have time and energy can make society a better place. Financial aid for need-eligible students makes it possible for these students to attend college and make a difference in their communities.

Supporting and Educating Children in Need

Lena Parker was a MacDonald Scholar (hereafter, referred to as a Scholar) at Davidson College. She is interested in public education and volunteered as a tutor, mentor, lead volunteer, and Girl Scout troop leader at Ada Jenkins Learn Works program, which provides educational support to children who are not doing well in school and are typically from poor families in the greater Charlotte metropolitan area. Connor Randol, a Scholar at Indiana University, worked at Wonder Lab, a program to inspire children to explore the wonders of science.

These students connected with children at risk and may have helped each one move toward a better life. There is considerable research on links between poverty and education. People who are poor tend to have less-educated children, and these children, in turn, become poor as they age without benefit of education. This is confirmed by *Poverty and Education*, a booklet published by UNESCO, the International Academy of Education, and the International Institute for Educational Planning, which states as follows: "It is widely agreed that the relationship between poverty and education operates in two directions: poor people are often unable to obtain access to an adequate education, and without an adequate education people are often constrained to a life of poverty."[1] It elaborates on this finding, stating, "Two consistent research findings in the social sciences relate to the relationship between economic and education variables, therefore between education and poverty. Educational research has consistently found home background (socio-economic status) to be an important determinant of educational outcomes, and economic research has shown that education strongly affects earnings."[2]

The question is thus one of how to facilitate education as a means of emerging from poverty: "For education to offer a route out of poverty on a substantial scale often requires special interventions or favorable economic circumstances. A large number of interventions have been implemented to overcome the negative impact of poor home background in countries around the world. These interventions include remedial education measures, nutritional support, social work in the community, attempts by school authorities to involve poor parents in their children's education, adult literacy campaigns, and anti-poverty policies, to name a few."[3] The booklet concludes, "Poor schools also often suffer from having fewer resources, due either to budget limits or the inequitable resource allocation among schools. Additional resources are important."[4]

Early intervention programs for poor preschool-age children appear to have a significant effect on the future lives of participants: "Whites who attended Head Start are, relative to their siblings who did not, significantly more likely to complete high school, attend college, and have higher earnings. African-Americans who participated in Head Start are less likely to have been booked or charged with a crime."[5]

Despite the overwhelming results of research on the beneficial impacts of quality early education, educational resources are not keeping pace with demand. In 2011, 48 percent of the nation's public school students qualified for free or reduced-price meals, a common measure of poverty. To qualify for these meals, a family of four could earn no more than $40,793 annually (2011).[6]

"A majority of students in public schools throughout the American South and West are low-income for the first time in at least four decades."[7] On average, the country spends about $10,300 annually per student, but that figure varies wildly among states and even within school districts. In 2011, for example, New York spent $19,076 for each student. States with some of the biggest proportions of poor children spend the least on each student. Mississippi, for example, spent $7,928 per student in 2011. In North Carolina, where Lena Parker and her fellow Scholars worked, the average per student expenditure was only $8,296 according to most recent data (2016),[8] which was still less than it was in 2008 ($8,867). Volunteer students, who do not have to work to make money while attending college, are helping fill the government funding gap to help young students from poor families. Their work helps people and the greater society.

Educating children in other countries also pays benefits to the world and those around us. An educated world is more likely to support economic trade, democratic institutions, and research and shared knowledge. Erick Deyden, a Scholar at the University of San Diego, organized and raised funds to supply backpacks filled with school supplies for hundreds of children in northern Mexico. As discussed earlier, Olivia Tait, a Scholar at Davidson College, raised funds and had a primary school constructed and operated in a village in Ethiopia.

Homelessness

Jacquie Morges was a Scholar at Davidson College. Her special interest was seeking solutions to homelessness, and she was actively involved with the National Coalition for the Homeless, Urban Ministry Center and Crisis Assistance, and the Salvation Army Shelter for Women. Before graduating from college, she made a documentary on homelessness in Charlotte, which inspired others to help those without shelter.

Miguel Abascal was a Scholar at the University of San Diego. On weekends he participated in Pancake Peeps, a program to feed and support the homeless in San Diego. Jacquie and Miguel are just two scholarship students who have worked to address one of America's chronic public issues.

Almost six hundred thousand people are homeless in the United States, according to one study. These include people living on the streets, in cars, in homeless shelters, or in subsidized transitional housing during a one-night national survey in January 2017.[9] This represents a rate of approximately seventeen people experiencing homelessness per every ten thousand people in the general population.[10] Of the total, about two hundred thousand were in families, and the remainder were individuals.

An estimated 15 percent, or about eighty-three thousand individuals, are considered chronically homeless. These are individuals who have a disability and have been homeless for a year or suffer from frequent homeless experiences. About 8 percent, or approximately forty-eight thousand of the homeless, are US veterans. About 50 percent of the homeless population is over the age of fifty.

An estimated 550,000 unaccompanied single youth under the age of twenty-four experience homelessness for more than a week at a time. An estimated 380,000 youth who have experienced homelessness are under the age of eighteen.

Between 2016 and 2017, homelessness increased nationally despite a good economy. The largest increases were among unaccompanied children and young adults, the chronic homeless, and people experiencing unsheltered homelessness.

There are several causes of homelessness. One is the lack of affordable housing for lower wage earners. In the 1970s there was typically an ample supply of inexpensive housing, but with escalating housing prices in recent years, an estimated eleven million low-income households pay at least 50 percent of their income for housing. Federal funds for a new subsidized housing supply are limited and inadequate to meet the needs. The federal budget for 2017 proposed a slight increase in homeless program funds but sharply decreased funds for other government-subsidized housing programs that historically contributed to homelessness prevention.

Another factor contributing to homelessness is medical conditions. An estimated 20 percent of homeless people on any given night suffer from mental illness, and an estimated 16 percent suffer from substance abuse. More than 10 percent of people who seek substance abuse or mental health treatment in the public health system are homeless. The recent issue of opioid abuse appears to be increasing the problem.

Mental illness in the homeless population often is untreated: "The most obvious effect of untreated mental illness is a steady—and often rapid—decline in mental health. Mental illness will not go away on its own, and the longer it persists, the harder it is to treat."[11]

Work by students to help homeless people will not solve the problem of homelessness in America. More affordable and available housing as well as better access to medical care, especially mental illness and substance abuse treatment, are needed. But individuals can make a difference to help individuals, especially during temporary bouts of homelessness. Helping one individual at a time to access services, food, and medical care may allow them and their families to rejoin a productive society and take advantage of economic opportunities.

Health Care

Jerry Chang joined the class of 2018 as a Scholar at Indiana University. He had a keen interest in finding a cure for diseases including cancer. Armed with scholarship funds to attend IU, Jerry was able to work at the Anschutz Medical Campus studying lung cancer. Maybe he will help find a cure someday.

Nina Mace was a Scholar at Davidson College. She volunteered at the Concord NC Community Free Clinic, providing assistance to those with health problems but inadequate funds to pay doctors.

Mary Lowenfield, also a Scholar at Davidson, secured grant funding from the Ministry of Hope to work with a mobile medical clinic in Malawi. All of these students made a difference in the lives of people.

The United States spends more on health care than any other country. According to the OECD, the Organisation for Economic Co-operation and Development, which includes thirty-four member countries with developed economies, the United States spends $8,713 per person annually, or 16.4 percent of its GDP, on health care—far higher than the OECD average of 8.9 percent.[12] On a per capita basis, the United States spends more than double the $3,453 average of all other OECD countries.

But the quality of medical care and results of high spending levels do not seem to be reflected in health care outcomes. The average life expectancy in the United States is 79.68 years, which ranks it as number forty-three and similar to Denmark, Puerto Rico, and Portugal. It is far behind countries like Japan, Switzerland, Israel, Australia, Italy, Sweden, Canada, France, and Spain.

In infant mortality, the United States ranks with Serbia and lags behind almost all European countries. The rate of infant mortality in the United

States is an estimated 5.8, which significantly lags behind countries like Cuba (4.4), the United Kingdom (4.3), the European Union as a whole (4.0), and South Korea (3.0) as well as dozens of other countries.[13]

According to the Commonwealth Fund Commission, in 2014, US health care ranked last when compared to Australia, Canada, France, Germany, the Netherlands, Norway, Sweden, Switzerland, and the United Kingdom. US specialists and availability to medical technology are likely first in the world, but treatment of poorer people, especially the uninsured and underinsured, results in poor performance averages.

There are fewer physicians per capita in the United States when compared to most OECD countries (2.6 versus 3.3). There are only 1.2 primary care physicians in the United States per 1,000 people, and the US population is aging and will require increased care in the future.

Students working with free medical clinics and local patient services will not solve America's problem of high-cost medical service and inadequate medical insurance coverage. But a low-income patient may receive the help in that moment that saves his life or allows her to return to work, support a family, and continue to be productive.

Medical science has made tremendous strides forward in recognizing diseases and curing previously incurable medical conditions. Research and funding by governments and private organizations like the Gates Foundation and Rotary International have virtually eliminated polio, for example. But there is much more to do, such as finding cures for cancer, dementia and Alzheimer's disease, and heart attacks. There is never enough money to hire the scientists and researchers to move these cures closer to reality, and student assistants free others to undertake and supervise more experiments, leading to a better chance of finding a cure.

Hunger

Alice Joson was a Scholar at Indiana University. She is concerned about hunger and food security for people in need. Alice worked at Mother Hubbard's Cupboard, which was founded by two mothers who were determined to make healthy food available to all regardless of income. Alice and her fellow Scholars at IU were leaders of a program that provided backpack meals to children in the surrounding Bloomington area whose families suffered from food insecurity and hunger.

Amy Lamb, while a Scholar at Davidson, worked extensively with Sow Much Good, an organization dedicated to promoting healthy lifestyles through food and nutrition. These students helped feed the poor and hungry.

The United States may be the wealthiest nation in the world and perhaps the most affluent nation in history, but there is still hunger in America. According to published statistics,[14] one in six people in America is hungry. Almost 14 percent of US households with children suffer from "food insecurity," defined by the US Department of Agriculture as being "uncertain of having, or unable to acquire, enough food to meet the needs of all their members."[15] Food insecurity exists in every county in the United States. Some states have significantly higher food insecurity rates, including Mississippi, Louisiana, Alabama, New Mexico, Arkansas, Kentucky, Maine, Indiana, Oklahoma, and North Carolina.

In 2013, 17.5 million households experienced food insecurity. Many people are increasingly relying on food banks. In 2016, 59 percent of food-insecure households received help from one of three major federal food assistance programs—Supplemental Nutrition Assistance Program, formerly called Food Stamps; the National School Lunch Program; and the Special Supplemental Nutrition Program for women, infants, and children.

About forty-nine million Americans struggle to secure adequate food. Over twenty million children receive free or reduced-price lunches because they are considered below the poverty line.

When people—and especially children—do not receive adequate nutrition, their cognitive and physical development are impaired, their ability to undertake tasks and be productive suffers, and their ability to learn and function fully in society is retarded.

Adequate food requires quality as well as quantity. Receiving proper nutrition and balanced meals is important, especially for children who are still growing and developing. Good nutrition appears essential to maintaining good health as well.

Students working in food banks and in food-resource organizations feeding the poor make a difference. They cannot solve hunger in America alone, but they can help families find enough to eat and ensure local households receive essential nutrition.

Poverty

Eli Kahn was a Scholar at Davidson. While at Davidson, he was active in many charitable ventures, including Lift Philadelphia, where he worked with residents from low-income backgrounds to secure employment, housing, and public benefits. After graduating from college, Eli joined the Foundation for the Carolinas, which helps other charities address local poverty and social needs.

Poverty is the leading cause of other maladies; it contributes directly to poor educational performance and advancement, homelessness, inadequate or unavailable medical care, and hunger. Working to help poor people who have the ambition, supportive circumstances and conditions, and work ethic to move out of poverty makes this country and every country a better place in so many ways. Not everyone can escape poverty despite their efforts to do so, but helping those who can take advantage of an opportunity offered is the most admirable activity imaginable.

There are many paths from poverty. Education provides a key path to upward mobility in the diverse society that constitutes America. But children from poor families who suffer from hunger or medical conditions have a difficult time advancing. Job training is another avenue out of poverty, especially when the economy is expanding and there are plenty of jobs to be filled. Increasingly, however, new jobs require technical skills that must be learned through college, community college, job training programs, or apprenticeships.

Good health is a requirement for a worker to perform at a high level. Access to medical treatment, including preventive care, is essential. Americans with below-average incomes are more likely than their counterparts in other countries to report not visiting a physician when sick, not getting a recommended medical test, treatment, or follow-up care; not filling a prescription; or not seeing a dentist.[16] This condition reduces the chance for successfully holding a job and earning sufficient income to escape poverty.

Even those who secure work and perform well may not escape poverty. The minimum US wage is $7.25 an hour. The average work year is about two thousand hours, so someone working full-time at minimum wage would earn only $14,500 a year. Even if the employee worked in a higher-wage state, made $10 an hour, and worked six days a week for fifty weeks a year, he or she would earn only $24,000 a year. That is below the federal poverty line for a family of four, and that does not account for any sick days or holidays (but does include a two-week paid vacation).

Without help, many Americans would not make it; they would live in poverty, be unable to secure adequate food, be forced to live with medical complications, and raise children who lack access to a quality education and a path out of poverty. It's pretty clear that the government is not capable of solving all of the related problems and conditions; harnessing the commitment and energy of students who are not constrained by debt and work-study requirements may be one part of the solution to poverty in America.

Engaged American students, freed from the need to work while in school and incurring less debt that requires repayment, are supporting needy residents, providing opportunities, filling in where the government fails to act, and changing the world—one person at a time. However, if resources were more available, the pool of students who are eligible and available to help others and address critical social issues likely includes millions throughout the country.

16

COMMUNITY ENGAGEMENT
AT UNIVERSITIES

AMERICAN UNIVERSITIES HAVE A LONG HISTORY OF ENGAGING WITH their surrounding communities to solve problems. They join forces, leveraging student manpower and creativity to mitigate local issues and conflicts. Harvard University, the first university established in the United States in 1638, initially focused on training ministers and sending them out into the colonies. A board of overseers was appointed for Harvard consisting of the governor and leaders of the surrounding communities. Both actions suggest a focus on the greater social good and the importance of connections between the university and communities.

In January 1900, Harvard opened Phillips Brooks House—a new building that, for the first time, provided a permanent home for religious and charitable organizations. Four years later, Harvard students founded the Phillips Brooks House Association (PBHA) to provide a focal point for student engagement in the community beyond the campus—placing student volunteers with Boston-area settlement houses, organizing clothing drives, and supporting the work of missionaries around the world. One of the earliest Phillips Brooks House volunteers was a young Harvard University student named Franklin Roosevelt. Today, PBHA still provides a physical and organizational base for more than seventy community service programs.

The University of North Carolina was the first public university in the United States, opening in 1795. The school's original purpose was to train future leaders of the state of North Carolina, thereby improving public service. Today, an estimated twenty-one thousand out of approximately thirty thousand students on campus are engaged in public service, according to the Carolina Center for Public Service (CCPS). Lynn Blanchard, the director of UNC's CCPS, commented, "When asked about what has had the most impact on them while in college, students often point beyond the campus. For them, community service is a defining experience, offering an opportunity to learn while making a difference in the lives of others."[1]

When I was a student at Indiana University in the late '60s, I was a member of the IU Student Foundation; we engaged in several community-based programs, including a campaign to restock community libraries with books. More recently, Indiana University has organized their many community outreach efforts under the banner of IU Corps.

Such community-outreach programs have become increasingly common at universities in recent years. Campus Compact, is a national coalition of college and university presidents whose mission is to "[advance] the public purposes of colleges and universities by deepening their ability to improve community life and to educate students for civic and social responsibility." Its vision statement proclaims, "Campus Compact envisions colleges and universities as vital agents and architects of a diverse democracy, committed to educating students for responsible citizenship in ways that both deepen their education and improve the quality of community life. We challenge all of higher education to make civic and community engagement an institutional priority."[2] The coalition was created in 1985 by the presidents of Brown, Georgetown, and Stanford Universities and the president of the Education Commission of the States. It has seen its membership grow from slightly more than 100 institutions in 1986 to more than 1,100. Based on surveys of its member institutions, Campus Compact estimates that between 2001 and 2006, the percentage of all students at its member colleges and universities who engaged in some form of community service during the year rose from 28 percent to 32 percent.[3]

The opportunities for community service that an institution offers have become an important factor for many high school students in their choice of colleges. To assist them in finding the right college, in 2005 the *Princeton Review* published "Colleges with a Conscience," a guide to eighty-one schools it rated as being among the leaders in this area. Steve Farmer, director of admissions at the University of North Carolina Chapel Hill told me that having community-based scholarships was a competitive advantage appealing to undecided but admitted students who often had many choices for which school to attend and an interest in community service opportunities.

A growing number of colleges and universities now include community service among the factors on which faculty members are evaluated. Campus Compact reports that between 2001 and 2006, the percentage of its member institutions that consider community engagement in their tenure and promotion decisions rose from 16 percent to 34 percent.[4]

The Carnegie Foundation for the Advancement of Teaching classifies universities as "community engaged." A survey of the community-engagement levels of universities is now conducted from Brown University's Swearer Center (formerly based at the New England Resource Center for Higher Education). The survey lists almost four hundred universities as "engaged" with their communities.[5]

The president's Higher Education Community Service Honor Roll recognizes institutions that support exemplary service programs and raise the visibility of effective practices in campus community partnerships.[6] The Corporation for National and Community Service first administered the award in 2006 in collaboration with the US Department of Education and the US Department of Housing and Urban Development as well as the American Council on Education, Campus Compact, and the Interfaith Youth Core. The last honor roll was published in 2015. According to the Corporation for National and Community service's website in 2018, the 2016 honor roll was still "under review."

Many universities have organized community service and community engagement departments, and several organizations, including *Princeton Review*, *Newsweek*, and *Washington Monthly*, have attempted to rank schools according to community service opportunities, but the rankings are subjective and typically not consistent. The American Association of Universities maintains a list of schools with community service programs.[7]

Community engagement happens at all kinds of schools, from Ivy League schools like Princeton to lower-cost public schools like California State University in San Marcos. It happens at big schools like the University of Michigan, where the Edward Ginsberg Center for Community Service and Learning typically supports 4,000 to 6,000 involved students annually. It happens at small schools like Davidson, with 1,800 students, where Stacey Riemer and staff direct 90 Bonner and MacDonald Scholars (mostly Bonner) and multiple community outreach programs throughout the year.

Universities that engage with local communities and organize, supervise, mentor, and provide community service opportunities for their students offer many benefits. They serve their students' desire to give back and help others, their programs and student volunteers help other nonstudents in need, and they provide essential services that are not otherwise available to area and community residents. And, importantly, these experiences broaden the education of young participating students by connecting them to others who often come from different backgrounds and cultures, with different needs and circumstances.

Campus Compact believes that "we build democracy through civic education and community development."[8] Thomas Jefferson connected the importance of education with virtuous behavior when he said, "I look to the diffusion of light and education as the resource most to be relied on for ameliorating the conditions, promoting the virtue and advancing the happiness of man."[9]

A few of the many schools with notable engagement organizations are listed below. The list is not intended to be comprehensive; I am sure there are many other schools that have active community engagement programs that are not listed in the various publications and websites I reviewed and that I am not otherwise not familiar with.

- Adelphi University (Center for Student Involvement)
- American University (Center for Community Engagement and Service)
- Auburn University (University Outreach)
- Azusa Pacific University (Center for Academic Service-Learning)
- Boston College (Volunteer and Service Learning Center)
- Brandeis University (The Waltham Group)
- Brown University (Howard R. Swearer Center for Public Service)
- California State University San Marcos (Division of Community Engagement)
- Case Western Reserve (Center for Civic Engagement and Learning)
- Clark University (Community Engagement and Volunteering Center)
- Cornell (Public Service Center)
- Creighton University (Schlegel Center for Service and Justice)
- Dartmouth College (Center for Social Impact)
- Davidson College (Center for Civic Engagement)

- George Washington University (Center for Civic Engagement and Public Service)
- Georgia Tech (Center for Student Engagement)
- Harvard University (Community Connections)
- Indiana University (IU Corps)
- Indiana State University (Center for Community Engagement)
- Loyola University, Chicago (Center for Experiential Learning)
- Loyola University, Maryland (Center for Community Service and Justice)
- Loyola Marymount University (Center for Service and Action)
- Marquette University (Center for Community Service)
- Massachusetts Institute of Technology (Public Service Center)
- Michigan State University (Center for Service-Learning and Civic Engagement)
- New York University (Office of Civic Engagement)
- Ohio State University (Office of Outreach and Engagement)
- Pepperdine University (Volunteer Center)
- Pitzer College (Community Engagement Center)
- Princeton University (The Pace Center for Civic Engagement)
- Purdue University (Office of Engagement)
- Rice University (Center for Civic Leadership)
- Rutgers University (Office of Community Affairs)
- Syracuse University (Mary Ann Shaw Center for Public and Community Service)
- Stanford University (Haas Center for Public Service)
- Stony Brook University (Office of Community Relations)
- Texas A&M University (AggieServe)
- Tufts University (Tisch College, the Leonard Carmichael Society)
- Tulane University (Center for Public Service)
- United States Coast Guard Academy
- University of Buffalo (Office of Government and Community Relations)
- University of California, Berkeley (Public Service Center)
- University of California, Los Angeles (UCLA in the Community)
- University of California, San Diego (Volunteer Connection)
- University of Chicago (University Community Service Center)
- University of Colorado, Boulder (Office of Outreach and Engagement)
- University of Denver (Center for Community Engagement and Service Learning)
- University of Florida (David and Wanda Brown Center for Leadership and Service)

- University of Idaho (Volunteer Center, Department of Student Involvement)
- University of Illinois, Urbana-Champaign (Office of Volunteer Programs)
- Iowa State University (Leadership and Service Center)
- University of Kansas (Center for Service Learning)
- University of Maryland (Leadership and Community Service-Learning)
- University of Michigan (Edward Ginsberg Center for Community Service and Learning)
- University of Minnesota, Twin Cities (Center for Community-Engaged Learning)
- University of North Carolina, Chapel Hill (Carolina Center for Public Service)
- University of Notre Dame (Center for Social Concerns)
- University of Oregon (Holden Center for Leadership and Community Engagement)
- University of Pennsylvania (Civic House)
- University of Pittsburgh (Office of PittServes)
- University of Rochester (Center for Community Leadership)
- University of San Diego (Mulvaney Center)
- University of San Francisco (Leo T. McCarthy Center)
- University of Southern California (The Volunteer Center)
- University of Texas, Austin (Longhorn Center for Community Engagement)
- University of Virginia (Learning in Action)
- University of Washington (Carlson Leadership and Public Service Center)
- University of Wisconsin, Madison (Morgridge Center for Public Service)
- Vanderbilt University (Office of Active Citizenship and Service)
- Virginia Polytechnic Institute (VT Engage)
- Washington University in St. Louis (Gephardt Institute for Civic and Community Engagement)
- William and Mary University (Office of Community Engagement)
- Yale University (Dwight Hall)

17

THE GINSBERG CENTER AND THE
UNIVERSITY OF MICHIGAN

THE UNIVERSITY OF MICHIGAN (UM) HAS A REPUTATION AS ONE OF the nation's top educational and public research institutions, with more than 275 degree programs. The university is also full of stories of students who both participate in service learning and community engagement and receive financial aid. In many cases, students are able to use some of their financial aid to support their work with communities. In addition to the large program of financial aid awarded to students based on need, Michigan alumni and other donors have established funds that provide scholarships and internships that allow students to receive training and guidance while they are being agents of positive change in the world.

Supplementing the financial aid work-study program that supports students doing service work, over the last several years donors have significantly increased funding for engagement activities. There are now specific grants, scholarships, fellowship funding, and paid internship opportunities for individual students engaging in service-learning and civic engagement projects.

At the core of this community engagement at the University of Michigan is the Edward Ginsberg Center, whose mission is to cultivate and stew-

The author thanks Julia Smilie and Julie Lubeck-Hofer for assistance with research and the preparation of drafts of this chapter. Julia is marketing and communications manager at the Ginsburg Center for Community Service and Learning. Julie is a University of Michigan graduate and was an event coordinator at the Ginsberg Center.

ard mutually beneficial partnerships between communities and the University of Michigan to advance social change for the public good. The center was created in memory of Edward Ginsberg, University of Michigan alum, former lawyer, and devoted community servant. Ginsberg Center staff have found that once students are involved, they develop a passion for service, often changing paths to incorporate community engagement in some way into their careers and going on to do impactful things.

With determination and hard work, students pursue, receive, and even create scholarships that change the trajectory of their lives, careers, and goals. The result is graduates who see the world, their peers, and their communities from different, broader, and deeper perspectives. Derick Johnson is one of those students. Derick grew up primarily in Royal Oak, about fifteen miles from the heart of Detroit. With no siblings and a father who, in Derick's words, "didn't want to be in the picture," it was just Derick and his mother against the world. A probation officer, Derick's mother worked long, stressful hours in a sometimes dangerous profession, earning just enough to make ends meet. "I didn't realize how dangerous her job was until I was maybe a freshman in high school, and I saw her bulletproof vest and it clicked," Derick says now, clearly still in awe of his mother's commitment to their well-being.[1]

A University of Michigan education looms like a promise for kids from all around the state. Derick was no exception. His journey toward UM is a story of tenacity and focus, all stemming from a seed planted in him at the age of ten, when he attended his first University of Michigan football game. On one fall afternoon, his uncle took him to a game at the "Big House." "My uncle played a huge part in why I wanted to go to Michigan initially," Derick says.

But as middle school went on and high school began, Derick lost his focus on college. Teenage interests—playing football, wrestling, playing video games—took on an increasingly prominent role in his life. He remained a fan of Michigan sports but says that at that time, "I was really smart, but I didn't care that much about school." He also recalls, "I knew I didn't have the grades to apply to Michigan, so I didn't. I was really upset with myself because I knew that if I had worked harder and did what I was supposed to do, I could have gotten accepted. So then I decided to do everything possible to be able to transfer to Michigan one day."

Derick attended community college and focused his energies on achieving good grades. In addition to the academics, Michigan's social and cultural aspects drew him in. Derick, who is black, grew up in the mostly white suburb of Royal Oak, but he also spent a great deal of time in Detroit, moving back and forth, he says, between the two cultures.

For a year and a half at community college, with the exception of two Bs, Derick pulled in all As. He applied to UM for the first time as a transfer student for the winter 2013 semester, but his high school grades simply didn't make the cut. Not one to give up on his goal or to be easily dissuaded, Derick applied again for fall 2014.

Late one night, as the rest of his house lay quiet, Derick decided to check on his admission status before turning in. He'd sent in his application weeks before and hadn't heard a thing. A quick log in to the University of Michigan admissions system and there, waiting for him, were the words he'd waited years to see. He'd been accepted to the University of Michigan. "All I remember seeing is 'Congratulations,' and a tear fell out of my eye, because I'd worked so hard to get in. My goal was finally completed," he says.

Derick hustled upstairs and woke his sleeping mother to tell her the news. "I basically knocked her door down to tell her," he says, adding that he then lifted her up out of bed into a giant hug. "She doesn't like the big hug," he says, "so I can only do it when I accomplish something really big." This definitely counted.

The joy for both of them was tremendous, but Derick's acceptance came with another sobering obstacle: finances. His mother couldn't conceive of how they could possibly afford Michigan's significant tuition and housing rates. Again, as focused as ever, Derick threw himself into researching financial aid options, including all the loans, grants, and scholarships Michigan could possibly offer. He felt confident that with enough aid—and only with enough aid—he could follow through on his dream.

Not surprisingly, in time Derick managed to piece together enough financial aid to make UM a reality, including some much-needed scholarships and grants. Derick Johnson was going to Michigan.

Once he was finally there, Derick thrived. He signed up as a tutor with America Reads, part of the Federal Work-Study Program, through University of Michigan's Ginsberg Center. As an America Reads tutor, Derick worked with kids in Detroit public schools, often teaching immigrant children for whom English was their second language, an experience he greatly enjoyed.

After graduation, Derick applied for teaching jobs in Central and South America. A private school in Honduras called, and Derick headed south to teach science and math to third graders in the city of Comayagua. While he's enjoying teaching for now, Derick has other long-term plans. He's currently working toward his master's degree in psychology.

Reflecting on his experience at Michigan, Derick recognizes that it was entirely dependent on receiving that much-needed financial aid. "There's no way I would have been able to get to Michigan if it weren't for financial support," he says now. "It's so important."

When it comes to scholarships, there may be no better example of paying it forward than Nadine Jawad. Born and raised in Dearborn, Michigan, to Lebanese parents—her father a refugee of the Lebanese Civil War—Nadine and her three siblings were the first generation in their family to go to college.

Like Derick Johnson, Nadine was focused on the University of Michigan for her education. She applied for early admission—and it was the only school she applied to. Her brother was there already, having been recruited by UM to play soccer, so she knew the campus.

Nadine was also drawn to Michigan for the sheer number of scholarship opportunities it offered. She comes from an extremely hard-working family, but her father had been laid off, then injured in a car accident that further diminished his earning capacity. And her mother's teaching career, once launched, still wouldn't generate nearly enough income for Nadine to attend UM. Fortunately, in addition to UM's financial resources, Nadine's hometown of Dearborn offered opportunities for local scholarships. "Dearborn is good at empowering students," she says. "I applied for upward of twelve scholarships and won six or seven of them. Winning those was the gateway to going to Michigan."

Nadine started out in Michigan's College of Literature, Science, and the Arts in fall 2014. During her first week at Michigan, she received an email from the Ginsberg Center announcing the Shuyi Li Scholarship for Community Service and Civic Engagement. The scholarship, funded by University of Michigan alum Shuyi Li, provided Nadine with $1,000 based on her commitment to community service as well as financial need. It also sparked something inside her. "That scholarship was the springboard for everything in my future," she says.[2]

The scholarship required that Nadine serve for a year on the Ginsberg Center's student advisory board, which voices the needs, concerns, and ideas of students as they pertain to the center's mission. She wound up keeping her seat for three years. "I asked to return the next year and the year after that. I stopped only when I ran for student body vice president," she says with a laugh.

Nadine—whose family had instilled in her a great belief in giving back—was inspired to start her own nonprofit, Books for a Benefit, which distributes books to those in need in Dearborn. "I'm the first woman in my family to go away to school," Nadine says. "I saw this discrepancy between first-generation college students and other immigrants. I believe that reading books really breaks down barriers. We collect and distribute gently used books to households in what I call book deserts in Southeast Michigan—families that may not have the capacity or the ability to get to a library." To date, Nadine estimates that Books for a Benefit has distributed more than one hundred thousand books, and the organization now has five part-time employees.

Nadine funds Books for a Benefit largely from local business and small crowd-funded donations. And once she knew how to raise money, she was inspired to take it one step further. Knowing her experiences couldn't have happened without the Shuyi Li scholarship, Nadine decided to follow in her donor's footsteps and set up a scholarship through the Ginsberg Center in her family's name.

Working from the foundation of the Muslim principle of *zakat*, which requires Muslims to donate 2.5 percent of their earnings to charity, Nadine asked her family to channel those funds into a scholarship named after her grandfather. "I loved what the Shuyi Li Scholarship did for me and what it brought to my life," she says. "Much of my family doesn't have a lot to give. But I said to them, 'You have to give something, so you might as well do something in the name of our grandfather. If everyone donated ten dollars, we could build this scholarship for one year." And that's exactly what the Jawad family did, sometimes in increments as small as five-dollar contributions. Whatever her family members could afford to give, they did.

The end result was the Ahmad K. Jawad Scholarship for Community Service and Social Action: $1,000 awarded to support a first-generation UM student who "lives a commitment to community service or social action and demonstrates financial need."

As for Nadine, she graduated from the Ford School of Public Policy in April 2017 with plans to attend medical school. "There's a direct correlation between the scholarship money I received, the experiences I had, and the trajectory of my studies. I still plan to become a physician."

Prior to graduating, Nadine won a Truman Scholarship, a graduate scholarship for those pursuing careers in public service. The funds paid for her housing and living expenses while working in Washington, DC, for the summer after graduation, interning with a public service organization through the Harry S. Truman Scholarship Foundation. Next, she'll head to Oxford University as a Rhodes Scholar.

The University of Michigan is committed to keeping education accessible and affordable for all families with need. The Ginsberg Center's work reinforces the university's mission to serve the people of Michigan and the world, and financial aid makes it possible for many students to serve. According to Ginsberg Center director Mary Jo Callan, "When we engage students in distinctive experiences on complex issues, we shape their development, so they may become citizens who will challenge the present and enrich the future."[3]

18

THE CAROLINA CENTER FOR
PUBLIC SERVICE AND THE UNIVERSITY
OF NORTH CAROLINA

A S THE FIRST PUBLIC UNIVERSITY TO OPEN ITS DOORS TO STUDENTS, the University of North Carolina at Chapel Hill (Carolina) has a long tradition of service to the public, and that commitment continues to maintain a central place in the life and reputation of Carolina today. Carolina's leadership and reputation for service and community engagement are well documented. The university was among the first to receive recognition from the Carnegie Foundation for the Advancement of Teaching in community engagement for curricular engagement and outreach and partnerships. From 2006 to 2015, the Corporation for National and Community Service administered the president's Higher Education Community Service Honor Roll to "recognize institutions that support exemplary service programs and raise the visibility of effective practices in campus community partnerships." Carolina was on the Honor Roll annually and in 2009 was recognized as a Presidential Award recipient in a ceremony at Carnegie Hall. In 2014, Carolina was named to the Honor Roll with Distinction in General Community Service. On a more individual level, more than 85 percent of the class of 2013 reported completing an average of ten hours a week in some form of volunteer activities during their four years at Carolina.

The author thanks Ryan Nilsen and Lynn Blanchard from the Carolina Center for Public Service (CCPS) for assistance with research and the preparation of drafts of this chapter. Lynn is director of CCPS. Ryan is senior program officer for community engagement. He works with the MacDonald Scholars at UNC, among his other responsibilities.

By most available indicators, the majority of students include service as part of their experience at Carolina, and there is significant institutional support on campus for students to engage in service and connect it with their academic work. The Carolina Center for Public Service (CCPS) is a pan-university public service center founded in 1999 with the mission of "engaging and supporting the faculty, students, and staff of the University of North Carolina at Chapel Hill in meeting the needs of North Carolina and beyond." The center addresses this mission by "connecting the energy and expertise of both the University and the community to provide students, faculty and staff with deep and transformative experiences."[1]

One significant way the center supports undergraduate students in their public service engagement is providing them with opportunities to integrate their service with their educational experiences at Carolina. Since 2009, the center has housed and provided staffing and financial support to the APPLES Service-Learning program, one of the oldest student-led service-learning organizations in the country, which regularly supports the university's offering of eighty to ninety academic service-learning courses each year along with alternative breaks, service-learning internships, social innovation fellowships, and a preorientation program for incoming first-year students.

The center also offers undergraduate students the opportunity to pursue designation as a Buckley Public Service Scholar (BPSS) on graduation. BPSS challenges participants to expand their understanding of service, connect academic and community-based experiences, and build their capacity to help effect change. The program provides students involved with public service a framework for pursuing their public service experiences and access to the Buckley Portfolio, an online tool that allows them to track their service hours while sharing information about upcoming opportunities with a network of like-minded students. As of April 2018, approximately 10 percent of undergraduate students were enrolled in BPSS at CCPS.

In 2008, service-learning and the related community-based learning were together identified as one of ten high-impact educational practices studied and promoted by the Association of American Colleges and Universities.[2] Increasingly, researchers and practitioners are exploring the value of integrating academic service-learning with other high-impact pedagogies and considering various models for supporting structured and developmental engagement over multiple terms in a student's undergraduate career.[3]

Through programs at CCPS, students can take advantage of many of these opportunities and are able to engage with communities largely because they have financial support that enables them to invest the required time and energy. Active participation in service-related efforts often transform a student's education and future direction.

Austin Gragson, for example, is a first-generation college student from rural Kernersville, North Carolina, who graduated from Carolina in 2017. Gragson qualified for Carolina Covenant and connected early to the CCPS through a presemester program for incoming first-year students that introduced them to service and community partners in the local area. Gragson found his own community through this program, quickly sought out leadership opportunities within the APPLES Service-Learning and Buckley Public Service Scholars programs, and decided to also apply for a work-study job at the center. He worked for four years in the center's office, taking on progressively more responsibility. The financial support he received through Covenant and work-study allowed him to pursue opportunities he otherwise would not have considered possible. Gragson developed a goal of working internationally and is now serving as a science educator in rural Liberia. He plans to attend graduate school for psychology when he returns to the United States.

Tiffany Turner, a 2018 Carolina graduate, is another model of how a student can take on significant service roles and accomplish great things when given adequate financial support. Over her four years as an undergraduate, as part of the Bonner Leaders Program, Turner worked at TABLE, a local organization providing healthy food aid to those experiencing food insecurity. Later, she brought various threads of her service and academic experiences together in serving as the executive director for the nonprofit Pupusas for Education, the sister venture of So Good Pupusas, a food truck and catering company started by a UNC alumna that uses its profits to provide scholarships to undocumented students. Turner received needed financial support as a MacDonald Scholar,[4] and she used her fellowship to expand fundraising efforts to offer more scholarships and build capacity to support the growing program. During the summer after graduation, Turner continued to work with Pupusas for Education to pilot a summit and fellowship program for undocumented students and then took a job with the American Heart Association in her hometown of Greensboro, North Carolina.

Gragson and Turner were able to take advantage of so many programs and high-impact educational experiences offered through departments like the Carolina Center for Public Service and the Campus Y largely because of the financial support they received through scholarships and work-study. For every student like Gragson and Turner, however, there are other students who have equal potential but must take jobs unrelated to their passions or future careers to help ease the financial burden of being a student.

For the last few years, CCPS has funded and organized scholarships requiring community service, and the results have been impressive. Community Service Scholars like Finn Loendorf have worked in a wide array of service activities, from hospital volunteering to voter and election engagement efforts. Loendorf, a physics major, began working with young people through Boomerang, a youth empowerment program with a mission to disrupt the school-to-prison pipeline through providing after school programing and alternative-to-suspension options. Others have participated in community gardens, theater programs, charity fundraising, outreach, resource sharing with people experiencing homelessness, and much more. One of the most valuable parts of the community-service scholarships model is its flexibility in allowing students to seek out and commit to activities and organizations that they care most deeply about.

The administrative and programmatic foundation of the Carolina Center for Public Service has been established over the last twenty years (or thirty in the case of the APPLES Service-Learning program). On this foundation, community-service scholarship programs will continue to exemplify reducing barriers and providing transformational learning experiences through service for generations of Carolina students to come.

19

THE MULVANEY CENTER AND THE
UNIVERSITY OF SAN DIEGO

COMPASSIONATE SERVICE AND COMMUNITY ENGAGEMENT ARE CORE values for the University of San Diego (USD) and the Mulvaney Center. For over three decades, the Karen and Tom Mulvaney Center for Community, Awareness and Social Action has partnered with students, faculty, staff, alumni, and community members to ensure that the USD community is part of the larger San Diego and global community and able to join in addressing some of humanity's most urgent issues. USD contributes more than 350,000 community engagement hours annually and is a nationally recognized leader in community engagement. It has been designated as a Changemaker Campus by Ashoka and as a Carnegie Classified Community Engagement Institution.[1] *Washington Monthly* has ranked the school fifth in the nation for community service participation and hours served, and Fair Trade University has named it first in California;[2] it was also one of eighty-one campuses included in Princeton Review's *Colleges with a Conscience*.[3]

But community engagement is not just about numbers—it is about creating sustainable relationships. In the words of Tom Mulvaney, "If something clicks, if we help one person to go out and make a difference in the world, then this is all worthwhile."[4] Through the generous support of many,

Some of the quotes and much of the material for this chapter was provided by Chris Nayve, associate vice president, community engagement, and director of the Karen and Tom Mulvaney Center for Community Awareness and Social Action at the University of San Diego.

and led by gifts from Karen and Tom Mulvaney and others, the Mulvaney Center has been able to expand the depth and scope of programs, creating educational opportunities, community connections, and global-immersion experiences found at few other institutions.

Past student scholarship recipients include Alexa McAneney, a senior majoring in biochemistry. When not in science classes and labs, McAneney serves as USD's site coordinator at Holy Family School, a nearby Catholic elementary school that serves an ethnically and economically diverse neighborhood. She tutors and organizes the tutoring program bringing USD students together with children who need some extra help and teachers.

McAneney observes, "Community service has been a very grounding experience for me. College can be a selfish thing: what school do I want to go to, what classes do I want to take, what subject do I want to major in, what career do I want to pursue. But there is more to life than that."[5]

Given USD's commitment to academic excellence, ethical conduct, and social justice, community service has always played an important role throughout the campus. Yet the university is determined to do more: to become a catalyst for positive change, a leader in social awareness and entrepreneurship, a model for community and global engagement, and a frontrunner in curriculum-based community service-learning and student leadership. As sociology professor Judy Liu notes, "This does not mean simply increasing the quantity of service learning programs, but instead merging academics, student life and external partnerships into an educational continuum and environment that incorporates new theories, praxis and paradigms."[6]

"Over the past five years we have seen a tremendous increase of involvement from students and faculty in our local and global communities," reflects Center for Community Service Learning (CSL) director Chris Nayve. "Much of this increase is due to our strategic initiatives that focused on differentiating USD as a place with an ecosystem for deep community engagement."[7] Some of the additional student resources come from scholarships for need-eligible students, which allow them the financial freedom to undertake community service and help others.

USD has partnered with the San Diego Microfinance Alliance and the Center for Community Service Learning to create the San Diego Microfinance Project, which provides loans to San Diego women. Steve Conroy, a business professor at USD who teaches related classes on microfinance and wealth creation, says, "We're the only university I'm aware of that has a micro-lending program here, at home, in San Diego [instead of in Africa or Asia]."[8]

USD's anchor partnerships are primarily local but also extend beyond the borders of the campus and the nation. For many years, the faculty and students have engaged in meaningful work locally, whether it was volunteering or developing service-learning courses while working closely with the Mulvaney Center or Changemaker Hub on campus. The work of organizations such as the university ministry with the Romero Immersion Programs, Justice in Mexico, or the Trans-border Institute in the Kroc School, which helps to build sustainable peace in Mexico and the border region, are great examples of how the school and its students can effectively leverage their position near an international border.

According to Nayve, "We must intentionally strengthen and deepen our partnership network and join communities as we work to enhance USD's role in the community. This will manifest in many ways since opportunities exist for USD to be more engaged locally in improving K–12 education, enhancing economic development, promoting health care, and serving as a catalyst for community development. This work will help USD emerge as the leading faith-based anchor university in the United States."[9]

Moving beyond the institution to examine real and effective sustainable change, one must acknowledge who at the university is responsible for the heavy lifting. It's not the centers across campus nor the policy makers; instead it's the select students who show up day after day and continue to lay groundwork for others to follow. For many, however, finding access to or the ability to remain in college has proven to be an almost insurmountable obstacle at times. The lack of affordability, unfortunately, prevents many students from ever tapping into their truest potential. The Mulvaney Center, backed by the generous support of philanthropic donors, seeks to change that narrative by providing scholarship funds.

There are few examples more profound than Robert Ornelaz, whose story exemplifies the transformative powers of education and how the access to it can alter one's life. Robert transferred to the University of San Diego in 2016 from the University of the Channel Islands; the transition was far from seamless. Originally from Palmdale, California, Robert came from humble beginnings. As one of seven children, he and his family members overcame tremendous adversity and challenging economic times.

Many have judged Robert by his physical appearance, misunderstanding who he truly is, because what he represents challenges many of the norms seen across college campuses. His arms and chest are covered in tattoos, and he has scars across his face, yet his smile and disposition are contagious to all who encounter him. He skips to the beat of his own drum and is an artist by trade; his determination to overcome any obstacle is apparent.

Since entering USD, Robert has had to work extremely hard to make ends meet. However, he has seen each challenge as an opportunity for growth. When he was without a place to live and money for food, he applied to become a residential assistant, and he now serves as an influential student leader to many of his peers and fellow underclassman. Thanks to the support of federal work-study programs, Robert has also been able to work as classroom tutor and mentor at Mark Twain Alternative High School, located in the nearby Linda Vista community. Through the Mulvaney Center's Youth Engagement Initiative program, he started as a tutor and after a year was elevated to the role of program coordinator. He now oversees all USD students working onsite.

Maria Coleman is a soon-to-be first-generation college graduate. She is a single mother of two young boys. A college education never seemed possible for her. But Maria, single-handedly raising two young boys while combatting poverty and homelessness, saw education as a tool for herself and her family to have a better life.

As an older student with considerable family responsibilities, Maria's transition into USD was difficult. However, like Robert, she epitomizes resilience. She approaches each day with fearlessness and drive because she knows that one day education will allow her to provide the best possible life for her sons. All of this, however, would not have been possible without the financial support of special programs through USD.

Maria is one of USD's Torero Renaissance Scholars (TRS), a special network of students, all of whom were at one point foster youth, homeless, or at risk of becoming homeless. Through the TRS program, Maria was given stable housing and summer employment—she was placed as an intern in the community through the Mulvaney Center. As a lover of the arts, Maria was able to spend her summers working in San Diego's New Americans Museum as a curator of art and assisting in the documentation of generational oral histories. During the school year, she serves as a bridge between the USD campus community and the New Americans Museum.

Adversity and resilience manifest in many ways across college campuses. Another student, this one much younger, who embodies passion and hard work is Valerie Jaimes. Val is a second-year student at USD. As the first in her family to go to college, she came to USD from her hometown of Santa Barbara, California, through USD's Summer Bridge Program. Thanks to the efforts of the Center for Student Support Services, Val was exposed to a community of other nontraditional students, many of whom had also overcome great odds to find themselves at college.

During her experience in Summer Bridge, prior to the start of her freshman year, Val was introduced to the Mulvaney Center, where she was hired on as a federal work-study tutor through the Youth Engagement Initiative program. Val now spends much of her week in a classroom at Linda Vista's Kit Carson Elementary School.

After completing her first year of college, Val applied and was accepted to the Summer Micah Fellowship, a unique and challenging immersive leadership and educational program hosted by the Mulvaney Center and their friends from St. Mary's College in the greater Oakland, California, area. She spent eight weeks living in Alameda, California, among a community of nearly five hundred homeless families. Through this paid community-engagement fellowship, Val was able to work with St. Anthony's, an organization in the Tenderloin District of San Francisco that serves thousands of meals a day to the city's homeless population.

Had it not been for financial assistance, Val admits, she would not have been able to afford the cost of USD's tuition. With scholarships, she was able to access a quality education while helping others.

Kimberly Riveros is a senior at the University of San Diego and one of the most civically engaged students on campus and in her community. Originally from the south side of San Diego, Kim, like Val, is a Chicana engaged woman and was also a Micah Fellow in the summer of 2017. She worked with young children in the lower-economic community of Fruitvale in Oakland.

Kim has always been an advocate for those who are neglected, especially with regard to the juvenile justice system. In San Diego, she is perhaps best known for her role as the student leader of the Mulvaney Center's Kearny Mesa Juvenile Hall program. Over the past three years she has been at USD, Kim has dedicated countless hours to building relationships with young incarcerated boys and girls. Most importantly, however, she has facilitated connections between hundreds of USD students and volunteers and young people in juvenile hall.

Kim, like Robert, Maria, and Val, is an example of what education and opportunity, coupled with financial assistance, can do to transform the lives of young people. Many take for granted the opportunity to receive a quality education. Those who have endured great challenges and deprivations in their life, however, are often best suited to connect with other less-fortunate individuals and affect the lives of many.

MY STORY

From Farmworker Boy to Pediatrician

Ramon Resa

I STRUGGLE TO FIND A BEGINNING FOR MY STORY. DO I START WITH MY first memories of picking cotton when I was three, or say something about the only picture I have of me as a baby, sitting in a dirt field looking abandoned? My son, Joshua tells me, "Start with your father," but I never knew my father, so what am I supposed to say about him? When people ask me about him, I simply say, "I don't have a father."

I do know who my mother is, but all she did was give birth to me and my siblings. She turned me and two of my brothers over to her mother, our "Ama" and to Ama's husband, "Apa." They raised us.

I'm standing in the middle of a cotton field. It's autumn, and the plants are taller than I am. The fog envelops the cotton field, and for a minute I feel panicky. I glance back to make sure my grandfather's behind me somewhere.

This is my job at age three, to pile up mounds of cotton. Every once in a while, I spook a cottontail. When he scampers away, I run after him as fast as my legs will take me. I go back to piling the cotton as high as I can so Apa will be proud of me. He comes up behind me and pats me on the head.

Ramon Resa strides the halls of Sierra View Medical Center in Porterville, California, where he's on staff.

This chapter is abridged from Ramon Resa, Out of the Fields: My Journey from Farmworker Boy to Pediatrician (Carlsbad, CA: Carlsbad Press, 2010). Reprinted with permission; reviewed and approved by the author. Photo by NashCO, originally printed in Mary MacVean, "Bringing Up Babies," Rotarian, December 2017.

Then he shoves me forward to go make another pile. "Get back to work!" Apa yells.

Three or four years later, I'm itchy, hurting, and cold. I've been cold all day. We get up before dawn. After our breakfast of eggs and tortillas, all of us kids and adults cram ourselves into our beat-up Chevy and set off in a caravan of cars filled with other relatives. The older kids squeeze into the front and back seats. We younger ones end up in the trunk with the lid partly tied down. The trunk is freezing cold. We bring our blankets with us and huddle together.

We arrive in no time at all. Climbing out of the car into the gloomy, overcast day is miserable. The cotton's still wet from the moisture in the air, so the contractor won't let us go into the fields until the sun dries the cotton. We're paid by the pound, and once the cotton's dry it'll weigh less, so he won't have to pay us as much.

When I am seven or eight, I graduate to my own sack. I'm still too young to pull a full-sized 10-foot sack, so Apa makes me one out of a flour sack. I strut around enjoying feeling it wrapped around me, and I pick with more purpose now that I'm no longer a child.

The first day of Christmas vacation! I'm eight years old and in second grade. Today I wake up earlier than on school days but not because I'm eager to enjoy every minute of vacation. Today we're going to be picking oranges in Porterville, 30 miles away.

I dread going outside, but I have to get my chores out of the way before breakfast. We're having one of those cold snaps when the morning temperature dips down to 30 degrees. My first job is to feed the rabbits. I reach into the cage and open the attached box with the litter of baby rabbits; they've frozen to death overnight. I don't have any gloves, and by the time I finish my hands are red and stiff. I still have to feed the pigs, chickens, and goats.

As I'm heading into the house to warm up before we have to leave, my feet crash through the ice in our yard. My tennis shoes are worn out. The soles are flapping loose and fill with ice and slush. I'm wearing my only good pair of socks, so I'm going to spend all day with wet feet.

One year runs into another, and after a while they all seem the same. Christmas vacation comes, and so does another season of pickling oranges. One year it's different. It rains. I have never seen so much rain. We have pans and pots collecting the water that seems to be dripping through our whole roof.

At first, I'm glad we don't have to work, but the rain keeps us pretty much confined to the house. There's nothing to do except watch TV. All the shows are about Christmas and presents and families gathering around the tree and opening tons of gifts—nothing like our house. The closer it gets to Christmas Day, the emptier I feel. There's nothing to look forward to. By this time, we usually have a Christmas tree with at least a few presents under it. Not this year. No crops means no Christmas.

We must have been through bleak winters before, but this is the first time I'm aware how little we have. I can tell that Apa and Ama feel terrible because they can't give us any presents, but they can't think about anything except keeping us fed and getting by one day at a time. We eat mostly beans, rice, and potatoes with tortillas. Ama had bought 100-pound sacks of beans, rice, and flour, but these are almost empty. We still have to make it through the rest of the winter. If the weather doesn't change soon, we'll lose the orange-harvesting season completely. And then I don't know what will happen.

When we get up the next morning (December 25) and open the front door, we're astonished to find a couple of boxes full of food and clothes on the step. This won't be such a terrible holiday after all. We wondered who left them and when.

Another disastrous year hits when I am in sixth grade, a couple of years after we move into our new house across from my school. The weather's too bad for us to work. It seems like we'll have to do without Christmas again.

By now I am not a kid anymore, and I know that we may lose our house if we can't make the mortgage payments. Our phone's already been cut off. We're getting notices that our gas and electricity may be disconnected if we don't make some sort of payment arrangement. If it were summer, I could do yard work. At this time of year there's nothing.

I feel responsible for helping the family, so when I hear that a new weekly paper is looking for delivery boys, I apply. I get five cents for every paper I sell. Within weeks, the paper shuts down. I'm lucky to break even. Joe and I manage to make a few bucks collecting discarded soda bottles.

During yet another poor harvest season a year or two later, I hear footsteps on our front walk on Christmas morning. When I open the door, my classmate Elaine's mom is standing there with some boxes. Elaine is Anglo, and she and I have been in the same class ever since kindergarten. I see her waiting in the car, and she waves to me.

"Merry Christmas!" her mom tells me. "Our church passes out food baskets to needy families, and we're dropping some things off for your family."

"Thank you," I tell her.

"You're welcome!" She walks back to her car. Elaine waves again as they drive off. I'm embarrassed that Elaine knows how poor we are. We do appreciate the food boxes, but I never tell her that.

When I look back at my childhood, I record the years by what crops we were harvesting, and how dire our circumstances by how bad the seasons were. A bad year for grapes meant no extras for school. A freeze or poor orange crop meant no Christmas.

A lot of the households in Goshen, California are like ours—farmworker families with lots of kids who live at the mercy of crops and weather. But my friend Eddy Jiménez, who I guess is my best friend, and his family are different. The Jiménez's have only four children. His dad works full time for the same farmer Apa used to work for until he got too old, and his mom works full time at our school cafeteria during the school year.

Eddy's family looks like the ones I see on TV—a mom and dad who live in a relatively nice house with hot water and an indoor bathroom, and four good-looking kids with clean, new clothes. Those TV families aren't anything like mine. For one thing, there are so many of us and we're so varied in age. I guess that Ama and Apa were pretty much obligated to take us in.

If our family isn't much like Eddy's or the ones I see on TV, neither is our house. The first place I remember living is a tiny clapboard house with a separate casita, a small shed, next to it.

The rooms are so tiny that there's no room for furniture, only mattresses that cover most of the floor space. The casita is a hangout for us boys and also where the older boys, Al and Bill, sleep. Everything in the casita, and what little furniture in the house, comes from the dump. The dump is our shopping center. We go there every week to get rid of stuff, but we usually come back with more junk than we take. Apa, not one to pass up a possible bargain, has us climb up and down the mounds of debris searching for something of value. If a chair has three legs, we salvage it because we have no problem finding a fourth leg. It doesn't matter if they don't match. We're not into décor, only function. Dishes, utensils, mattresses, couches—we load it all up and take it home.

We have no indoor bathroom, only a ramshackle old outhouse. The outhouse is stifling hot and foul smelling in the summer and freezing in the winter. The many crevices in the old wood are perfect hiding places for black widows. Great-aunt Natalia, one of Ama's sisters, got bitten on her behind.

When I'm in third grade, we move from our old house into a newly built one right across from Goshen Elementary School. We've never had anything new, so this is one of the most exciting things that's ever happened to us. We have a yard, a bathroom with a toilet, and hot-and-cold running water.

The living room is small and cluttered. The walls are covered with religious pictures and fake flowers. Five of us boys sleep in one room. Four girls share another bedroom. We all have to share the one bathroom, so mornings are a real zoo.

With so many of us, we always have people milling around. The chores never end—tending the garden, caring for our meat animals, repairing tools for the next day's work.

Alcoholism is rampant in our family. Most of the neighbor kids are also our relatives, and they're constantly getting beaten up by their drunken fathers. My cousin, Ricky's, father once came at him with a knife. Another time, his dad threatened Ricky with a gun. When I see things like that, I wonder if maybe I'm lucky not to have a father.

Grapes are my least favorite crop. The harvest starts in late summer, so the grape fields are like ovens. The work is also dirty, because the juice from the grapes makes the dust stick to us like glue. On a typical day, I can fill a hundred trays. At 7½ cents a tray, I make $7.50 after a full day of backbreaking work in the 100 degree+ August heat.

Most of the growers and their foremen look at us as second-class citizens, but that's how they've been raised to think. Although Apa's been living in the United States for decades, he's still considered a "guest worker." He grew up in a small Mexican town near Juarez, in a society where the bosses are god and control your life. Ever since he's been here, he's kept the subservient manner he learned long ago.

Sometimes when we arrive in the morning, the foreman tells us the rate is eight cents a tray. Then, toward the end of the day, he says it'll be only seven cents. One day, one grower calls immigration just before the harvest is finished. Most of the other workers are undocumented, so they scatter and end up not getting paid at all. But when he refuses to pay us, too, Rosa stands up to him. "We're not illegal!" she yells at him. He goes into the house and comes back with a shotgun. "Get off my property!" he threatens. She stands her ground and eventually he pays us what he owes.

Goshen Elementary School is a couple blocks west of Highway 99 near the edge of town. The teachers there do the best they can. There's no involvement by parents since 95 percent of them are farmworkers who have no education.

I go to Goshen from kindergarten through eighth grade. I remember in kindergarten we were kept separate from other classes by a chain-link fence. Because we speak Spanish at home and because I stuttered, they felt I was not ready for first grade. Eventually, I was allowed into first grade because my kindergarten teacher, Mrs. Barrios, came to my defense.

Although Mrs. Barrios was the first teacher who helped me, it's my second-grade teacher, Mrs. Lambers, who really inspires me. She tells me I don't have to be like my parents and work in the fields all my life. She tells me I'm smart and that I need to go to college so I can get a good job. I don't know what "college" is. But somehow the word stays with me.

[I remember when my fourth grade teacher] Mrs. Tobin calls us up to get our report cards at the end of the day. I receive straight As. I'm stunned. I've never gotten all As before. Pride wells up in me. When I head home that afternoon, I feel such a warm glow inside. She's [Ama] going to be so proud of me! She'll probably get on the phone right away and call everyone, even my mother. After all, my getting straight As is a momentous achievement.

When I walk into the house, she's sitting at our yellow metal dining table smoking a cigarette. The TV is tuned to a Mexican telenovela. When I approach her, she looks surprised. I usually keep my distance so she won't make me run errands when I would rather read. I hand her my report card and hold my breath waiting for her reaction. "Mijo," she'll say. I am so proud of you." But she does nothing. She just stares down at the card.

I say, "Ama, I got all As." She gives me a blank look. I realize she doesn't know what "all As" means.

"All As means I'm smart. Nobody else got all As."

"Oh." After a few moments, she hands me back the card without another comment or glance. This was the first time I realized that I wasn't going to get much encouragement from my family to dream of achieving more in life than becoming a farmworker.

All of my buddies have taken to calling me "Bullwinkle" or "Professor," after the cartoons. They think reading is a waste of time and can't understand why it fascinates me. My family thinks I'm odd because ever since I learned to read, I read whatever I can get my hands on.

I get straight As for the rest of fourth grade and every year from then on until I graduate.

I end up with the highest grade point average in my eighth grade class. I am looking forward to graduation but also feeling apprehensive and nervous about giving the valedictorian's speech. Several weeks before the big day, I'm told to report to Mr. Sims's [the principal] office. "Good morning, Raymond. I guess you're wondering why I asked you to come in."

"Yes."

"Well, it's about graduation day. I know you're our best student, and you've done a great job here, and we're proud of you. Well, I'll get to the point. We're going to have Elaine give the valedictorian's speech. She's right behind you grade-wise, and we feel she will do a better job because people will understand her better."

I've stopped listening. I say, "I understand," and I leave his office. Actually, I think I do understand. But that doesn't stop me from being pissed off.

A few weeks later, the guidance counselors from Redwood High School in Visalia arrive to advise us on what courses to take. I know I want to go to college, and I'm going to ask about college prep courses. I learn that Mr. Moss, who was my older brothers' counselor, will be mine, too.

When Elaine and I are ushered into Mr. Moss's presence, I see a big Anglo man, over six foot four and maybe 250 pounds. He has our transcripts on the desk in front of him. "So, you two are the top students," he says. "Is that right?"

"Yes," we answer.

He turns to Elaine first. "So Elaine, what are you interested in studying?"

"Nothing."

"Aren't you interested in college?"

She shrugs. "No."

"Well, with your grades, you should be." He tries to convince her to think about college, and Elaine reluctantly agrees to consider it.

Then he turns to me. "Raymond, I know your brothers, and they're doing really well in woodshop. We'll sign you up for the same classes they had."

"I'm interested in going to college, and I want to take college prep courses."

"I don't think college would be a good idea for you, it'll be really hard and you won't like it. Why don't you just take woodshop? It was good enough for your brothers."

I wonder why he is so insistent that Elaine should go to college, but when I tell him I want to, he tells me the complete opposite. For once, I don't back down.

Finally, he says, "I'll put you in the college prep courses on trial. But if you have any trouble, I'll pull you out of them immediately." I didn't say anything. I've won this battle.

September 1968—my first day at Redwood High School! I've never seen so many people! There were only about 40 of us in my graduating class. Now I'm going to be in a class of 500. And almost all the kids in my classes are white. I see only a few Mexican kids like me.

My classes for the first semester are French, Algebra, college-prep English, world geography, and some other required classes—plus running cross country. I am running cross country because I have the endurance to run three-mile races. Besides, cross country is a family tradition. Bill, Al, Domingo, and Milly all ran cross country. The team is made up of 90 percent Mexicans.

A couple of weeks into freshman year, I start hanging around with a group of other Mexican kids who are also thinking of going to college. Until now, my family has been my whole world. Being in high school is exciting and challenging. I like belonging to my circle of new friends.

During the summer between my freshman and sophomore year, I enroll in summer school. I don't know why Ama and Apa are willing to let me out of field work, but they do. After summer school ends, I go back to irrigating [fields] with Mercy. This time I start getting paid by the hour. I make the same wage he does, $1.75 an hour. I'm thrilled to be getting an actual paycheck with my name on it. Even though I have to give most of it to Ama, it feels like a lot of money.

I can't even think about dating. First, I need a car, and second, I need money. I have to save whatever Ama lets me keep so I can pay for my school expenses. Whenever my gang wants to go out for pizza or to a movie, I make an excuse to get out of going.

My sophomore and junior years go by in a blur, punctuated by summers spent irrigating. At times, I become depressed. The blue moods come on more frequently. I feel like giving up on everything because I'm not going to amount to anything anyway. I start feeling that no one will blame me if I didn't make it to college after all.

Even though Mr. Moss realizes that I'm not going to fail my college-prep courses, he makes no effort to spur me on, and he still refuses to give me any information.

I do find a woman who is 100 percent behind me. Her name is Pat and her daughter, Paula, is in my class. Pat works at the school district office. She has a college education and is one of the few Mexican role models I have. She is the only person I can begin to share my feelings with. When I tell her about my struggles and every time I bring up going to college, Ama tells me I can't go, Pat replies, "Nonsense! Of course you'll go to college."

Only a few weeks into the [first] semester in my senior year, I got a note from the principal's office telling me instead of going to my 1:30 [p.m.] class I'm to go to one of the meeting rooms. When I mention this to the group at lunch, I learn all of us have gotten the same notice. We have no idea what it's about.

We settle ourselves into the meeting room and wait to see what will happen next. The door opens and two men come in. They're obviously Mexican.

"My name is Roberto Rubalcava," the older man says. "I'm the director of the Educational Opportunities Program at the University of California at Santa Cruz. And this is Noe Lozano. Noe graduated from here at Redwood and is a psychology major at Santa Cruz." Rubalcava tells us, "We're seen your grades, and I'm telling you right now that you all qualify for admission to the UC system. But it seems that nobody's bothered to inform you of this fact." He's right. The only advice our counselors give us is to go to COS [community college].

Noe begins by telling us that, like many of us, he comes from a farm-worker family. Just as I am wondering how a farmworker kid like him can afford a place like Santa Cruz, he adds "I bet you're all wondering how I can afford college, given my parents' economic status. The answer is Cal grants and scholarships." The grants are based on family income, and if it's very low, the grant will pay the whole cost of college minus the student's summer earnings.

It's late fall 1971, and my application to Santa Cruz is almost complete. I have three strong recommendations. I've done my best with the financial statement. I'm almost finished with my essay. The next time Linda visits, we go over my application and she says everything looks good. "Now take it home and get your guardians to sign it," she tells me.

That's the final hurdle I have to face. When I show her [Ama] the form, she looks puzzled. "What's this?"

"My college application. It's for the University of California at Santa Cruz. I have a chance to go to college. For free."

She explodes. "What about us? Who's going to take care of us if you go away? You can't leave! After we raised you, this is how you reward us! Ungrateful son! Thinking only of yourself!" The criticisms and accusations continue. "I'm not signing anything!"

My only choices are to forge her signature and sign it myself, or to have one of the girls do it. I ask Elia.

One day in early spring, Domingo stops by with my mail. [He] hands me a regular-sized business envelope. It's from Santa Cruz. My heart sinks. I've been thinking that if I were accepted I would receive a thick, full-sized envelope full of forms, but if they turned me down, all I'd get would be a one-page letter. Like the one I'm now holding.

I slide my finger under the adhesive and open it. The letter's from Roberto, congratulating me on being accepted to Santa Cruz! "I know you will be receiving your official acceptance in the next couple of days, but I couldn't wait to let you know. Domingo," I say quietly. "I am going to Santa Cruz."

[A few months later.] Finally! I just turned 19, and I'm about to head off to Santa Cruz. Ernie and I have been assigned to room together; now we have to figure out how we're going to get to Santa Cruz. Mercy offers to drive us in his van. As usually happens whenever our family goes on a trip in a vehicle, something breaks down. This time the van gets a flat near Pacheco Pass, but Mercy is carrying some spare retreads, so we're not stopped for long.

We have a couple days to settle in before classes start. We've been given temporary meal tickets. Dinner includes lots of pasta, various drinks, and fruit. I have never seen so much food. I can eat as much as I want and even have seconds. At home, I always felt hungry and was concerned about taking too much and not leaving enough for others. Here, I don't have to think about that anymore.

The next day we go to the financial aid office. I am astonished to see a lot of white students in line. I had no idea that there were white students who needed aid, too. I had taken it for granted that every white student had money. Obviously, I was mistaken.

Late that winter, a family crisis occurs that changes the course of my life. My favorite aunt, Helen, had gone to see a doctor about a mass in her breast. He told her she had breast cancer and would die without treatment. Although she started radiation treatment, the doctor treated her with such contempt that she decided she would rather die than be subjected to more of his callous behavior. She stopped going to treatments and died several months later.

Helen was the nicest aunt I could ever have had. I never want anyone to go through what she went through. I'm going to become a doctor.

[After Christmas] I can't wait for the winter quarter to start. Debbie [my new girlfriend] and I go to an outdoor reception on campus. A lot of professors and advisors are present, and many students are taking advantage of the opportunity to seek career guidance. When I see my advisor's free, I approach him with Debbie at my side. "I've decided to change to pre-med and try for medical school," I tell him. "How do I go about doing this?"

"I think you should stay with being a psych major," he replies. "Premed's too difficult. Besides your people need psychologists as much as they need doctors."

I can tell immediately he doesn't remember who I am. Nor does he have my records with him, so why is he making a snap judgment that I'm not qualified? Debbie is equally shocked because we just overheard him encouraging a couple of Anglo students to think about going into medicine. He even told them that Santa Cruz had a great record of getting students into medical school.

Now that I've decided to become a doctor, I realize that I'm a year behind other pre-med students because I made the decision so late. I am going to have to take most of the science courses in sequence. This will mean a heavy workload.

I start my sophomore year as a biology major. This is going to be my make-or-break year, and I soon find that the pre-med curriculum is as hard as I thought it would be. I have to take chemistry, physics, and calculus in the fall quarter and more chemistry as well as other courses in the winter and spring. Debbie's love and support keep me from going insane.

During the summer between my junior and senior year, [we] get a month-long grant to provide medical information to the farmworkers at the Woodville migrant camp near Porterville[, California,] and several other camps in the [San Joaquin] Valley. Unfortunately, we weren't able to accomplish much for the migrants. We're threatened with legal action when we try to get them decent medical care. The county clinic refuses to see them. I take an elderly man to the Tulare clinic. They turn us away so we have to drive him all the way to the Porterville clinic.

My experience on the grant strengthens my resolve to become a doctor because, during that whole time, we encounter not a single Mexican doctor in any of the town clinics we go to. All of the doctors we met were white, male, and arrogant.

In addition to our senior-year coursework in the fall and winter quarters, all of us in our pre-med group have to take the Medical College Admission Test (MCAT) and start filling out our applications to schools. When I sum up my reasons for wanting to be a doctor in the essay I have to submit with my application, I mention my background [and] the work-my-butt-off work ethic I developed from being a farmworker. I also tear into the medical establishment and write about how racist and uncaring it is toward minorities and the poor. I promise after I finish my medical training, I'll return to my home area so I can serve the poor and mentor others.

The three major schools I apply to are the University of Minnesota, the University of California at Irvine, and the University of Washington. Some of my relatives are amazed I'm not satisfied with what I've accomplished already. I tell them I need to spend four more years in medical school. Ama says, "But when are you going to get a job? Most of the guys have good cars and nice houses because they didn't waste time away at some fancy college."

[Subsequently] I receive the following letter.

Dear Ramon,

We would like to congratulate you on your acceptance to UC Irvine Medical School. You will be receiving your official letter soon, but because Irvine starts at the end of June, we feel we must get working on your financial aid.

We're in a real time bind. Commencement's the second week of June, and Irvine starts just a week later. [In between, Debbie and I plan to get married.] The wedding date was set for the afternoon of Saturday, June 19, 1976 at the house in Sanger[, California,] where I first met Debbie's family on Christmas Day three-and-a-half years ago.

My first two years of medical school turn into what I think of as the zombie years. Anatomy, microbiology, and neurology. Every day I feel like giving in to my anguish because I'm so far behind. No matter what I do, I can't catch up. I'm on the verge of giving up and going home a loser when out of the blue I receive a letter from Aunt Lucinda. She writes, "I knew you were smart and you would make something of yourself someday. I thought you would grow up to work in a store like JCPenney and wear a shirt and tie. But for you to be a doctor, I never imagined that. I can't believe my 'little brother' is going to be a doctor. I am so proud of you."

Her letter makes me resolve to stick around. I can't let her down.

By the second year, several of my minority classmates have dropped out. Each day, I have to struggle to survive. I cling to the hope that I can make it through to the end of the first two years. If I can make it through to my clinical rotations, where we will be actually working with patients, things will get easier.

[After barely surviving the first two years] I'm excited to be starting clinical rotations, because to me this is what medicine's all about—seeing and helping people with their ailments. We leave the Irvine campus to first- and second-year students and join fourth-year students, interns, and residents. Over the next two or three years, we'll spend six weeks in each of the hospital's departments getting experience in the various specialties.

Clinical rotations are hard and exhausting because they take up almost every waking hour. We're on call for 36 hours at a time, and we get saddled with most of the scat work, like doing the 2 a.m. blood draws and preparing all the lab reports for morning rounds. For us minority students, patients and even staff sometimes mistake us for janitors or orderlies. We'll be asked to clean up patients' rooms or to get hold of a doctor. Neither the patients nor the staff are used to seeing black, Mexican, or female medical students.

When I start my obstetric-gynecological (OB-GYN) rotation, I'm not sure how I'll feel, but I do know I've always wanted to help bring a new baby into the world. My first delivery is a Mexican woman in her 20s. She has a couple other kids; that means she's actually more experienced than I am. She does her best to help me along; we manage to bring a baby girl into the world.

It turns out that OB-GYN is preparation for my finding my true calling. The moment I begin my pediatrics rotation, I know I've found my calling. I grew up surrounded by infants and children in my family. The day I see my first clinic patient, I know I'm never going to be bored. When I walk in, the mom is holding a cute four-month-old baby girl in her lap. I lay her down, and she coos and laughs during the whole exam as I find her tickle spots. This doesn't feel at all like work.

In the fall of my final year, we [Debbie and I] decide it's time to have a baby. At first, we weren't concerned, but as months go by we start feeling frustrated. Then, in January 1981, she's late. We buy a pregnancy test kit. [It's] positive. We're going to be parents!

Match Day is an ordeal that all American medical students face toward the end of their last year of medical school. I interview for the pediatric programs [including] a program of the UC San Francisco Medical School that's based in Fresno. Fresno is only an hour from Goshen and [near] Sanger because [Debbie's] aunt and uncle are still in Sanger. Her parents would be only three hours away. On Match Day, my top pick [Fresno] has matched me to its program.

Life is finally good. Joe helps us move by driving the U-Haul to Fresno, while we follow in the Toyota pickup we just bought. I'm very proud of it because it's the first vehicle I've ever owned.

Debbie's Aunt Beth has a friend who owns a small house for rent less than three blocks from VMC [Valley Medical Center, where I will work]. The neighborhood is a bit seedy, but I consider it a step up compared to Goshen.

The biggest change in our lives now is that I finally have a paying job. My salary is the most money I've ever made. The problem is, I've forgotten about my student loans. When I receive my first payment notice, I realize that they're going to take a significant part of my salary each month. Still, looking at the overall picture, I can't be too upset. After all, where would I be if I hadn't borrowed that money in the first place? I know when I open my practice a few years from now, I'll be earning many times what I owe in loans.

It's September 24, 1981—a day I'll never forget. We see our little girl for the first time. My eight-pound daughter looks right at me and my heart is hers forever. When I hold her for the first time, all my troubles fade away. I go back to Debbie's bed, and together we admire our beautiful little Marina.

A few months before I finish my residency, Lindsay District Hospital recruits me to open an office in Porterville. [I] meet with Hugh Olson, the hospital's CEO, and we reach an agreement that includes a guarantee of my first year's salary. Plus they'll pay our moving expenses and even assign

Shirley Powell, their assistant administrator, as my liaison to help set up my office.

Early August 1985, I open up my office. The sign reads: Ramon Resa, MD Pediatrics. For the first time since we can remember, we have no worries. I'm on top of the world. We take our first real vacation and go to Hawaii.

We return to find a major upheaval at Lindsay District Hospital. Hugh Olsen's been fired, and the new CEO refuses to honor the contract I signed only a few weeks earlier. Hugh Olsen gives me an introduction to the manager of the Bank of the Sierra in Lindsay. The next day the area manager informs me he's been authorized to advance me $50,000! That is enough to see me through the first six months. Six months later my practice is solvent.

Less than a year after I open my practice, Debbie and I feel we're established enough to buy a house. She's pregnant again, and we want to have our own place for our family. We find a house in the hills in Springfield. I go straight to the Bank of the Sierras for the financing; within weeks the house is ours.

Debbie's second pregnancy is much easier. Josh makes his appearance at Lindsay Hospital on December 9, 1986.

Around the time Josh is born, Jimmy Howell, a long-time Rotary member, invites me to a meeting. When I'm invited to join, about three or four months after I start attending, I'm more than glad to accept. [A few years later I become president of the local Rotary Club.]

It's during my presidency that the Big Freeze of 1990 hits just a few days before Christmas. It ultimately wrecks almost $800 million in agricultural damage and puts many farmworkers in our area out of work. Because of my background, I relate to their suffering, and I decide to tell my fellow Rotary members my story.

I suggest we help our farmworkers survive the freeze by buying and giving out rice, beans, and flour—staples that go a long way and last a long time. My fellow Rotarians overwhelm me with their generosity.

Despite all the successes I've achieved—my thriving practice, my family, my standing in the community, and my great experiences with Rotary—my old insecurities aren't entirely eradicated. Deep down, I don't feel I deserve any of it. I start taking out my fear and anger on Debbie and the kids. Until now, I've resisted therapy because I'm afraid to admit I need help.

I finally agree to see a psychologist, but only to keep Debbie from walking out. Over time, we see "Mike" both individually and as a couple. [Eventually] I start opening up. I am able to talk more. I understand how much of my childhood and especially my anger toward my mother and grandparents are still affecting me.

One night, I reach the end of the line. I'm in so much anguish that I call Shirley. "I need help now," I tell her. "I need to see your pastor." It's almost midnight, but he says he can come over right away. After talking with him for hours, I get down on my knees and pray. I feel a weight lifted off my shoulders. I pray for forgiveness, and I receive it.

In the years since those dark days came to an end, my life has been so different. I get angry but I don't stay angry.

My life is good. I reached goals I never could have imagined when I was a little Mexican kid picking cotton, oranges and grapes and swimming in ditches full of chemicals. I have a beautiful house with a big swimming pool. Josh and Marina grew up; they're both adults now. Marina went to UC Santa Cruz and graduated with a major in theatre. She's now an actress and therapist in Los Angeles.

Josh graduated from Stanford University with a degree in biology. He graduated from UCSF Medical School and is a board-certified pediatrician. He is a pediatric oncology fellow at Sloan Kettering in New York.

I never had another recurrence of depression. I now know that I have too much to live for. Debbie stuck with me through all the problems and never stopped believing in me.

I understand why I suffered for so many years from depressive moods and "imposter syndrome." Coming from a family in which it was a minor miracle to graduate from high school, who would have ever thought I could become a doctor? I marvel. This little farmworker boy, I remind myself, has earned his good fortune.

CONCLUSION

What Must Be Done

THE HIGHER EDUCATION SYSTEM THAT PROVIDES A PATH FOR AMER-icans to obtain a college education and secure good employment is broken. With the extraordinary costs of attending most universities, only the rich can afford an education, unless a student can secure considerable financial aid. Some students from poor families receive scholarships and grants, but many others rely heavily on loans to finance all or part of their education. Students from middle-class families often do not qualify for need-based grants yet also do not have the financial resources to pay the costs of attending school. Student loans, with compounding interest, become unaffordable and impossible to pay off. The comparatively low increases in typical wage gains cannot keep pace with compounding student debt. Some loan recipients are trapped for the rest of their lives, forever burdened by debt that will exceed their ability to pay.

Parents who cosigned student loans often find they cannot afford retirement, as student debt consumes their savings. Aging workers who worked and saved their entire adult lives delay retirement; many cannot enjoy their old age. Borrowers do not support the economy, which is largely dependent on consumer spending. Home purchases are deferred, families delayed, and other purchases curtailed.

The two primary proposals that are debated nationally include (1) reducing available financial aid to reduce the level of federal spending and obligation and (2) making college free. Neither is sustainable. Withholding access to education will almost certainly diminish the nation's ability to compete globally and limit future economic growth, and the mammoth federal budget deficits make adding new entitlement programs extremely difficult.

Some have argued that it would be desirable to get the federal government out of the student loan business and leave it to private lenders. They generally argue that schools can raise tuition because the federal government is compliant in providing more financial aid including loans to cover the increased cost. This logic ignores the causes of why college costs so much and would almost certainly lead to higher levels of student debt, with private loans compounding sooner and at higher interest rates. More student debt and less access to a university education are not desirable social goals.

Some argue for free public education. Typically they estimate the cost to be $90 billion, which is the total spent on public college tuition and fees. This ignores the obvious consequences of making education free: more people will attend college and stay longer—hey, it's free. Increased enrollment comes from added current nonattendees, transfers from expensive private schools, and no financial imperative to proceed quickly to a degree. It subsidizes both rich and poor kids, raising the question of why the son or daughter of a wealthy family should be subsidized by the taxpayer.

In addition to cost issues, it will likely result in a two-tiered education system. Public schools, overburdened with higher student populations and without commensurate financial resources, most likely will deliver an inferior education. Elite private schools will deliver high-quality education but at a high price. The rich get a good education and the poor an inferior one. This seems to be the case where such policies have been implemented. Again, this does not seem like wise social policy. So what's the pragmatic solution?

For the past four decades, the higher education model has followed a consistent path to arrive where it is today. As operating and facility costs increased and enrollment rose, state and federal support for schools fell behind. Schools raised tuition, but wages and income have not kept pace. The federal government provided more student assistance to help close the school affordability gap, but there is not enough gift or scholarship money, so more students rely on more loans. This model is no longer sustainable.

Alternative education models need to be discussed. A physical university with classrooms, dedicated facilities, and entertainment venues including a range of athletic facilities may no longer be affordable for many or most of the student population. Perhaps future schools will rely more on technology, automation, and artificial intelligence, as is the trend in business. There is no clear answer, and the stakes—an educated population unburdened by extreme debt—are high. Let the debate began.

In the near term, any plan to address the problem of enabling access to education while reducing the level and sustainability of student debt should include the following elements:

1. More funding for student grants
   i. Increased federal grant funding, possibly tied to a formula that rewards states that meet education funding thresholds and universities who keep tuition increases in check.
   ii. Increased state funding. If states elect not to support their universities, then federal funds should be less available in those states. Why should the US taxpayer make up for what state taxpayers are unwilling to support?
   iii. Increased funding should be limited for schools with high student loan default rates or low graduation rates.
   iv. Additional funding should be available to schools that keep tuition increases in check.
   v. A cooperative program should be developed with participating states that would provide full tuition funding at community colleges for two years for eligible students. This actually would not cost that much because community college tuition is typically low, and the new funds would apply only after other grants are counted, including PELL grants. The New York State Excelsior program provides assistance to New York State residents from families earning no more than $125,000 annually.[1]
   vi. Private scholarship donations should be encouraged through either tax credits or a federal or state match. Donations may be more forthcoming as a tax credit instead of a deduction on federal taxes. Donations to state public schools should be credited on the applicable state income taxes.
   vii. A national marketing program should be launched to encourage more donors to give scholarship money to universities and colleges.
2. Greater and clearer eligibility for loan forgiveness due to public service
   i. Public service requirements to achieve loan forgiveness should be made clearer and more obvious to potential participants.
   ii. The eligible list of employers should be expanded.
   iii. Retroactively, the US government should evaluate whether existing debtors did have qualifying service employment even if they failed to provide timely paperwork.

3. Better financial literacy tools for borrowers and guarantors

    i. Greater borrower literacy tools should be developed and implemented. Many student borrowers are overwhelmed by the paperwork required to finance a college education. Indiana University recently introduced a template to show clearly what the student borrower is committing to and the future repayment obligations. When confronted with this level of financial magnitude, the students on average borrowed less money than originally requested and were able to source funds elsewhere.[2] The program has subsequently become state law in Indiana. It should be required in all student loan application processes.

    ii. The borrower should also be shown the calculations of what their future wages might be if they pursue their intended degree. Comparing future debt payments with possible future wages is important for informed decision-making.

    iii. Coborrowers or guarantors should be provided the same information and asked to demonstrate their financial ability to pay off the loans in light of their income, expenses, retirement plans, and health.

4. Schools share the responsibility for loan defaults

    i. Schools should share accountability for loan defaults. Currently, if a school encourages students to take out loans when the students are unlikely to succeed, the school has no liability. There should be shared liability, especially if the loan default rate exceeds reasonable levels.

    ii. Most defaults are on loans with a balance of less than $5,000. This is typically because the student was not prepared for college and dropped out early in their studies. The first $5,000 of default should be the responsibility of the school. This would eliminate most defaults and make schools more careful about encouraging students to borrow money.

5. Bankruptcy and for-profit schools

    i. Student loans should not be exempt from bankruptcy actions. If someone is truly broke, why does it matter if their debt is student loans or credit cards?

    ii. Private, for-profit schools should be rigorously evaluated with regard to past loan policies and performance. Schools in this category typically have the highest loan amounts and highest default rates. Those with the poorest performance should be banned from future participation in government loan programs.

6. Community service requirement
    i. Governments and donors should require community service by most grant recipients. Helping others is potentially a big benefit to society and fills in gaps left by government cutbacks and inadequate funding. It also provides meaningful learning experiences to students.
    ii. Universities should establish community service outreach programs if they do not already have them. The programs should include training, mentoring, and coordination with community needs and organizations. Staff and faculty should be involved and committed.
7. Administrative cost controls
    i. Governments and universities should reexamine the necessity of administrative costs incurred in operating the schools. Too much money is being spent on noneducational tasks, driving up tuition costs. Perhaps more flexible regulations and reporting could reduce some university costs. The US Department of Education should review their administrative requirements and reports with a view to reducing administrative costs. A financial incentive system to reward schools that are able to reduce or limit tuition increases should be considered.
8. Assistance to those currently in debt
    i. For students currently in debt, a financial match program should be evaluated (e.g., for every $1,000 of principal paid in an agreed time period—say, three years—the government would credit $1,000 toward their federal debt balance.
9. Immediate action
    i. While government policy makers debate what to do, individuals should step up and support colleges and universities with donations to scholarship funds.

Doing nothing is a slow form of national suicide. The country is on the path to realize a less-educated public, heavily indebted consumers unable to participate fully in the economy, and a society where future opportunity is increasingly based on parental income.

APPENDIXES
MORE STORIES OF HOPE AND
INSPIRATION

APPENDIX A

Finding a Purpose after Prison

Martin Leyva

B EING SENTENCED TO PRISON WASN'T THE MOST TERRIFYING EXPERI-
ence of Martin Leyva's life. When you're arrested for the first time at
age thirteen and you spend the next two decades in and out of jail and
prison, it's easy to become accustomed to life behind bars.

No, terrifying for Leyva was stepping on to a college campus for the
first time. "I didn't speak the language, I didn't look like anybody else, I
didn't feel like anybody else," Leyva said of starting classes at Santa Barbara
City College, Santa Barbara, California, in 2007.

It didn't take long for Leyva to realize he wasn't alone in those feelings,
that there were others on campus who could relate to his struggles with
alcohol, drugs, and incarceration. It soon became Leyva's mission to help
those who faced struggles similar to his own. A mentor in prison told him
as much during what Leyva vowed would be his final stretch locked up.

"My elder said, 'When you get out of prison, you help the people. Help
the people,'" said Leyva, who was released in April 2007. "I always think to
myself, 'I have to help the people. Whoever my path crosses, I'm going to
help them out.'"

This chapter by Eric Breier was first published by CSUSM NewsCenter on August 23, 2017, as
"Finding a Purpose after Prison," https://news.csusm.edu/finding-a-purpose-after-prison/.
Reprinted with permission from the publisher, the author, and Mr. Leyva.

"I've been clean and sober going on fifteen years," said Leyva, who is forty-four years old and was recently named a Sally Casanova Scholar, an award that helps students explore and prepare for doctoral programs.

"I'm no longer on probation. I'm not on parole. I go to sleep at night knowing I've helped another person and I've done some good. And I wake up with the ambition to go out and continue that work. It's my routine. Helping another person is helping myself."

"I Became My Environment"

It was the summer between sixth and seventh grade. A friend asked Leyva if he wanted to smoke pot in a creek where kids in his neighborhood often hung out. "No, I can't do that," Leyva told his friend. "But I'll go with you." Seeing his friend and another acquaintance smoking, Leyva changed his mind. "Why not?" he said.

Santa Barbara is often referred to as the American Riviera, home to upscale boutique stores and restaurants, multimillion-dollar homes, and a favorite for celebrities seeking a getaway from Los Angeles. But the Santa Barbara that Leyva knew was nothing like the idyllic beach-side setting most envision. "I was born around drugs and violence," he said. "I had a loving mother, but she worked a lot. I had no good male role models. My male role models were into negative things. I became my environment."

While Leyva was accustomed to the chaos of his neighborhood, something felt different when he got home after smoking pot for the first time. He felt free of the turmoil and the chaos faded. "I attached my drugs and my drinking to emotions," Leyva said. "If I was sad or angry or anxious, I taught myself at a very young age, just use drugs and it will go away. But it never goes away. It just gets temporarily covered up."

It wasn't long after getting high for the first time that Leyva had another first, one that would define his life for the next twenty-plus years. At thirteen, he was arrested for possession of a stolen moped. A friend stole the moped, but it was Leyva who was caught while cruising around on it. The arrest, coupled with his drug and alcohol use, began a spiral that was difficult to escape. There was a DUI. An arrest for gun sales. Parole violations.

Leyva's substance abuse became so bad that his mother began to view his incarceration almost as a blessing: "I must have been in my mid-twenties and my mom said, 'I actually like it when you're in jail because I know you're sleeping and I know you're eating,'" he said. "It makes me emotional just thinking about it."

Clean and Sober

Leyva stopped drinking about a year before he went to prison for the final time in 2004. He kicked his drug habit shortly before beginning his sentence on a robbery charge. He remained clean and sober while locked up, no easy task given the proliferation of drugs in prison. "It's so easy to stay high in prison," he said. "Any drug you could want. People even make their own alcohol. It's a big issue in the prison system. As long as you have the money to pay for it, you can stay high."

Leyva said he made a conscious decision to stay clean in prison, and he stuck to it. It wasn't the only conscious decision he was making to improve his life—he also was determined to make this the last time he would ever be locked up. The words of his prison elder, "Help the people," were a guiding force, and a newspaper article he received from his mother shortly before his release in April 2007 provided a final push toward change.

The story detailed the death of fifteen-year-old Luis Angel Linares who was stabbed in the middle of the day on Santa Barbara's renowned State Street. A fourteen year old was charged with the murder, which was part of large gang brawl. Leyva had never been a gang member, but the story resonated all the same.

"I said, 'I can go home and continue being part of the problem—even by staying silent—or I can go home and do something to help the young people in the community,'" he said. "That article really put me in a different place. I didn't know what I was going to do, I didn't know how I was going to do it, but I was going to do something positive when I got out."

A New Life

Less than five months after his release from prison, Leyva walked on to a college campus for the first time. It was a short stay. Leyva got off the bus at Santa Barbara City College and just stared at the buildings. He began pacing while he continued to eye the administration and student services buildings. When the next bus rolled up to the stop, Leyva got on. "I can't do this," he told himself. But the next day, his niece, also a student at Santa

Barbara City College, told him to get in the car. She was going to drive him to school.

Leyva met with an academic adviser, who suggested a drug and alcohol treatment certificate program. Reading his class material was like reading his autobiography. "I was thinking about my neighborhood, my family dynamics, the people I met in prison," Leyva said. "Everything I was reading was about me. And I fell in love with education."

Considered a high-risk parole offender as he began college, Leyva was required to report to the parole office twice a month. Each time he was there, he saw two men he recognized from Santa Barbara City College. Eventually, he approached one of the men. Leyva told him about the anxiety he felt at school, the feeling of not belonging, of not wanting to raise his hand in class for fear of being labeled stupid. That's when Leyva learned he wasn't alone in those feelings. Together, they approached the third person they had seen at the parole office, and he, too, echoed their sentiments.

By the end of the semester, Leyva approached the administration about starting a formal support group for formerly incarcerated men and women. By the summer of 2008, the group had its first cohort of the Transitions Program, whose mission would be to provide access to higher education for formerly incarcerated individuals and create a smooth transition from prison to community college.

Making Transitions

Santa Barbara City College recently graduated its tenth Transitions Program cohort. Leyva has helped launch a program at Mira Costa College and is hoping to do the same at Palomar College (both in San Diego). "Martin [Leyva] aspires to erase the margins and empower society's underdog by helping them become successful through higher education," said Dr. Xuan Santos, an assistant professor of sociology who has known Leyva for more than ten years.

"As a graduate student, Martin has worked tirelessly to bring the Transitions Program to North San Diego County as more men and women experience mass incarceration and the tentacles of the Prison Industrial Complex. As more people are re-entering society, we are looking for felony-friendly employers and institutions of higher learning to become OGs—opportunity givers."

His mother, once relieved when her son was incarcerated so that she knew he would have meals and a bed, now tells Leyva, "I don't have to worry about you anymore." She knows he doesn't drink. She knows he doesn't use. She's been at restaurants with Leyva and seen strangers approach to shake his hand and thank him.

"Ten years ago, right out of prison trying to figure out what I was going to do, I couldn't look in the mirror and say, 'You're a good man. I love you.' Today, I look in the mirror and say, 'You have a purpose in life. You love yourself and you love others.'"

APPENDIX B

From Night Watchman to College Success

DeCarlos Hickson

For DeCarlos Hickson, a rising senior at UNC Chapel Hill, being creative and turning his passion for art into a career has always been his dream. "I've been into creativity, the arts, and things like that. So from a young age I've always been into visual arts and storytelling. That's always been my first love," he says. Several aspects of his childhood fostered this dream, from his happy and easygoing disposition and overall positive experiences growing up to the support network around him.

Growing up, DeCarlos moved frequently and lived in several places in the city of Durham, North Carolina. Although his family moved many times, mostly in response to unfavorable financial circumstances, his mother provided stability in his life, allowing him to have a childhood filled with good memories.

"My mom, she showed me by example what a strong and good person is. She was always thinking about everyone. She was always working to provide for me and my brother, always making sure we had what we needed. She worked really hard." Despite her hard work, the family still endured financial struggles. From this experience, DeCarlos learned at an early age about the need to persevere in spite of adversity and financial constraints: "It made me conscious of materials and money. I saw those who had it and

The author thanks University of North Carolina at Chapel Hill graduate student Lacey Lumpkin for assistance with research and the preparation of drafts of this appendix. Lacey interviewed Mr. Hickson in June and July 2018 in Chapel Hill, North Carolina. He is quoted from these interviews here.

realized what I didn't have." Those struggles didn't stop his mother from pushing her children to dream big and pursue those dreams, he says: "My mom, she always instilled in us that we can do whatever we want to do, and we could be whatever we want to be. So, for me, that's something I really believed."

In addition to his mother, DeCarlos credits his uncle for being a positive role model: "I really looked up to him. He was a role model of what a strong man should be. That was something that really meant a lot to me because my dad wasn't around. My uncle was like my mother; he had a strong work ethic."

DeCarlos noticed something about their hard work, though: "I picked up on the difference between working hard and working smart. Not to say that the role models around me were not working smart, but I could definitely see that there's a way to be more efficient, because you can definitely work hard and not have nearly as much to show for it as some other people who don't seem to work nearly as hard."

Like many Americans growing up in challenging financial situations, DeCarlos speaks of being conscious of not having enough money and needing more money for the things he wanted. DeCarlos realized, like his mother and uncle, he also needed to adopt a strong work ethic to move ahead; he wanted things to go differently for him.

DeCarlos wanted to work for himself and someday own his own business: "Later on in life is when I started to desire to be my own boss. I slowly started to think about if I could start my own business. Because I want to create what I want to create. I didn't see people doing that. All my family members, they were just working at other people's businesses. So I wasn't even aware that that was a thing—that you could work for yourself. That's the dream right there—work for yourself and be able to hire other people. This is what America is all about."

The path to reaching that dream, however, was not so clear. In high school, DeCarlos didn't think much about the importance of a college education. No one in his family had ever attended college, so it was natural to focus just on high school activities. He cruised through high school with the belief that he would be successful without a college education. He was anxious to get a job and make some money.

After high school, DeCarlos set out to make his dreams a reality but found that it was more difficult than he thought: "I was thinking I was going to be able to kind of get my own little thing going. . . . You get a taste of the real world. It's difficult especially if you don't have an education because even if you're trying to do your own things it's still what people want to see. It [college] just really helps you to move forward."

DeCarlos secured a job as a security guard, but while working the graveyard shift, he quickly realized he wanted a change. "This is not where I want to be," DeCarlos would think.

His job as a security guard was not very glamorous or stimulating, but it paid the bills. A typical shift would start at eleven o'clock at night: "There was me and one other officer. Every other hour we would take tours." While the job did not challenge him much, he did take pride in doing it well. "You would go to the mechanical rooms, and you would check temperature gauges . . . make sure the temperature did not get too high," he says. "You spent a lot of time by yourself. You see the other officer passing by for like five minutes. The total time you probably saw each other was maybe an hour." The solitude provided time for DeCarlos to ponder what he wanted to do with his future: "I spent a lot of time by myself. So—there I would do a lot of thinking about life. I came to the conclusion that I had a lot more in me than this. It was never what I wanted to do. It was more like a pit stop. It was one of those things where I was like, 'I have to figure something out. I want to do more than just walk around in circles all night.'"

Not everything about the job was bad; there were some gratifying moments. He also was able to find inspiration from people around him. DeCarlos discovered a mentor in the company's director of human resources, who gave him advice that would start him on his path to getting a college degree.

Visitors also provided meaningful connections. "I got to meet a lot of people. I met some pretty awesome people," he says. "It was a Japanese-owned company, so a lot of times people would come from Japan and other areas. We would get to talk to some executives. That was really cool. That was really what exposed me to the global thing. I could see how passionate they were about what they did, and I wanted that for myself. That was one of the things that drew me in to the HR director; I saw how passionate he was. What they had, I wanted that. That was an eye opener. That void was there, and I definitely wanted that to be filled."

The exposure he received guided him to expand his mindset even further and pursue more knowledge about the world and all of its possibilities: "Sometimes you have to experience other cultures to really get that awakening and get out there. It's really so important to broaden your horizons. A lot of times you'll stay in your little bubble until you find out there is all this over there. I definitely want to get a chance to just spread out and just really put myself out there. There's so much to see and do, and there are so many different cultures I would like to experience. As much as experiencing other cultures adds value to you, you also add value to those other cultures."

In 2014, DeCarlos decided to enroll in Durham Technical Community College (Durham Tech). Even though he was wary of schools, he was determined to change his situation: "Everywhere that I go, I see that education is a factor. You can't escape it." He still wanted to go into business for himself, and he recognized that having an education could help with that.

He also thought there was room for personal improvement and knowledge, and going to college could be beneficial. When he was growing up, his family had been die-hard Tar Heel fans: "UNC has always been like the Harvard of my family. I never thought that I would go there because of money issues. I just didn't think it was possible." So finding out about C-STEP (Carolina Student Transfer Excellence Program) and seeing there was a bridge to UNC, he decided to enroll in Durham Tech. He thought it might be a gamble, but he decided to take his chances. With the advice from his mentor to "work, work, work," DeCarlos set out to change his life.

The HR director was not his only supporter throughout this process. He also found great encouragement from his mother. When he asked if she thought he should try the school route, her response was, "Absolutely!"

"I was shocked to see how supportive she was," he said. "She always felt like I could do whatever I wanted to do. Thanks to her support, that really gave me the push that I needed." She convinced him that the four years would go by fast.

With self-guided determination, DeCarlos thrived. "I was just really like this time when I do school, I'm going to put everything that I can put into it. And the grades reflected that work," he recounts. Schoolwork wasn't the only work he had to deal with; in addition to being a student, he was still employed as a security guard. "I was working full time, working overtime just to try to pay bills while taking on a full course load. So I would get off of work after working third shift and go straight to school. I was getting four hours of sleep. I wouldn't recommend it, but I really wanted to change my situation."

Though the schedule was grueling, DeCarlos found that it turned out to be the right move. "I loved Durham Tech," he expresses. "It was awesome. I got to experience some amazing things. I met some amazing people."

This will to succeed paid off, and after a few years at Durham Tech, DeCarlos was off to UNC, where he transferred in as a junior. Even though he had a path highlighted to gain admission to UNC, he was still unsure of how his education would be financed. His advisors in C-STEP informed him about different scholarships UNC offered, including the Covenant, so he hoped one of those would come through. His doubts about his ability to afford UNC changed when he received his financial aid package and learned he was eligible to become a Covenant Scholar. DeCarlos knew that if he did not receive Covenant, he would not be able to attend UNC. So when he found out he was awarded a full scholarship, all the pressure was lifted off of his shoulders.

"When you see all those zeros and commas, literally I was sweating bullets," he admits. "All this hard work I put in, and it all comes down to if I can find some money. I did not want to do the loan thing because I have been down that path before, and that was terrible for me. So when I got the Covenant scholarship, I was just elated, jumping for joy, and then I could finally enjoy graduating from Durham Tech."

When DeCarlos mentions a previous unpleasant encounter with student loans, he is referring to a time when he had enrolled in a for-profit art school, before Durham Tech. "They made everything sound really good," he says. "It was one of those things where they promise you the world. A lot of pain came from that. A lot of stressful things. It definitely made my financial situation really tough. That was one of the things that really put me behind in life. But fortunately, I was able to not let that break me down. I still had hope." His mother's lessons and the example she had set helped him through this time. "That was one of the things I got from my mom," he says. "She was like, 'Don't ever stop. Don't ever give up just because one thing didn't work out. You don't stop there. Just keep working.'"

"I didn't know at the time that they [the art school] got me to take out some loans. It ended up coming back to haunt me even to go to UNC." To enroll at UNC, DeCarlos needed transcripts from all schools he had attended, but this school was withholding his transcript until he was able to pay off some of his loans: "I had to work two jobs while I was at Durham Tech, trying to keep my GPA up, just to get that. I'm still paying on those loans. Fortunately, I let that school go within a short amount of time, but it was still enough where I feel it in my pockets."

That experience had such a negative impact on him, as it does many students, that it would have deterred him from entering UNC if he had not received a financial aid package made up of gift aid: "I didn't want to do that again. Even though UNC is a phenomenal school and it's like my dream school, I did not want to go that route this time because I know what that looks like. I can't even express how grateful I am for the Covenant scholarship because I wouldn't be here without it."

Through the help of the Covenant Scholarship, DeCarlos was able to put himself on a path to achieve his dreams. That lifelong interest in visual arts manifested into him becoming a communications major with a concentration in media production. He beams with excitement while talking about the department he has come to love. With the goal of one day having his own animation studio, DeCarlos is set on soaking up all the information he can about how that business works. He is also taking advantage of all the tools UNC offers to build his portfolio and put himself into the position to get his work more visible.

He attributes his ability to follow his chosen career path to the Covenant Scholarship: "Initially, I was going to choose the safe route and do business, even though art has always been this thing that has always been with me. That's always been my dream of doing art and storytelling. Initially, when I was going into this I was like, 'No, this is my second chance.' And I was like, 'I can't mess this up. I can't afford to mess this up.' When I found out that I was a Covenant Scholar and I had all these people supporting me, saying that you can do whatever you want to do—you need to do what you're passionate about. That's what gave me the courage to say you know what, I'm going to really do this and put myself out there."

DeCarlos doesn't even like to think about where his life would be today without the financial support from scholarships. He knows not receiving that opportunity would have meant either missing out on attending college or taking out an extraordinary amount of loans. It also would have meant not being able to follow his dreams of pursuing a career in the arts and media and owning his own business.

Grateful for all the help he has received, DeCarlos wants to pay it forward. One of the ways he set out to do this was by joining the Scholarship Ambassador Program. As an ambassador, he is able to reach out to alumni and donors to inform them about the great things happening at UNC and how their contributions are helping to achieve these things. He also has returned to the C-STEP program to talk to incoming students from Durham Tech to share his experiences and offer his support.

Receiving funding has fundamentally changed DeCarlo's life, providing opportunity and harnessing inherent skills to pursue his long-held dreams. When asked about his feelings about the future, his response was, "I feel like I can do whatever I want to do now. It's at that point where it's just like, you know, hard work does pay off, and I'm definitely seeing that. I feel like the future is very bright. I'm just excited for it," he shared with a giggle and large smile.

Scholarship programs provide hope and enthusiasm for the future to students who don't otherwise have a path to success. Often people work hard but lack the financial and psychological support and direction they need to see that hard work pay off. This can cause their belief in themselves to lapse and their efforts to fail. Opportunities are forever lost.

Scholarships do not only provide someone like DeCarlos with a way to fund an education; more importantly, they also provide one with an avenue to pursue a life that brings joy, opportunity, and a future of unlimited options, as long as one works hard and perseveres. Everything DeCarlos talked about in regard to his dreams has been made possible because donors funded scholarships for need-eligible students at UNC.

APPENDIX C

Overcoming Adversity to Earn a Degree

Riley Bender

R ILEY BENDER GREW UP IN ORANGE COUNTY, CALIFORNIA, BUT IT'S difficult for her to pinpoint a specific city. There was Anaheim, Costa Mesa, Fullerton, Irvine, Newport Beach, Santa Ana, and Tustin. The list is seemingly endless.

There were periods of being homeless when her mom would park their station wagon near the Newport Harbor docks. The longest stay she had anywhere was living on a 42-foot boat in Newport Harbor.

Being raised by a single mom working to make ends meet financially meant frequent moves, which led to Riley and her younger sister, Jordan, shuffling through numerous schools. They were even homeschooled for a time, which Riley says was less about schooling and more about hikes and writing poems. She jokes that the biggest skill she picked up during that period was learning how to rhyme.

Riley's grades were so dismal that she ended up at a continuation school as a high school junior. But ask Riley about the 180-degree turn her life has taken and she is hesitant to talk about her many successes. "I still feel this thing where I can't talk about how well I'm doing above a whisper because it feels like it will just vanish into thin air," Riley said.

So she doesn't boast about being a few months away from graduating from Cal State San Marcos with a bachelor's in human development. She

This appendix by Eric Breier was first published by CSUSM News Center on February 26, 2018, as "Overcoming Adversity to Earn Degree," https://news.csusm.edu/riley-bender/. Reprinted with permission from the publisher, the author, and Ms. Riley.

doesn't brag about being on the dean's list every semester. Or about earning the Orientation Team Leader of the Year Award. Or about being the president of the Human Development Club and the co-founder and president of the Tau Sigma Honor Society.

Instead, she expresses gratitude to the people who helped her along the way—from her mom to her siblings to her professors to fellow students—all the while remaining somewhat mystified at how she reached this point.

The Struggles

Riley's transient youth never seemed abnormal. Struggling financially simply meant moving often. And the constant moves made it difficult to get help in school.

Riley's father had an intermittent presence in her life, as he struggled with alcoholism and drug addiction. Most of her memories of him are from visits to rehab centers or hospitals. He died when she was 16.

Her mother, Coco, had a difficult upbringing—pregnant at 15, married by 16, never having a chance to pursue education. Coco was determined to give her three daughters the opportunities she never had, and she worked numerous jobs in an effort to provide for the family, from cleaning houses to working at Riley's elementary school. But finances were always precarious. "Being poor is expensive," Riley said. "It's difficult and debts accumulate. We don't have a system that's set up to fully support people who are struggling with poverty."

Riley still marvels at the irony of her time at a Newport Beach elementary school. The school was a stone's throw from the ocean in one of the wealthiest cities in the nation, but her family was temporarily living in her mom's station wagon. "My mom would pick us up in our home and we'd drive and park our home somewhere," she said. Riley credits her mom for always making their lives feel normal.

Despite Riley's struggles in school, Coco's mantra never changed: Go to college. "You have to break that cycle," Coco said, "and breaking that cycle means you have to go to college." But figuring out how to get there was another matter, especially when Riley was floundering in school.

Though Riley struggled throughout her K–12 education, her mom's persistent refrain—*Go to college*—resonated. Riley moved to North San Diego County to live with her older sister, Kelly, who is nineteen years her senior.

The Turning Point

Riley still isn't sure exactly why things changed when she transferred to California State University at San Marcos. She didn't even think she could afford to attend a four-year university. Kelly, having navigated the path to CSUSM two decades earlier, insisted that Riley would get financial aid. It was something Riley had never before considered.

Poverty and debt had made Coco wary of sharing personal financial information, and Riley was always told to never provide her Social Security Number for fear it might be used against her in some way. When Riley started filling out the Free Application for Federal Student Aid form, she stopped as soon as her Social Security Number was requested. She called Coco, who again warned against providing it.

But Riley decided there was little to lose at that point. Completing the application proved a sound decision as she received grant money to cover the entire cost of tuition. "I was just dumbfounded," she said. "Not only was I not getting arrested for some debt that we didn't pay when I was thirteen, but they were giving me money."

Riley was cognizant of how isolating it can potentially be for commuter students and transfer students at a four-year university. "The fact that I was still able to get involved and create a support system felt so incredible to me," she said. Not only did Riley get involved in student organizations, she saw dramatic improvement in her academic results. Her grades skyrocketed.

"Riley impressed me the first time I met her at an HD Club meeting," said Tracy Hall, a lecturer in CSUSM's Human Development department and faculty co-adviser of the HD Club. "What impresses me the most is her positive outlook on life and her enthusiasm for wanting to do well and be someone who is making a positive difference in people's lives. She has had to overcome many obstacles in her life, and to come this far is a testament to who she is."

The Future

Riley will attend graduate school next fall to study marriage and family therapy. Going through the application process made her cringe as she saw some of the grades that are no longer reflective of the student she has become. But she is learning to appreciate the adversity and struggles she went through to reach this point.

ACKNOWLEDGMENTS

I AM VERY APPRECIATIVE OF AND THANKFUL TO THE FOLLOWING PEO-
ple who supported and encouraged me in life and while I was researching
and writing this book. Many have worked with me to formulate and implement community scholarship programs that now support more than one
hundred university students each year.

My sons, Andrew and Ross MacDonald, and daughter-in-law, Davida
Baxter MacDonald, continue to inspire me and give me hope for the future.

Students who helped research and write parts of this book and interview
its subjects, including Samantha Young (IU), Lacey Lumpkin (UNC), and
Alivia McAtee (Davidson).

Indiana University Press, including Gary Dunham, who encouraged me
and published this book.

Universities who have adopted the MacDonald Scholars program and
who recruit, mentor, and guide students to help others.

David Davis, MCD Design, for the cover design.

Indiana University

Emily Arth	Lauren Robel
David Johnson	Brandon Shurr
Michael McRobbie	Curt Simic
Abby O'Neal	The Bloomington Faculty Council

Davidson College

Eileen Keeley	Carol Quillen

University of San Diego

Allen Baytop	Austin Galy
Sandra Ciallella	Chris Nayve

University of North Carolina

Lynn Blanchard	Terri Hegeman
Tricia Daisley	Emil Malizia
Shawne Grabbs	Noreen McDonald
Kevin Guskiewicz	Shirley Ort
David Routh	

University of Michigan

Mary Jo Callan	Heidi Kirby
Mike Flood (alumni)	

NOTES

1. The Rising Level of Student Debt and Societal Implications

1. Zack Friedman, "Student Loan Debt Statistics in 2018: A $1.5 Trillion Crisis," *Forbes*, June 13, 2018, https://www.forbes.com/sites/zackfriedman/2018/06/13/student-loan-debt-statistics-2018.

2. Abigail Hess, "Here's How Much the Average Student Loan Borrower Owes When They Graduate," CNBC, last modified February 15, 2018, https://www.cnbc.com/2018/02/15/heres-how-much-the-average-student-loan-borrower-owes-when-they-graduate.html.

3. "Real Student Debt Stories," Student Debt Crisis, accessed January 17, 2019, http://studentdebtcrisis.org/read-student-debt-stories/. Last names and posting dates have been omitted.

4. Sallie Mae and Ipsos, "How America Pays for College 2019," Sallie Mae, accessed April 15, 2020, https://www.salliemae.com/about/leading-research/how-america-pays-for-college/; Sallie Mae and Ipsos Public Affairs, "How America Pays for Graduate School 2017," Sallie Mae, accessed April 15, 2020, https://www.salliemae.com/assets/Research/HAPGS/HAPGRAD_SchoolReport.pdf.

5. Hess, "Average Student Loan Borrower."

6. Elissa Nadworny, "Teachers with Student Debt: These Are Their Stories," NPR, last modified July 26, 2017, http://www.npr.org/sections/ed/2017/07/26/537258324/teachers-with-student-debt-these-are-their-stories.

7. Kim Clark, "A Record Number of People Aren't Paying Back Their Student Loans," *Money*, March 14, 2017, http://money.com/money/4701506/student-loan-defaults-record-2016/.

8. "Real Student Debt Stories." Last name and date of posting have been omitted.

9. "Trends in Student Aid: Highlights," College Board, accessed January 17, 2019, https://trends.collegeboard.org/student-aid/figures-tables/five-year-federal-student-loan-default-rates-institution-type-over-time.

10. Ibid.

11. "Real Student Debt Stories." Last name and date of posting have been omitted.

12. "Trends in Student Aid."

13. Sandra Black, Amy Filipek, Jason Furman, Laura Giuliano, and Ayushi Narayan, "Student Loans and College Quality: Effects on Borrowers and the Economy," VOX, last modified August 4, 2016, http://voxeu.org/article/student-loans-and-college-quality-effects-borrowers-and-economy.

14. "United States Department of Education," Wikipedia, accessed April 6, 2020, https://en.wikipedia.org/w/index.php?title=United_States_Department_of_Education&oldid=937302603.

15. Kaitlin Mulhere, "For-Profit College Students Are Defaulting on Their Loans at an Alarming Rate," *Time*, January 12, 2018, http://time.com/money/5099019/for-profit-college -student-loan-default/.

16. Adam Looney and Constantine Yannelis, "A Crisis in Student Loans? How Changes in the Characteristics of Borrowers and in the Institutions They Attend Contributed to Rising Loan Defaults," *Brookings Papers on Economic Activity* (Fall 2015): 28–29.

17. "Student Loan Delinquency and Default," Federal Student Aid, accessed January 17, 2019, https://studentaid.ed.gov/sa/repay-loans/default.

18. Black et al., "Student Loans."

19. Ray A. Smith, "How to Get Millennials to Buy Jewelry," *Wall Street Journal*, June 20, 2018, A11.

20. "Choose the Federal Student Loan Repayment Plan That's Best for You," Federal Student Aid, accessed April 24, 2020, https://studentaid.ed.gov/sa/repay-loans/understand /plans.

21. Ibid.

22. Nadworny, "Teachers with Student Debt."

3. Betrayed by the Dream Factory

1. Blake Ellis, "Forty Million Americans Now Have Student Loan Debt," CNN Money Moves, September 10, 2014, https://money.cnn.com/2014/09/10/pf/college/student-loans/.

2. Institute for College Access and Success, *Tenth Annual Report: Student Debt and the Class of 2014*, October 2015, https://ticas.org/wp-content/uploads/legacy-files/pub_files /classof2014.pdf.

3. Federal Student Aid, "Income-Driven Repayment Plans," StudentAid.gov, accessed June 15, 2020, https://studentaid.gov/manage-loans/repayment/plans/income-driven.

4. Samual Garner, "A Fair Shot for Everyone to Attend College," Press Conference for Elizabeth Warren, May 15, 2014, https://www.youtube.com/watch?v=JuUmwvviAPY.

4. College as an Investment

1. Ascent Student Loans, "College Students Taking on More Financial Responsibility While Lacking Confidence in the Value of Their Education," Ascent, last modified July 12, 2018, https://ascentstudentloans.com/blog/2018/07/12/college-students-taking-financial -responsibility-lacking-confidence-value-education/.

2. "Seek UT," University of Texas System, accessed August 29, 2018, https://seekut .utsystem.edu/seekuttool.

5. Why College Costs So Much

1. "Trends in College Pricing," College Board, table 2, accessed April 6, 2020, https:// research.collegeboard.org/trends/college-pricing/figures-tables/average-published-charges -sector-over-time/.

2. "National Average Wage Index," Social Security Administration, accessed January 17, 2019, https://www.ssa.gov/oact/cola/AWI.html.

3. "Consumer Price Index Data from 1913 to 2020," US Bureau of Labor Statistics, accessed April 6, 2020, https://www.usinflationcalculator.com/inflation/consumer-price-index -and-annual-percent-changes-from-1913-to-2008/.

4. "Digest of Education Statistics 2016," National Center for Education Statistics, Institute of Education Sciences, US Department of Education, table 330.10, accessed May 10, 2020, https://nces.ed.gov/programs/digest/d16/tables/dt16_330.10.asp.

5. For tuition, see "Digest of Education Statistics 2017," National Center for Education Statistics, Institute of Education Sciences, US Department of Education, table 330.10, accessed May 10, 2020, https://nces.ed.gov/programs/digest/d17/tables/dt17_330.10.asp. For wages, see "National Average Wage Index," year 2017 in the table "National Average Wage Indexing Series, 1951–2018." For consumer price index, see "Consumer Price Index US City Average (1982–2016)," year 2018 in the table "Historical Consumer Price Index for All Urban Consumers: US City Average" all items, by month (August).

6. "Trends in Higher Education: Tuition and Fees and Room and Board over Time," College Board, accessed January 17, 2019, https://trends.collegeboard.org/college-pricing/figures-tables/tuition-fees-room-and-board-over-time, table 2.

7. Jordan Weissman, "A Truly Devastating Graph on State Higher Education Spending," *Atlantic*, March 20, 2013, https://www.theatlantic.com/business/archive/2013/03/a-truly-devastating-graph-on-state-higher-education-spending/274199/.

8. Rick Seltzer, "'Anemic' State Funding Growth," *Inside Higher Ed*, January 22, 2018, https://www.insidehighered.com/news/2018/01/22/state-support-higher-ed-grows-16-percent-2018.

9. "Digest of Education Statistics 2018," National Center for Education Statistics, Institute of Education Sciences, US Department of Education, table 333.10, accessed May 10, 2020, https://nces.ed.gov/programs/digest/d18/tables/dt18_333.10.asp.

10. Ibid.

11. Ibid., table 334.10, https://nces.ed.gov/programs/digest/d18/tables/dt18_334.10.asp.

12. "Annual Financial Report 2015–2016," Indiana University, accessed January 25, 2019, https://www.in.gov/che/files/fy2016.pdf.

13. "Comprehensive Annual Financial Report," University of North Carolina at Chapel Hill, accessed January 25, 2019, https://finance.unc.edu/files/2018/12/2018-CAFR.pdf#page=48.

14. "The Federal Role in Education," US Department of Education, last modified May 25, 2017, https://www2.ed.gov/about/overview/fed/role.html.

15. The Civil Rights Act of 1964 protects people from discrimination based on race, color, or national origin in programs or activities that receive federal financial assistance, including the US Department of Education.

16. The Higher Education Act of 1965 was signed into effect by President Lyndon Johnson with the intention of "strengthening the educational resources of colleges and universities to provide financial assistance for students in postsecondary and higher education." The act increased the amount of federal monies distributed to universities.

17. The Higher Education Amendments of 1972 prohibited discrimination on the basis of sex in institutions of higher education.

18. "Digest of Education Statistics 2018," table 303.10, https://nces.ed.gov/programs/digest/d18/tables/dt18_303.10.asp.

19. "Federal and State Funding of Higher Education: A Changing Landscape," Pew Charitable Trusts, last modified June 11, 2015, https://www.pewtrusts.org/en/research-and-analysis/issue-briefs/2015/06/federal-and-state-funding-of-higher-education.

20. *The Federal Pell Grant Program End-of-Year Report, 2011–2012*, table "Historical Pell Grant Maximum Awards: 1993–2015," accessed April 6, 2020, https://www.lanecc.edu/sites /default/files/budget/financial_aid_award_levels.pdf.

21. Paul F. Campos, "The Real Reason College Tuition Costs So Much," *New York Times*, April 4, 2015, https://www.nytimes.com/2015/04/05/opinion/sunday/the-real-reason-college -tuition-costs-so-much.html.

22. Tunku Varadarajan, "College Bloat Meets 'The Blade,'" *Wall Street Journal*, December 15, 2018, A11.

23. "Chronicle Data," Chronicle Data, accessed January 17, 2019, https://data.chronicle .com.

24. "Facing Facts: Faculty Salary Increases Do Not Equal Student Tuition Hikes," California Faculty Association, last modified February 24, 2016, https://www.calfac.org/headline /facing-facts-faculty-salary-increases-do-not-equal-student-tuition-hikes.

25. Ibid.

26. "Digest of Education Statistics 2018," table 315.20, https://nces.ed.gov/programs/digest /d18/tables/dt18_315.20.asp.

27. John W. Schoen, "Why Does a College Degree Cost So Much?" CNBC, last modified December 8, 2016, https://www.cnbc.com/2015/06/16/why-college-costs-are-so-high-and -rising.html.

28. Steven Hurlburt and Michael McGarrah, "Cost Savings or Cost Shifting? The Relationship between Part-Time Contingent Faculty and Institutional Spending," Delta Cost Project and TIAA Institute, last modified November 2016, https://www.deltacostproject.org/sites /default/files/products/Cost-Savings-or-Cost-Shifting-Contingent-Faculty-November -2016_0.pdf.

29. "Facing Facts: Faculty Salary Increases Do Not Equal Student Tuition Hikes."

30. Campos, "The Real Reason."

31. Ibid.

32. "Digest of Education Statistics 2018," table 334.10.

33. Hurlburt and McGarrah, "Cost Savings."

34. Kellie Woodhouse, "Who's to Blame for Rising Tuition?" *Inside Higher Ed*, May 5, 2015, https://www.insidehighered.com/news/2015/05/05/report-says-administrative-bloat -construction-booms-not-largely-responsible-tuition.

35. Mark Snyder, "Saban Passes Harbaugh as Highest-Paid Coach," *Detroit Free Press*, May 2, 2017, https://www.freep.com/story/sports/college/university-michigan/wolverines /2017/05/02/jim-harbaugh-nick-saban/101193540/.

36. "NCAA Salaries," *USA Today*, accessed January 17, 2019, http://sports.usatoday.com /ncaa/salaries/mens-basketball/coach/.

37. Will Hobson and Steven Rich, "Why Students Foot the Bill for College Sports, and How Some Are Fighting Back," *Washington Post*, November 30, 2015, https://www .washingtonpost.com/sports/why-students-foot-the-bill-for-college-sports-and-how-some -are-fighting-back/2015/11/30/7ca47476-8d3e-11e5-ae1f-af46b7df8483_story.html?utm_term =.df1c9b56f933.

38. Ibid.

39. Jonathan Meer and Harvey Rosen, "The Impact of Athletic Performance on Alumni Giving: An Analysis of Micro Data" (CEPS Working Paper No. 162, Princeton University, March 2008), https://www.princeton.edu/ceps/workingpapers/162rosen.pdf; Sean Silverthorne, "The Flutie Effect: How Athletic Success Boosts College Applications," *Forbes*, April

29, 2013, https://www.forbes.com/sites/hbsworkingknowledge/2013/04/29/the-flutie-effect
-how-athletic-success-boosts-college-applications/.

40. "The Higher Education Capital Improvement Fund Act Statute," New Jersey Educational Facilities Authority, State of New Jersey, accessed January 17, 2019, https://www.nj.gov
/njefa/pdf/NJEFA%20Statute%202019.pdf.

41. Woodhouse, "Who's to Blame for Rising Tuition?"

42. John Caulfield, "5 Ways Universities Use New Buildings to Stay Competitive," *Building
Design and Construction*, April 13, 2016, https://www.bdcnetwork.com/5-ways-universities
-use-new-buildings-stay-competitive.

43. Melissa Korn, "Top Colleges Are Enrolling More Students from Low-Income Homes,"
Wall Street Journal, December 17, 2018, https://www.wsj.com/articles/number-of-low-income
-students-at-top-colleges-begins-to-rise-11545042601.

44. Jie Zong and Jeanne Batalova, "International Students in the United States," Migration
Policy Institute, last modified May 9, 2018, https://www.migrationpolicy.org/article
/international-students-united-states.

6. The History of Financial Aid for College Students

1. "Higher Education Act Media Kit," LBJ Presidential Library, accessed February 25,
2017, http://www.lbjlibrary.org/mediakits/highereducation/.

2. Matthew B. Fuller, "A History of Financial Aid to Students," *Journal of Student Financial Aid* 44, no. 1 (2014): 43–45.

3. Ron Chernow, *Alexander Hamilton* (Toronto: Penguin Books, 2004), 36–37.

4. Fuller, "A History of Financial Aid," 48–50.

5. Ibid., 53.

6. Ibid., 53–54.

7. Higher Education Act of 1965, Pub. L. No. 89-329 (see Government Publishing Office,
accessed April 27, 2020, https://www.gpo.gov/fdsys/pkg/STATUTE-79/pdf/STATUTE-79
-Pg1219.pdf).

8. "Types of Financial Aid," Federal Student Aid, accessed February 25, 2017, https://
studentaid.ed.gov/sa/types.

9. College Board, *Trends in Student Aid 2019*, Trends in Higher Education Series, accessed May 4, 2020, https://research.collegeboard.org/pdf/trends-student-aid-2019-full
-report.pdf; see table 1, p. 9, and fig. 1, p. 10.

10. "Wondering How the Amount of Your Federal Student Aid Is Determined?," Federal
Student Aid, accessed February 25, 2017, https://studentaid.ed.gov/sa/fafsa/next-steps/how
-calculated.

11. "You Must Meet Certain Requirements to Qualify for Federal Student Aid (Grants,
Work-Study, and Loans)," Federal Student Aid, accessed February 25, 2017, https://studentaid
.ed.gov/sa/eligibility/basic-criteria.

12. "Federal Grants Are Money to Help Pay for College or Career School," Federal Student
Aid, accessed February 25, 2017, https://studentaid.ed.gov/sa/types/grants-scholarships.

13. Fuller, "A History of Financial Aid," 54.

14. "Federal Pell Grants Are Usually Awarded Only to Undergraduate Students," Federal
Student Aid, accessed February 25, 2017, https://studentaid.ed.gov/sa/types/grants
-scholarships/pell.

15. Ibid.

16. "Trend Generator," National Center for Education Statistics, Institute of Education Sciences, US Department of Education, accessed February 25, 2017, https://nces.ed.gov/ipeds/trendgenerator/.

17. "A Federal Supplemental Educational Opportunity Grant (FSEOG) Is a Grant for Undergraduate Students with Exceptional Financial Need," Federal Student Aid, accessed February 25, 2017, https://studentaid.ed.gov/sa/types/grants-scholarships/fseog.

18. College Board, *Trends in Student Aid 2019*.

19. "A TEACH Grant Can Help You Pay for College If You Plan to Become a Teacher in a High-Need Field in a Low-Income Area," Federal Student Aid, accessed February 25, 2017, https://studentaid.ed.gov/sa/types/grants-scholarships/teach.

20. "If Your Parent or Guardian Died as a Result of Military Service in Iraq or Afghanistan, You May Be Eligible for an Iraq and Afghanistan Service Grant," Federal Student Aid, accessed February 25, 2017, https://studentaid.ed.gov/sa/types/grants-scholarships/iraq-afghanistan-service.

21. College Board, *Trends in Student Aid 2019*.

22. Ibid.

23. "Federal Student Loans for College or Career School Are an Investment in Your Future," Federal Student Aid, accessed February 25, 2017, https://studentaid.ed.gov/sa/types/loans.

24. "The US Department of Education Offers Low-Interest Loans to Eligible Students to Help Cover the Cost of College or Career School," Federal Student Aid, accessed February 25, 2017, https://studentaid.ed.gov/sa/types/loans/subsidized-unsubsidized.

25. Ibid.

26. "Direct PLUS Loans Are Federal Loans That Graduate or Professional Students and Parents of Dependent Undergraduate Students Can Use to Help Pay for College or Career School," Federal Student Aid, accessed February 25, 2017, https://studentaid.ed.gov/sa/types/loans/plus.

27. "Student Loan Consolidation," Federal Student Aid, accessed February 25, 2017, https://studentaid.gov/manage-loans/consolidation.

28. "The Federal Perkins Loan Program Provided Money for College or Career School for Students with Financial Need," Federal Student Aid, accessed February 25, 2017, https://studentaid.ed.gov/sa/types/loans/perkins.

29. "Federal Student Loans for College or Career School."

30. College Board, *Trends in Student Aid 2019*.

31. Ibid.

32. Ibid.

33. Barack Obama, "Remarks by the President on College Affordability—Buffalo, NY," last modified August 22, 2013, https://obamawhitehouse.archives.gov/the-press-office/2013/08/22/remarks-president-college-affordability-buffalo-ny.

34. Jillian Berman, "Ted Cruz Invokes His Student Loans, but Will He Help Others with Theirs?" *MarketWatch*, March 23, 2015, https://www.marketwatch.com/story/ted-cruz-man-of-the-people-blocked-a-bill-to-lower-student-loan-rates-2015-03-23.

35. "Transcript: Marco Rubio's Republican Response," ABC News, last modified February 12, 2013, http://abcnews.go.com/Politics/transcript-marco-rubios-state-union-response/story?id=18484413.

7. What Schools Are Doing to Reduce Student Debt

1. Board of Governors of the Federal Reserve System, "Report on the Economic Well-Being of US Households in 2015," Federal Reserve, last updated November 18, 2016, https://www.federalreserve.gov/econresdata/2016-economic-well-being-of-us-households-in-2015-education-debt-student-loans.htm.

2. "Price of Attending an Undergraduate Institution," National Center for Education Statistics, Institute of Education Sciences, US Department of Education, last modified April 2019, https://nces.ed.gov/programs/coe/indicator_cua.asp.

3. "Fast Facts," National Center for Education Statistics, Institute of Education Sciences, US Department of Education, accessed May 23, 2018, https://nces.ed.gov/fastfacts/display.asp?id=76.

4. "Digest of Education Statistics 2018," National Center for Education Statistics, Institute of Education Sciences, US Department of Education, table 331.95, accessed April 8, 2020, https://nces.ed.gov/programs/digest/d18/tables/dt18_331.95.asp.

5. "Digest of Education Statistics 2019," National Center for Education Statistics, Institute of Education Sciences, US Department of Education, table 331.35, accessed May 4, 2020, https://nces.ed.gov/programs/digest/d19/tables/dt19_331.35.asp.

6. "Financial Aid: A Commitment to Need-Based Financial Aid," Pomona College, accessed April 27, 2020, https://www.pomona.edu/financial-aid.

7. "How Aid Works," Columbia Financial Aid and Educational Financing, accessed June 1, 2018, https://cc-seas.financialaid.columbia.edu/how/aid/works.

8. "Financial Aid," Office of Student Financial Aid and Scholarships, Vanderbilt University, accessed June 1, 2018, https://www.vanderbilt.edu/financialaid/.

9. "The Davidson Trust," Davidson College, accessed May 21, 2018, https://www.davidson.edu/about/distinctly-davidson/the-davidson-trust.

10. Ibid.

11. Interview with Clark Ross by Alivia McAtee, 2017 (Davidson College).

12. "Davidson College Receives $25 Million for the Davidson Trust," *Philanthropy News Digest*, May 20, 2012, https://philanthropynewsdigest.org/news/davidson-college-receives-25-million-gift-from-alumnus.14. Interview with Helen Duffy by Alivia McAtee, 2017 (Davidson College).

15. Interview with Zoe Hall by Alivia McAtee, 2017 (Davidson College).

16. "President Quillen."

17. "Dinner at Davidson: Perspectives on a Decade of the Davidson Trust," Davidson College, News, last modified March 15, 2017, https://www.davidson.edu/news/2017/03/15/dinner-davidson-perspectives-decade-davidson-trust.

18. "Carolina Covenant," Scholarships and Student Aid, University of North Carolina at Chapel Hill, accessed May 14, 2018, https://carolinacovenant.unc.edu/about-the-covenant/.

19. Ibid.

20. "2018–2019 Impact Report: The Carolina Covenant," University of North Carolina at Chapel Hill, accessed April 8, 2020, https://campaign.unc.edu/carolina-covenant-impact-report/.

21. Ibid.

22. Interview with Terri Hegeman by Lacey Lumpkin, 2018.

23. Ibid.

24. Ibid.

25. "BOG Caps Tuition Revenues Used for Financial Aid," *Carolina Alumni Review*, August 4, 2004, https://alumni.unc.edu/news/bog-caps-tuition-revenues-used-for-financial -aid/.

26. "The Carolina Edge," University of North Carolina at Chapel Hill, accessed May 17, 2019, https://campaign.unc.edu/funding-priority/the-carolina-edge/.

27. Interview with Terri Hegeman by Lacey Lumpkin, 2018.

28. University Communications, "Covenant Scholar Invests in His Future," University of North Carolina at Chapel Hill, Dynamic Minds, accessed June 4, 2018, https://www.unc.edu /discover/covenant-scholar-invests-in-his-future/.

29. "Scholar Profile: Marquis Peacock," Carolina Covenant, accessed June 4, 2018, https:// carolinacovenant.unc.edu/?scholar=marquis-peacock. This page is no longer available.

30. Farran Powell and Emma Kerr, "Schools That Meet Full Financial Need with No Loans," *US News & World Report*, September 30, 2019, https://www.usnews.com/education /best-colleges/paying-for-college/articles/2018-09-18/18-schools-that-meet-full-financial -need-with-no-loans.

31. "Princeton's Endowment: Funding for Future Generations," Princeton University, accessed June 4, 2018, http://giving.princeton.edu/endowment.

32. "Facts and Figures," Princeton University, accessed June 4, 2018, https://www .princeton.edu/meet-princeton/facts-figures.

33. "Princeton's Endowment."

34. "How Princeton's Aid Program Works," Princeton University, accessed June 4, 2018, https://admission.princeton.edu/cost-aid/how-princetons-aid-program-works.

35. Ibid.

36. "Making It Possible," Princeton University, accessed June 4, 2018, https://pr.princeton .edu/aid/pdf/1314/PU-Making-It-Possible.pdf.

37. "Financial Aid Program Provides Access, Affordability," Princeton University, last modified July 28, 2008, https://www.princeton.edu/news/2008/07/28/financial-aid-program -provides-access-affordability.

38. Office of Admission and the Office of Communications, "Affordable Princeton: Financial Aid Allows Students to Graduate Debt Free," Princeton University, last modified March 31, 2016, https://www.princeton.edu/news/2016/03/31/affordable-princeton-financial-aid -allows-students-graduate-debt-free.

39. Ibid.

40. Ibid.

41. Ibid.

42. Eric Quiñones, "Graduates of First 'No Loan' Class Look to Future," Princeton University, News, last modified May 24, 2005, https://www.princeton.edu/news/2005/05/24 /graduates-first-no-loan-class-look-future.

43. Peter Reuell, "Leveling the Playing Field," *Harvard Gazette*, June 12, 2018, https://news .harvard.edu/gazette/story/2018/06/creating-a-more-diverse-harvard-with-need-blind -financial-aid/.

44. Ibid.

45. Ibid.

46. Ibid.

47. Ibid.

48. Ibid.

49. Ibid.

50. "Kenneth Griffin Makes Largest Gift in Harvard College History," *Harvard Gazette*, February 19, 2014, https://news.harvard.edu/gazette/story/2014/02/kenneth-griffin-makes -largest-gift-in-harvard-college-history/.

51. "Brown Launches Campaign to Eliminate Loans from University Undergraduate Financial Aid Packages," Brown University, last modified September 20, 2017, https://news .brown.edu/articles/2017/09/promise.

52. Powell and Kerr, "Schools That Meet Full Financial Need."

53. "With a 13.4 Percent Return, Brown University's Endowment Grows to $3.5 Billion," Brown University, last modified October 3, 2017, https://news.brown.edu/articles/2017/10 /endowment.

54. Ibid.

55. "The Brown Promise," Brown University, accessed June 5, 2018, https://brunonia .brown.edu/giving/browntogether/info/brown-promise.

56. Ibid.

57. "Brown Launches Campaign."

58. "The Brown Promise."

59. Mark S. Schlissel, "President Schlissel on Go Blue Guarantee," University of Michigan, streamed live on August 24, 2018, YouTube video, 0:43, https://www.youtube.com/watch ?time_continue=43&v=5GpKFoIDAAI.

60. Powell and Kerr, "Schools That Meet Full Financial Need."

61. "UVA Answers Frequently Asked Questions about Access UVA," *University of Virginia Magazine*, accessed June 5, 2018, http://uvamagazine.org/articles/u.va._answers _frequently_asked_questions_about_accessuva.

62. Mason Adams, "Admissions Director Notes Success and Future Opportunities to Draw More Applicants," *Virginia Tech Daily*, April 22, 2019, https://vtnews.vt.edu/articles /2019/04/provost-espinoza-admissions.html.

63. "Centennial Scholars Program—What We Do," James Madison University, accessed June 8, 2018, https://www.jmu.edu/centscholars/whatwedo.shtml.

8. The Importance of Philanthropy

1. *Merriam-Webster*, s.v. "philanthropy," accessed July 18, 2018, https://www.merriam -webster.com/dictionary/philanthropy.

2. "Support the Museum," Smithsonian National Postal Museum, accessed July 23, 2018, https://postalmuseum.si.edu/support/support-us.php.

3. John R. Thelin and Richard W. Trollinger, *Philanthropy and American Higher Education* (New York: Palgrave Macmillan, 2014), 1.

4. Ibid., 2.

5. Ibid. 9–10.

6. Ibid., 16, 108.

7. Ibid., 16.

8. Ibid., 10.

9. Shelley Strickland, "Partners in Writing and Rewriting History: Philanthropy and Higher Education," *International Journal of Educational Advancement* 7, no. 2 (June 2007): 104–16.

10. "Charitable Giving and Universities and Colleges," Association of American Universities, March 2014, https://www.aau.edu/sites/default/files/AAU%20Files/Key%20Issues /Taxation%20%26%20Finance/Charitable-Gifts-FINAL.pdf.

11. Thelin and Trollinger, *Philanthropy*, 96.

12. Ibid., 95.

13. Mark Dodgson, "How Philanthropy Could Change Higher Education Funding," *The Conversation*, February 28, 2018, https://theconversation.com/how-philanthropy-could-change-higher-education-funding-92260.

14. "Colleges and Universities Raise Record $40.30 Billion in 2015," Council for Aid to Education (press release), last modified January 27, 2016, https://cae.org/images/uploads/pdf/VSE_2015_Press_Release.pdf.

15. Alyssa Rossodivita, "Philanthropy in Public Higher Education," Learning to Give, accessed 2017, https://www.learningtogive.org/resources/philanthropy-public-higher-education.

16. James Michael Langley, "Cultivating a Culture of Philanthropy: New Approaches to New Realities," *AGB Trusteeship Magazine*, July/August 2014, https://agb.org/trusteeship-issue/cultivating-a-culture-of-philanthropy-july-august-2014/.

17. Judith R. Fox, "Commentaries: The Importance of Philanthropy to Education," *PhilanthropyNYU*, December 11, 2013, http://www.philanthropynyu.com/polIssueStory.cfm?doc_id=253. Page no longer available.

18. Ibid.

19. Bruce Matthews, "Higher Education Cuts Reinforces Importance of Philanthropy," Campbell and Company, last modified March 22, 2013, https://www.campbellcompany.com/news/bid/105291/Higher-Education-Cuts-Reinforces-Importance-of-Philanthropy.

20. Ibid.

21. Dwight Burlingame, *Philanthropy in America: A Comprehensive Historical Encyclopedia*, 3 vols. (Santa Barbara, CA: ABC-CLIO, 2004), quoted in Matt Kelly, "UVA Professor Uncovers the Rich History of Philanthropy in America," *UVA Today*, January 23, 2012, https://news.virginia.edu/content/uva-professor-uncovers-rich-history-philanthropy-america.

22. Ibid.

23. Ibid.

24. Grace Camblos, *Giving Is Good for the Soul: The Life and Legacy of Charles and Shirley Weiss* (Chapel Hill: University of North Carolina at Chapel Hill, 2012), 66.

25. Ibid., 68.

26. Ibid., 69.

27. Ibid.

28. "Philanthropic Partnership Benefits Students and Companies," The Ohio State University, last modified October 27, 2017, https://engineering.osu.edu/news/2017/10/philanthropic-partnership-benefits-students-and-companies.

29. Ibid.

30. "Philanthropy in Action," Penn State College of Education, accessed August 5, 2018, https://ed.psu.edu/giving-broken/philanthropy-in-action.

31. Ibid.

32. Strickland, "Partners in Writing," 104–16.

33. Mark Dodgson and David Gann, "Universities Need Philanthropy but Must Resist Hidden Agendas," World Economic Forum, last modified February 15, 2018, https://www.weforum.org/agenda/2018/02/universities-need-philanthropy-but-must-resist-hidden-agendas/.

10. John Kuykendall and Davidson College

1. This and subsequent information is from an interview with John Kuykendall by Alivia McAtee on August 30, 2017 (Davidson, North Carolina).

2. This and subsequent information is from an interview with Eli Kahn by Alivia McAtee on August 8, 2017 (Charlotte, North Carolina).

15. Unmet Social Needs and Inadequate Funding

1. Servaas van der Berg, *Poverty and Education* (UNESCO, International Institute for Educational, and Planning International Academy of Education, 2008), 1, https://unesdoc .unesco.org/ark:/48223/pf0000181754.locale=en.

2. Ibid., ii.

3. Ibid., 20.

4. Ibid., 23.

5. Eliana Garces, Duncan Thomas, and Janet Currie, "Longer-Term Effects of Head Start," *American Economic Review* 92, no. 4 (September 2002): 999–1012. This quote is taken from the article abstract.

6. Lyndsey Layton, "Study: Poor Children Are Now the Majority in American Public Schools in South, West," *Washington Post*, October 16, 2013, https://www.washingtonpost. com/local/education/2013/10/16/34eb4984–35bb-11e3–8a0e-4e2cf80831fc_story.html?utm _term=.563d3ff456cc.

7. Ibid.

8. "Facts and Figures 2015–2016," North Carolina Government, accessed April 10, 2020, https://files.nc.gov/dpi/documents/fbs/resources/data/factsfigures/2015–16figures.pdf.

9. "2016's Shocking Homelessness Statistics," Social Solutions, accessed January 17, 2019, https://www.socialsolutions.com/blog/2016-homelessness-statistics/.

10. "The State of Homelessness in America," National Alliance to End Homelessness, accessed January 17, 2019, https://endhomelessness.org/homelessness-in-america/homelessness -statistics/state-of-homelessness-report-legacy/.

11. Joel L. Young, "Untreated Mental Illness," *Psychology Today*, December 30, 2015, https://www.psychologytoday.com/us/blog/when-your-adult-child-breaks-your-heart /201512/untreated-mental-illness.

12. "The US Health Care System: An International Perspective," Department for Professional Employees, accessed January 17, 2019, https://dpeaflcio.org/programs-publications /issue-fact-sheets/the-u-s-health-care-system-an-international-perspective/.

13. "The World Factbook," Central Intelligence Agency, accessed January 17, 2019, https:// www.cia.gov/library/publications/the-world-factbook/rankorder/2091rank.html.

14. "11 Facts about Hunger in the US," DoSomething.org, accessed January 17, 2019, https://www.dosomething.org/facts/11-facts-about-hunger-us.

15. "Food Security Status of US Households in 2018," US Department of Agriculture, Economic Research Service, accessed May 4, 2020, https://www.ers.usda.gov/topics/food -nutrition-assistance/food-security-in-the-us/key-statistics-graphics.aspx#foodsecure.

16. "The US Health Care System."

16. Community Engagement at Universities

1. Interview with Scott MacDonald on January 15, 2018 (Chapel Hill, North Carolina).
2. "Mission and Vision," Campus Compact, accessed January 17, 2019, https://compact.org/who-we-are/mission-and-vision/.
3. "Campus Compact," Campus Compact, accessed January 17, 2019, https://compact.org/.
4. "AAU Campus Community Service Directory," Association of American Universities, accessed January 17, 2019, https://www.aau.edu/education-service/service/aau-campus-community-service-directory.
5. "Carnegie Selects Colleges and Universities for 2015 Community Engagement Classification," Carnegie Foundation for the Advancement of Teaching, last modified January 7, 2015, https://www.carnegiefoundation.org/newsroom/news-releases/carnegie-selects-colleges-universities-2015-community-engagement-classification/.
6. "President's Higher Education Community Service Honor Roll," Corporation for National and Community Service, accessed January 17, 2019, https://www.nationalservice.gov/special-initiatives/honor-roll/.
7. "AAU Campus Community Service Directory."
8. "Campus Compact Overview," Campus Compact, accessed January 17, 2019, https://compact.org/who-we-are/.
9. Thomas Jefferson to Cornelius Camden Blatchly, 1822, ME 15:399, accessed February 9, 2019, https://founders.archives.gov/documents/Jefferson/98-01-02-3106.

17. The Ginsberg Center and the University of Michigan

1. This and subsequent information is from an interview by Julia Smilie on June 26, 2018 (Ann Arbor, Michigan).
2. This and subsequent information is from an interview by Julia Smilie on June 27, 2018 (Ann Arbor, Michigan).
3. From an interview by Julia Smilie on April 16, 2018 (Ann Arbor, Michigan).

18. The Carolina Center for Public Service and the University of North Carolina

1. "About CCPS," Carolina Center for Public Service, accessed January 17, 2019, https://ccps.unc.edu/about/.
2. George D. Kuh, "High-Impact Educational Practices: What They Are, Who Has Access to Them, and Why They Matter" (Washington, DC: Association of American Colleges and Universities, 2008), 1. Excerpt available at https://www.aacu.org/leap/hips.
3. Robert G. Bringle, "Hybrid High-Impact Pedagogies: Integrating Service-Learning with Three Other High-Impact Pedagogies," *Michigan Journal of Community Service Learning* (Fall 2017): 49–63, https://quod.lib.umich.edu/cgi/p/pod/dod-idx/hybrid-high-impact-pedagogies-integrating-service-learning.pdf?c=mjcsloa;idno=3239521.0024.105;format=pdf.
4. "The Concept," MacDonald Scholars, accessed January 17, 2019, http://macdonaldscholars.com/program/.

19. The Mulvaney Center and the University of San Diego

1. University of San Diego, "CSL at USD: A Report on Community Service Learning at the University of San Diego, 2012–2013," 2–4.
2. Ibid.

3. Princeton Review, *Colleges with a Conscience: 81 Great Schools with Outstanding Community Involvement*, College Admissions Guides (New York: Random House, 2005), 186.

4. "Mulvaney Center: Making Community Connections for 30 Years," University of San Diego, USD News Center, January 26, 2018, https://www.sandiego.edu/news/detail.php ?_focus=65985.

5. University of San Diego, "CSL at USD," 16.

6. Ibid., 2.

7. Interview with Chris Nayve on March 15, 2018 (San Diego, California).

8. University of San Diego, "CSL at USD," 15.

9. "Envisioning 2024 Pathways," University of San Diego, accessed April 16, 2020, https://www.sandiego.edu/envisioning-2024/pathways/anchor-institution.php.

Conclusion: What Must Be Done

1. "Tuition-Free Degree Program: The Excelsior Scholarship," New York State, accessed January 15, 2020, https://www.ny.gov/programs/tuition-free-degree-program-excelsior -scholarship.

2. Libby Nelson, "Indiana University Used This One Weird Trick to Cut Student Debt," *Vox*, July 26, 2015, https://www.vox.com/2015/7/26/9041283/indiana-university-debt-letters.

Scott MacDonald is the author of *Think Like a Dog: How Dogs Teach Us to Be Happy in Life and Successful at Work* (IUP, 2019). He has had a successful career working on commercial real estate projects throughout the world. He has been CEO or president of several companies, including Investa Property Group in Sydney, Australia; New Plan Excel in New York City; Center America Property Trust in Houston, Texas; and the affiliated companies of Trizec Hahn in San Diego, California. He was a longtime advisor to Morgan Stanley Real Estate Funds in London and New York.